An Unnatural Pursuit

Also by Simon Gray

Fiction
COLMAIN
SIMPLE PEOPLE
LITTLE PORTIA
A COMEBACK FOR STARK

Stage plays
WISE CHILD
DUTCH UNCLE
THE IDIOT
SPOILED
BUTLEY
OTHERWISE ENGAGED
DOG DAYS
MOLLY
THE REAR COLUMN
CLOSE OF PLAY
STAGE STRUCK
QUARTERMAINE'S TERMS
TARTUFFE
CHAPTER 17
THE COMMON PURSUIT

Television plays
AWAY WITH THE LADIES
THE CARAMEL CRISIS
DEATH OF A TEDDY BEAR
PIG IN A POKE
MAN IN A SIDE-CAR
PLAINTIFFS AND DEFENDANTS
TWO SUNDAYS

AN UNNATURAL PURSUIT
and other pieces

SIMON GRAY

faber and faber
LONDON · BOSTON

First published in 1985
by Faber and Faber Limited
3 Queen Square London WC1N 3AU

Filmset by Wilmaset Birkenhead
Printed in Great Britain by
Butler & Tanner Ltd
Frome Somerset
All rights reserved

British Library Cataloguing in Publication Data

Gray, Simon
An unnatural pursuit: the journal of a production
1. Theatre—Great Britain—Production and
direction
I. Title
792′.0232′0924   PN2053
ISBN 0–571–13719–9
ISBN 0–571–13757–1

This book is dedicated to the Cast and
Company of the Lyric, Hammersmith,
production of *The Common Pursuit*,
without whom it could not have appeared.

Contents

Illustrations

The photographs of the poster designs were taken by the artist, Carlos Sapochnik. The *Time Out* photograph was taken by Bob Workman. Donald Cooper took all the other photographs.

Acknowledgements

I should like to thank Sarah Moorehead, without whose efficiency, constructive contributions and moral support this book would probably not have appeared.

For permission to reproduce extracts and reviews the publishers gratefully acknowledge the following:

Methuen London Ltd for 'Flops and Other Fragments' from *A Night at the Theatre* edited by Ronald Harwood (1982) and 'Memories of Lopez' from *Summer Days: Writers on Cricket* edited by Michael Meyer (1981), and for extracts from *The Common Pursuit* by Simon Gray (1984); Robson Books for 'My Cambridge' from *My Cambridge* edited by Ronald Hayman (1977); the *Sunday Times* for 'The Pursuit of F. R. Leavis' by Simon Gray (21 October 1984); *The Times Literary Supplement* for 'Confessions of a TV Playwright' (19 September 1968) by Simon Gray; and to *Wisden Cricket Monthly* for 'My Place in Cricket History' by Simon Gray (October 1979).

Foreword

Harold Pinter

How I managed to get through this book without a fag I don't know.

The author did mention that he intended to keep a diary of the production, but I hadn't taken it seriously. In fact I had forgotten all about it. We got on with the rehearsals, put the play on the stage, threw it at various audiences, discussed its future with the management, watched the last performance, had a few drinks, had supper at the Trattoo. I was just about to sit back and reflect upon the whole damn thing when this manuscript arrived, saving me the trouble of reflection. Well . . . not really.

Our perceptions of the endeavour, while closely allied, could never be identical. The author stands alone on a sheer cliff. Others can sympathize, but none can share his unique brand of vertigo. Certainly I had no idea that, after a day's hard labour, Simon would be up until all hours speaking into a machine. No wonder he looked like a particularly rough night on so many mornings.

However, he's got it right; even if some of it makes uncomfortable reading. In setting down what is often referred to as 'the naked truth', he shows himself no mercy. (In the light of this, it seems to me, none of the other protagonists can complain of harsh treatment.) Actually he's not nearly such a pain as his self-portrait would have you believe. In the course of our association on *The Common Pursuit*, I sometimes heard him offer the most extraordinarily helpful observations on subjects like life, putting on plays, and death.

This journal is a remarkable account of a remarkable experience.

Introduction

About a year ago, I had lunch with a friend who asked me why I didn't write a book about my experiences in the theatre along the lines of a short article I'd once done called *Flops and Other Fragments*. (The title surely defines the nature of the piece.)* I replied that I'd now and then yearned to do a diary of a production from the playwright's point of view – or, at least, from this playwright's point of view – from the moment the play was finished through to the play's opening and its critical and public reception. (The two aren't necessarily the same.) He said, well, why don't you? I said I wasn't sure that I'd ever write another play, or at least a play that would be thought worth producing, but agreed that if I did and it was, I would. I did write another play; it was thought worth producing, and I did keep a diary – if reporting into a tape recorder counts as keeping a diary. What follows isn't a transcript of the tapes – there were nearly twenty hours of me talking to myself after all, much of it incomprehensible to anyone except me, some of it incomprehensible to me as well. I've therefore used the tapes as a kind of *aide-mémoire*, amending the grammar of almost every sentence I've included, condensing passages that contained more information than anyone could possibly want, cutting out details that even I could see were boring. Nevertheless, I've done my best to follow the story of the production accurately. I don't believe that any of my reconstruction has distorted the nature of the experience itself – a view corroborated by my wishing, on reading it through, that the experience had been different. I haven't altered, in other words, except for the sake of coherence and speed. Now

* It was published in a collection of essays edited by Ronald Harwood, called *A Night in the Theatre*, published by Methuen, and is reprinted here on p. 189.

and then – and on one occasion particularly – I have left a passage exactly as I spoke it, on the grounds that a truer truth was communicated by a lunatic or drunken syntax than would have been communicated by rendering it merely comprehensible.

For me, the main revelation of the transcripts is that I habitually speak in a language that makes only partial sense. From which I gather that I am mainly understood in conversation through my gestures, and the play of my features. If I *am* understood, that is, by any except those closest to me, who probably understand me only too well, even when I'm silent.

I

An Unnatural Pursuit

The Play

A few days after I'd finished the last draft I made the following notes on the characters, the plot and the structure. Realizing that in their original context they tended to hold up the story of the production, but still thinking it might nevertheless be helpful to give the reader some sense of *The Common Pursuit* (and for easy reference), I have decided to place them here. I have kept them as written, and also left in some further commentary from the transcripts.

26 November

Spent the day reading the play, making revisions, testing it scene by scene. Like a pudding? But one doesn't test a pudding scene by scene. Also tried to find out what it's about. I never know until after the last draft, after the *first* version of the last draft, and then I'm not always sure. Not that it matters, there are lots of others, critics, etc., around to tell one what it's about. If anything at all, of course.* I think it's a play about friendship, though. English, middle-class, Cambridge-educated friendship. Which might well be, from several points of view, a play about nothing at all. If I'd set it in a working man's club, a factory, an insurance office or possibly even a green room† (I'm less sure about that) it would clearly be about something – i.e. real life.

---

* The Most Influential Critic in San Francisco began his radio review of one of my plays – rather a poignant one too, I thought – by bawling out, 'Ladies and gentlemen, the play's the thing, as Shakespeare put it. But ladies and gentlemen, there isn't a play here! No play at all, ladies and gentlemen.' (I quote from memory so may have got a phrase or two wrong.)

† The 'green room' is the room backstage to which the actors can retire when not performing, or between the acts, for cups of coffee and tea. It isn't unlike a university common room, except that the conversation tends to be of a higher intellectual standard.

But middle class and Cambridge educated is unreal, or anyway impermissible life, élitist, incestuous, who-cares kind of life. Why should theatregoers, theatre critics, want to know about privileged undergraduates – especially ones who become literary careerists, involve themselves in small-scale magazines, tangle with the Arts Council, commit adultery, become impotent, get divorced and even, in one case, end up butchered by a bit of rough trade in élitist rooms in Trinity? All this is liable to be found a trifle remote, at least by theatre critics and London audiences, who hunger for reality as they know it. But we are, I console myself, what we are. Which is why we write what we write. A bit of a conundrum that. I think I've only just scratched its surface here. But I mustn't get paranoid about the reviews before the play hits the boards. Time enough for that afterwards. One of the offstage characters, rather an endearing one, ends up as a theatre critic. Another instance of the play's unreality. Nobody ever does *that*, as we all know.

But the characters seem OK to me. At least I believe in them all. This afternoon I made the following notes about them.

Stuart

The spine of the play, serious about literature, prepared to suffer for it – up to a point. A Cambridge johnnie, all right. In love with Marigold. Genuinely in love, genuinely loving. An astringent and passionate man, with the strength and charm to hold his friends to him – almost. Finally, as it turns out, easy to deceive. An egoist, too vain, as he admitted in an earlier draft, to run a literary magazine successfully, even a small one. Even a small one demands efficiency, a respect for money, crude calculations, etc.

Martin

The rich orphan. Shy, loving, loyal, adorer of cats, desperate for friends, a traitor. A traitor precisely because he comes to understand (the only one of the group to do so) what precisely he wants from life, and who he's prepared to sacrifice to get it. He burrows into other lives from within, probably unconsciously, at first. He ends triumphant, matter-of-factly and ruefully so. A man finally at ease in the world. With the usual shadows. I believe I've seen lots like him all my life, but most particularly in the early stages at my public school, Westminster, where I always felt like an outsider – to do with my being an evacuee during the war, coming back to a middle-class education as a jug-eared, nasal-accented Canadian, envious particularly of the shyly charming Martins who ended up as monitors, and who were occasionally and therefore reluctantly compelled to inflict pain on one.

Humphry

Two of my friends, both homosexuals, have been murdered by casual pick-ups. Humphry is based on neither, although I used facts from both their lives (and other lives) in tracing his career. The important fact about Humphry is not his homosexuality but his over-developed critical (and self-critical) faculty which grows into contempt (and above all self-contempt), destroying whatever creative powers he might have. His murder is really a form of suicide. A man capable of deep affection, which he can show only critically. Almost wilfully unhappy. Brave.

Nick

Again a very *English* type, buoyantly and humorously on the make, a kind of (self-aware) mascot of the others, coarsely – unlike Martin – devious, always expecting, no, assuming, that he'll be forgiven. The most overtly ambitious, though for nothing (as he really recognizes) of value. Simply getting on and on in the literary world, then no doubt in the television world, just as he would have got on in any world, selling cars perhaps, or as a lawyer. His compulsive smoking is, I presume, an indication of his active, minute-by-minute self-waste. Is he the first character in theatre history to smoke himself to death (well, almost) on stage? A substantial claim. Although all Nick's friends are the ones we see on stage, his natural companion through life is his offstage rival, Harrop, nicknamed 'Nappies', a balding, homosexless derivative poet who is as competitive as Nick (ending up, or middling out, as theatre critic on *The Sunday Times*). So perhaps Nick, who is, I suspect, heterosexless, is a perpetual adolescent, looking for someone to play bloodless competitive sports with.

Peter

Devoted to the sexual act. (Why? Perhaps because he enjoys it. Then why with so many different women?) Begins his sexual career at Cambridge, with pick-ups, easy lays, etc., which becomes as much a habit, really, as Nick's chain-smoking until he falls in love at last (or thinks he does) and wrecks a marriage no better or worse than the one he replaces it with. A generous, hopeless, extravagant soul, doomed to a lifetime of academic self-peddling. A polar opposite of Humphry, who therefore loves him. Like Humphry, he also despises and destroys his own intelligence. Not based on anyone specifically, though I've known one or two people of his sort. I wish more academics had his sweetness of nature, his endless tolerance. There was an exchange in one of the early drafts that went something like this:

PETER: [*having described the mess he's in the middle of making of his life, marriage, etc.*] I don't blame anyone. Not even myself.
STUART: [*I think*] You've always been remarkably tolerant.

(But Stuart – if it was Stuart who said that – would have meant it ironically, and would nevertheless have missed the point. A truly tolerant man doesn't blame himself either.)

McTavish

A rowdily self-righteous Scot, who has rooms above Stuart's at Cambridge. His function is to interrupt. In the play's first scene, he bursts into the room to demand something back, though it's not clear what, as Stuart isn't there. He returns in Act Two, the Epilogue in fact, just after Stuart's return, to demand it again. What he wants, making a magnificent and moralizing fuss about it, is his butter back, having lent it to Stuart a few days before. He is referred to at various other points in the play by his nickname, or rather nicknames: 'McButterback', 'McButtocks', 'McButterbum', etc., although nobody can remember how he came by them. So he has a bit of an intervening offstage life. He once, in a long-ago but not completely forgotten draft, had a scene in the middle of the first act with Stuart and Martin, which I enjoyed writing. But I finally forced myself to cut it. It had no real purpose. Or at least discernible purpose. So there he is, in the first and last scenes, ferociously self-important, ferociously recriminating, ferociously Scots.

[Marigold]

The absence of information about Marigold is explained in the diary.

Plot

There isn't one. Lots of *incidents*, of course. Stuart struggling to save his magazine; Stuart renouncing his magazine to marry Marigold, who is pregnant. Marigold, not realizing Stuart's intentions, having an abortion. Then Stuart married, constantly in one kind of debt or another to Martin, being rendered impotent (by circumstances or merely by me?), getting cuckolded, getting divorced, ending up as a successful literary biographer only too willing to plug his book on Nick's programme. Martin, the old friend and humble ally, being virtually responsible for everything that happens to Stuart. Peter working away at his infidelities, being (an irony intended here) saviour of the magazine that Stuart anyway relinquishes, while betraying his own career, his marriage, etc. Humphry, provoking himself into getting hit by Peter, getting himself murdered. Old Nick, scrambling up the greasy pole into an early grave. I suppose all these people are talented in a way, but in the end their talent doesn't amount to much, i.e. Dr Johnson on Levett: 'To see that single talent well employed.' But no – Martin has a distinct talent for business; Stuart possibly finding and employing his real talent at the play's end, has written 'a good book' – but how good a book?

But let's face it, there really isn't a plot. Simply happenings. Love affairs, abortions, adulteries, treacheries, compromises, lingering deaths, sudden deaths. The routine stuff of English social comedy, in fact.

Further thoughts. The beginning and the ending are crucial to the play's structure. The last scene (the Epilogue) goes back to the first scene, a few minutes on, the rest of the play covering some fifteen – or is it seventeen? – can't quite work it out – years of the characters' lives. The first scene ends with a gramophone playing Wagner. The Epilogue opens with the gramophone still playing the same piece of Wagner, a bit further into it. The thought of seeing people as they were; then seeing them as they become; and finally seeing them as they had been; and the image of a gramophone playing the same piece of music; were the source of the play. Both the idea and the image have haunted me, pestered might be a better word, for years.

Another source is an old friend, Ian Hamilton, editor twenty years ago of that small but potent Oxford literary magazine, *The Review* and subsequently editor of the much grander, more cosmopolitan *The New Review*. He suggested I write a play about his editorial experiences, and furnished me with useful details once I got started. A further source was a television piece I wrote years ago called *Two Sundays*, which alternated scenes between two boys at a public school on a specific Sunday with the same two men in their forties, on a Sunday therefore some twenty-five years on, a gramophone being one of the devices that connected the two couples. The audience wasn't meant to know, I was never quite sure myself, which boy became which man. The real point, though, was time, change, lack of change. When I finished *Two Sundays*, I suspected I hadn't quite finished with it, there was something else there. Which is what we've got now. This is probably of no interest to anyone except myself. But then one likes to be got right. Up to a point, of course. Never to be got *completely* right – otherwise who would 'scape whipping and so forth?* (See *Hamlet*.)

---

* I didn't escape whipping on this one. Several reviewers claimed that I'd stolen the revolving-time effect from Harold Pinter's *Betrayal*, which was written quite a few years after *Two Sundays*.

The Journal

25 November 1983

I finished the play at six this morning, having worked through half the night. I'd also worked through three packages of cigarettes and half a bottle of malt whisky. But the main thing is that it's finished. Olé!

Of course when I say finished, I don't actually mean *finished*. What I mean, actually, is that I've finished the first version of the last draft. If this one goes as the others went, I'll be correcting and revising from about tomorrow night through to the first public performance, or even through to the official first night. This isn't because I'm a perfectionist, but because I get so many things wrong that it takes me the length of rehearsals to notice them all. I wish I wrote plays as Harold does, complete as texts when the ink is still wet on the last words. Or had the panache of Tom Stoppard, who virtually writes his plays in rehearsal, so I'm told. I suppose I'm one of the routine ones. What inspiration I have goes into getting it not quite right in the first place. Still, for the time being I've finished to this extent: the play has a first and a second act. They seem to belong to each other. So olé! Olé with reservations. Let's put it that way.

So at six this morning I numbered the pages, packed and shaped them into a completed-looking pile, toasted myself with a further gulp of whisky and a few more cigarettes, gloated. This, for me, is the only moment of pure happiness I ever experience in the playwriting business. I wish there was some ceremony, some physical ceremony, to express it – picking it up, turning it upside down, slapping its rump, dishing out cigars. But then there'd also be the alternatives, like having to rush it straight into an oxygen tent, or wrapping up its still little form and handing it back to myself, with a muttered: 'Believe me, it's better this way.'

Outside was the dawn and a bit more. Birds knocking about, light, no doubt dew, so forth. I called Hazel from under my desk, where she'd spent the night at my feet, and got up to fetch her lead. I fell over, not quite to the floor full stretch, but to my hands and knees. For a few seconds, or minutes even, Hazel and I were snout to snout. She hates it when this happens, the main distinction between us being, from her point of view, that I'm meant to be upright on two, she's meant to be down there on four. I clambered to my feet by means of the desk and the chair, took a few uncertain steps. (This is beginning to sound like Dick Francis.) Very odd, being so clear-headed, so exhilarated, so triumphant, and yet to have one's knees buckle under one. When I got my balance about right, we went out.

A middle-aged woman was coming up the pavement towards me, full of early-morning virtue and business ahead. A matron in a hospital? A policewoman? What, at six in the morning? Or had *she* just finished a play? They're all over the place these days, playwrights, and there's no knowing what they look like, what sex even. I prepared to give her a salute, spirit to spirit abroad in the dawn, but as I raised my arm she tacked quickly away, to the other side of the street. I suppose that as I was unshaven, my clothes shapeless, my gait unsteady, I looked a bit like a tramp. A tramp who'd just stolen a dog. But nobody would want to steal Hazel except somebody who already loved her. Perhaps we looked as if we were eloping.

Walked through Highgate woods. Very beautiful. Made it home. Went to bed an hour or so before everybody else started getting up.

27 November

Oh Christ. Just noticed I left Marigold off my list of characters. (For list of characters see previous section.) The only woman in the play, and what in lit. crit. essays they call 'the catalyst'. And yet Grahame McTavish, two brief scenes and about five lines, got on my list. What does this mean? It reminds me of *The Rear Column*. Five men who occupy the stage all evening and one woman, a Black girl, who has two minutes or so at the beginning of the third act, stripped to the waist, tied to a post, no dialogue. One afternoon in the New York rehearsal, as she was being tethered by the neck, I heard myself crying out, 'And they say I can't write parts for women!' As a matter of fact, I've written quite a few parts for women. My first television play, *Death of a Teddy Bear*, was about a woman entirely, really; so was *Molly* – actually *Death of a Teddy Bear* transformed into a stage play, and not nearly as good as the original. So I suppose that doesn't count. But *Man in a Side-Car* was also about a woman. And lots of other women, in all my plays *Close of Play* has a woman in the lead, originally to be played by Peggy Ashcroft.* And yet, resist the accusation though I will, the fact remains that I completely forgot Marigold, the only woman in the new play. What shall I say about her?†

28 November

Read through the play again. Made one or two corrections. Worry a bit about Stuart's revelation of impotence (Act Two, Scene One). Speech seems laboured, the conclusion too set up. Pleased, though, with the cats motif, Martin's love of them, ownership of them, cheerful dispatching of them when they become inconvenient. On the whole felt OK. Decided to telephone Harold, let him know that 'something' was on the way, but stressed that it was only work in progress, wouldn't mind some advice. This ploy fooled neither of us. He knows I mean business, or at least want it.

28 November

Evening. A few hours after phoning Harold I read through the play again. Still felt OK, if a trifle tremulous. Tonight I'd like to go out in a top hat, my nose reddened, and swivel around the lampposts. This may be my last chance to celebrate. Soon somebody else

---

* *Close of Play* was done at the National. Rehearsals were interrupted by a series of illnesses and accidents, so that at one point it seemed that we ought to be running a shuttle service between the theatre and the hospital. Then there was the six weeks' strike. And then, as a kind of afterthought, just when we were poised to go ahead, Peggy Ashcroft, who had begun rehearsals with a broken ankle, had to have an emergency operation on her knee, and was forced to withdraw from the production. Almost the greatest regret of my professional life is that she didn't perform in *Close of Play*, a part I would have written especially for her if I'd had the nerve.
† I didn't say anything about her. I think the reason becomes clear further on, during my first conversation about the play with Harold Pinter.

(Harold) will have read it and it'll be on its way – perhaps to nowhere in particular.

A few hours later

Didn't read through the play again, but dipped into it, reading a few pages, jumping, reading a few more. Saw urgent need, on every page I looked at, for revision. Began to make corrections but gave it up, as tomorrow I have to make photocopies, one of which will go to Harold. I'd like it to look spruce. Some of the dialogue is distinctly leaden. Made me think yearningly of the chap once known on Broadway as 'Doc', because he began his career doctoring other people's plays. Always a bad moment for the playwright when he came into rehearsal and found 'Doc' ensconced in an aisle seat, a pad on his knees, working on some salvaging one-liners. Or was it really a good moment, knowing that his play was receiving the best medical attention? 'Doc' must have picked up a few tips in his turn, as he went on to become Neil Simon, most successful living American playwright. Is anyone called in to doctor his plays, I wonder, now that he writes them instead of doctoring them?

28–29 November

Read the play through again after all. See further problems, notably Grahame McTavish, Marigold, great sections of speeches here and there. But cling to the view that it's OK. That is, taken as a whole.

Thursday, 30 November

I spent the day correcting and amending little passages, typing out the pages to keep them neat, then getting the play photocopied. I didn't go into College, (Queen Mary, down the Mile End Road) although I was meant to be teaching. In the evening I took the play around to Harold's. I was in a highly sensitive state, possibly even hysterical.

I had arranged to meet him in his studio at the bottom of the garden of his Holland Park house, which has a separate entrance on a parallel street. For some reason I still can't fathom, I went to the main house and was received by Antonia. I met her surprise with an attempt at insouciance, made the usual enquiries, answered the usual enquiries, and then allowed myself to be gestured towards the studio. I have made this journey many times before, in both directions. How, then, did I manage to walk straight into the trellis gate that separates the house garden from the studio patio, virtually straight through it in fact, kicking out a lump or two of wood in the process? Harold, alerted (with good reason) by Antonia that I was on my way, came out to greet me as I was bent double, trying to pack some of the wood back. I expect he wondered what I was up to. I didn't try to explain, except with half-gestures and a grunt. We went into the studio, had a few drinks. I talked almost all the time, my mind ranging freely over the play in the blue shoulder bag, my tongue dealing with quite other topics, many other topics. When I decided the time had come to leave, I swung the blue shoulder bag back over my shoulder, and made for the door. I suppose I would have left without handing the play over if Harold hadn't asked for it. He said he would read it tomorrow. We would meet in the evening, at L'Epicure, to discuss it. So that's that.

Friday, 1 December

Had lunch with David Jones, to consider approaches to a film version of *The Rector's Daughter*, which I've been longing to do for years. David Jones, who likes the book as much as I do, wants to direct it. It was a useful lunch, even though a lot of the time my attention was straying to images of Harold — at that very moment reading the play; or sitting glumly with it on his lap, having read it. I went home and hung about waiting for our dinner date, feeling slightly sick. I was also worried about our having chosen L'Epicure, because traditionally that's where we go to celebrate after (a) he's liked a play, and (b) made it clear that he'd like to direct it. In this case, it seemed to me, we'd taken a serious risk. Challenged the gods. So forth. Just before I left to meet him, he telephoned, sensitive to the kind of state I'd be in. One of the advantages of working with a fellow playwright is that he knows about the vanities, the timidities, the sheer terror attendant on sending a play out for the first time. He said that he was very excited, loved its structure, be of good cheer, only had four points to discuss. I set off for L'Epicure in highish spirits, that sank a bit on the tube, as I began to wonder what the four points were.

It occurred to me that there are only five scenes in the play. Perhaps he really meant that four of them were wrong. But would he actually say, 'Be of good cheer. Only four of your five scenes are wrong'? By the time I got to the restaurant I'd worked myself into a bit of a frenzy, made worse by his being, for almost the first time in my long experience of him, late. He is almost obsessively punctual. I had to wait for twenty extremely bad minutes, chain-smoking, staring towards the door, checking my watch, starting to my feet, had I got the restaurant wrong, had he funked it, made the mistake of rereading it, etc.

When he arrived, having been delayed by a protracted meeting to do with his cricket club, the Gaieties we got off to a sensational start by his proclaiming that he was delighted with the play. He already seemed to have grasped it. Grasped, I mean, not only its structure, what it was about, that sort of thing, but lots of its details, even to remembering quite a few of the lines. All on one reading. I kept him lingering around the compliments for as long as I decently could, then let him get to the four points. Which were as follows:

1 Old Grahame McTavish. An intrusion, one that doesn't belong within the play's world. Also he doesn't think that the part, whittled down to a few lines of Scots bluster, justified hiring an actor. He also feels that the idea embodied in McTavish is already done in various offstage characters. The name seems to him a give-away: farcical and unconvincing. Or was it I who made that point? Anyway, McTavish's got to go. I knew it.

2 Marigold. Or specifically, the scene in which she tells Stuart she's had an abortion. In Harold's view, too portentously a 'scene', signalling itself as a solemn piece of theatre instead of maintaining the tone already established, which is not, I hope, at all solemn.

3 Marigold again. This time the later scene, in which she tells Stuart and Martin that she's pregnant. Harold feels the same about this as about the earlier scene, in other words, portentous. This led us on to a discussion of her character as a whole. He feels that she has more life, individual life, in the first short scene

than in her two major ones, where she is being rather ceremonially presented as 'woman', with her 'womanly' nature, 'womanly' virtues. I admitted that I'd always had a slightly numb feeling about those two scenes, but didn't admit that I had actually forgotten her when drawing up my list of characters the other evening. He tried to persuade me to have another look at her, to find her in the particular rather than in the general. I put up some resistance, not because I didn't think he was right, but because I wasn't sure I could face going back to a section of the play on such large terms. He said they weren't large, that the structure of the scenes was fine, it was really just a question of finding a slightly different line in the dialogue. In the end I agreed to give it a go. What worries me is that I might go on to rewrite the whole play, drafts on drafts of it. I'm a compulsive. He knows that. Anyway, I reminded him that I was.

4 Stuart. Act Two, Scene One. Really, Stuart's explanation to Martin as to why he wants to quit Martin's publishing firm. Harold feels that Stuart has thought his speeches out too clearly, which therefore makes them seem rehearsed. My defence was that the speech actually has been rehearsed. There's a line, I pointed out, in which Stuart says he's 'thought it all out' while sitting on the hospital steps after his visit to the dying poet, Hubert Parkin (an offstage figure who dogs Stuart's life). Harold looked suddenly alert. 'Where is this line? I don't remember a line like that.' I showed him in my copy. He checked in his, where there wasn't a line, only a white smear, where a line might have been. Of course I realize it doesn't matter whether the line was there or not. The fact that Stuart says that he's 'thought out' what he wants to say doesn't mean that he's rehearsed his speech cadence by cadence. The truth is, I realized, looking at it with Harold then and looking at it several times since, that it's a rather dead, or more likely, over-written exchange, in which nothing is left to chance, no unexpected thought, no uncertainty. The wrong pulse in the rhythms. He ended rather oddly by drawing attention to Stuart's long speech about Martina, the cat, but didn't amplify, perhaps because he's not yet sure what it is he's drawing my attention to. There's nothing wrong with the speech itself, as far as I can see.

So there were the four points, none of them involving many hours work, all of them crucial. In making them, Harold had already begun to direct the play. So there we were, half-way through dinner, beaming away at each other, about to embark on a new production. This fairly prolonged lyrical passage ended when we began to discuss dates, his availability and mine. When it comes to putting a play of mine on, I'm always available, but he's committed to writing a film for Joe Losey,* so can't begin until the late summer of next year. Suits me perfectly, apart from not being anything like soon enough. Then we discussed a producer.

I was slightly surprised that we should need to, having assumed that we would go, as we've always done (except once, when we went to the National), to Michael Codron, who after all has produced all my West End plays. But Harold's view was that Michael wouldn't want to do it. He would love the play but would find it uncommercial. First of all he would think its world too enclosed and secondly it isn't a vehicle for stars, and Michael, like most West End producers these days, prefers to go into a theatre with a star or two.† Everything Harold said made sense, but I still felt I had an obligation to offer the play to Michael anyway both because of our past association; and because he's the best producer in the West End. Also, as I pointed out to Harold, if it weren't for Michael, I would never have written stage plays at all, which perhaps means that he has a lot to answer for, and deserves all he gets; even a crack at my latest. We left it that I'd get in touch with Michael tomorrow – today – tomorrow, depending on what time it is. Today. Later today. Also that we'd ask him to decide quickly. Within a week would be nice. Harold asked me, by the way, to report to Michael his prediction of Michael's response.

Saturday, 3 December

I phoned Michael up – he was in the country – to tell him that I'd written a new play and that I'd bring it around on Monday. He said he was going to Boston on Tuesday for Tom Stoppard's *The*

* Joe Losey became ill just before we began rehearsals and died during them.
† But not more. Too expensive.

Real Thing, and that he would read it on the plane. He would phone me soon after he arrived. He sounded quite excited, I thought, until I passed on Harold's prediction. Then he sounded apprehensive.

Sunday, 4 December

Beryl (my wife) has ricked her back, and is confined to bed. Every movement hurts. We decided that I shouldn't take Lucy back to school (she is a weekly boarder just outside Haslemere) as it would mean leaving Beryl on her own for four hours or so, immobile. I'll take Lucy back tomorrow, then go straight on to Michael's office.

Monday, 5 December

Sitting on the train on my way back from delivering Lucy to Haslemere, with Michael's copy of the play in my shoulder bag, I suddenly noticed an elderly man in the seat diametrically opposite. He reminded me of my father, although in every respect except one quite unlike him. The central character of *Close of Play*, Jasper, was based on my father. Jasper is in fact dead (my father died a year or so before I wrote the play) but is forced to endure, as if alive, a traditional English Sunday, helpless in his favourite armchair as his three sons and their wives fall to pieces in the usual English middle-class style, sometimes blaming him, sometimes appealing to him for help and sobbing at his feet for forgiveness, but basically ignoring him as they squabble around him. In other words I'd stuck him in Hell, which turns out to be 'life, old life itself'.*

When I went in on the first day of rehearsal Michael Redgrave, who was playing Jasper, was sitting in a chair, his jaw out-thrust, which gave me a slight chill as I had been going to suggest that he thrust his jaw out in performance, this being my father's most striking characteristic. I'd remembered it all the way through writing the play. My son thrusts his jaw out, by the way; so do both my brothers. I do it myself. All the male Grays do it, when tired. Sometimes, when we're all together in a room, we look like a gang of antique simians, particularly if our right hands are also, as they

---

* This phrase, which recurs throughout the diaries, is a quotation from *The Common Pursuit* (Stuart to Marigold, Act One, Scene Two).

frequently are, resting in our left armpits. The point I'm coming to is that the elderly man sitting diametrically opposite was doing both these things, sitting with his jaw stuck out, his right hand tucked into his left armpit, thus taking me back through Michael Redgrave to the image of my father, especially in the last months of his life, his jaw almost permanently thrust out in fatigue, despair, defeat. The elderly man on the train looked as if he, too, were in some state of despair or defeat. He had cheap rings on his fingers, but his shoes weren't properly laced and his trousers were stained. When we got into Waterloo, I passed him on the platform, and glanced casually down at his large, brown, almost empty, from the way he was carrying it, suitcase. The name 'James Gray' (my father's name was James) was painted on it in bold white letters, which gave me one of those hair-raising moments in life that I'm on the whole sure no one actually wants to be without, but never particularly wants at the moments when they come.

Michael Codron had just got back from an Equity meeting when I arrived. He came out of his office to greet me, then escorted me into it. I took out of my blue shoulder bag the large brown envelope and handed it to him. He received it gingerly, almost as if puzzled, seeming to weigh it in his hands, putting it on his desk, picking it up again, putting it down. All the time he kept saying, in a slightly strangled voice, 'Well, I very much *want* to like it. I do *want* to like it. I do *hope* I like it.' The accumulation of repetitions, along with his peculiar physical relationship with the envelope, as if it contained a relic both sacred and disgusting, had a rather pole-axing effect on me. I felt that he'd already lost his preliminary skirmish with attempting to like it. We had a briefish conversation about this and that, with both this and that seeming to lead us back to mild recriminations from both sides about our behaviour to each other in past productions. Michael said he sometimes felt that we (Harold and I) didn't sufficiently realize that as producer he very much wanted to produce. That is, to take part in the casting, the discussions on set design, all that kind of thing. In short, that's why he was in the business of producing. What Americans would call the 'creative' part of producing.* 'But why didn't you tell me this

---

* Though, unlike Michael, most American producers' idea of 'creative' producing is to fire people, preferably actors. They can't think of anything else to do with them once they've hired them. My first experience of this came during a Broadway

before?' I asked at one point. He gave me the look that I suppose the question deserved, and took me in to see David, his partner, whom I've known over many years, and who had previously never failed to give me a cheery welcome. He was on the telephone. He greeted me by raising his hand and then turning his back on me.* I left with Michael promising to read the play on the plane to Boston, and to phone me as soon as he arrived, but really with the words, 'I do want to like it, do hope to like it' ringing hollowly in my ears.

I went home, put a hot-water bottle or two under Beryl's back, phoned Harold and gave him the facts and some of the flavour of my conversation with Michael. I explained, too, about Michael's wanting actively to be a producer, not simply to be the money behind an already designed package. Harold said, 'Well, he's never said anything like that to me' and I said, remembering Michael's look when I'd said much the same, that I suspected Michael assumed that he shouldn't have had to say it, we ought to have known.

Tuesday

Michael now ensconced in Boston. Hasn't phoned.

Wednesday

Spent the day working on the text, along the lines discussed with Harold. Finally killed off Grahame McTavish. Minded a *bit*. Nothing from Michael in Boston. Hate waiting for the telephone to ring. I think I can work out what its silence means.

---

production of one of my early plays. I was driven straight from the airport to the rehearsal room, where, jet-lagged and slightly drunk, I sat through the first act. The producer, who actually *was* short and squat and smoking a cigar, sat down beside me and asked me what I thought. Lacking any thought, having been mainly comatose, I said vaguely that perhaps one of the actors, looking at a cluster of them in a corner and arbitrarily indicating the one who was closest, possibly needed a bit of attention. 'Want me to fire him?' he asked, rising eagerly to his feet. What he was trying to do, of course, was to resolve his professional identity crisis creatively.
* I learnt later from Michael that David was having a most difficult conversation, and didn't even take in whoever it was Michael had brought into his office.

Thursday

Had a *nuit blanche* fuming at Michael for not having phoned, then attempted to exonerate him on comforting grounds, i.e. his plane had crashed, he'd been mugged, *The Real Thing* was a disaster, etc., before finally making it to sleep at about 9 am. Michael then phoned. Not from Boston, but from London. He'd postponed his Boston trip because he'd been ill, was leaving for Boston in an hour or so. His first words were, 'Harold's quite right. I like it hugely, *hugely*, but I don't think it's commercial.' Not because the world of the play's too confined, but because he doesn't see how, given six equal parts, we could attract any stars. He doesn't want to be part of it if we insist on starting it off in the West End, but would like to be part of it if we'll consider going with a young and unstarry cast to the Lyric, Hammersmith, or Greenwich, from which we might get ourselves wooed or invited into the West End. What did I feel? I said I'd think about it and discuss it with Harold, but could see his point, and trusted his judgement.

My real feelings were, actually, mainly of resentment that he hadn't (a) insisted on buying the play immediately, on any terms; with a view to putting it on at any theatre of my choice, on any terms; (b) which amounts to the same thing, that he hadn't talked about the play at length, analysing its structure, revelling in its characters and dialogue, and generally showering it (me) with compliments. Nevertheless, I suspect Michael's right. We probably won't get a star or two, of the kind that people will pay to see whatever the reviews are like. And unspoken between Michael and myself is the knowledge that my plays generally get bad reviews,* with the probability that this one will fare worse than usual.

I telephoned Harold to give him a summary of my talk with Michael. We agreed to meet very shortly and consider it properly. He's not opposed to Greenwich or Hammersmith in principle. He wasn't of course surprised by Michael's rather ambivalent reaction – as it conformed precisely to his prediction.

* *Butley*, for instance, got mainly poor reviews, but had Alan Bates in the lead, and did very well. It's now generally assumed that it got good reviews, an assumption that I do nothing to discourage, especially as it's now actually beginning to get some.

Friday

Beryl has at last read the play, having put off doing so until she'd finished a piece of work of her own – or until she could actually face up to the months ahead, the obsessiveness, the bouts of paranoia concluding in grim, denunciatory *post mortems*. I was out when she read it, and she was out when I got back, so she left her views on the telephone answering machine. She has a number of what she calls 'wifely worries' to do with the literary world as the play presents it, and of how 'they'll' take it. She's particularly concerned over the joke about 'Nappies' Harrop being appointed theatre critic on *The Sunday Times* because of his 'lack of qualifications'. She felt I was asking for trouble. When she got back, I assured her that it was such a minor part of the evening, really coming down to one line, and that line *en passant* – and besides, reverting to a traditional tack, I wrote what I wrote and had to stand by it, the whole kit and caboodle – we'd wait and see how it went in previews – one could always adjust it.

Weekend

Nothing of interest. Several desultory conversations with Harold. We're meeting before Michael gets back from Boston.

Monday, Tuesday, Wednesday

Mainly working on a draft of *The Rector's Daughter*, but also looked at the play, going over the scenes discussed with Harold. Grahame McTavish gone. (Actually a few days ago. I think I've recorded that butchery.) Stuart's resignation speeches to Martin rewritten. I've encouraged Marigold to take me by surprise in her dialogue.

Thursday

Creepy. Creepy, creepy, creepy. I give two long seminars at Queen Mary on Thursday afternoons, one on something called 'Practical Criticism', which in effect means reading a poem or a passage from a poem or a piece of prose with students, and then going through it to find out what we think about it, who likes it, why? I always try to do something I've forgotten, or best of all, don't know, so that I'm as new to it as they are, which helps us both. I've often found myself liking or, if not liking, admiring poetry I've got into the comfortable habit of assuming I hate. This afternoon it was a lump from *Paradise Lost*. My established view of *Paradise Lost* is that it's a gigantic and exhausting bluff, reminding me of that Scots preacher who used to write in the margins of his sermons, 'Weak point here. Shout like hell.' But this afternoon I happened to hit on a passage from Book 2 – I can't be bothered to go on with this. Because what I really want to talk about is what happened after the seminar. No, it was after the *second* seminar, when we read bits of plays, examine them as if they were being rehearsed for production, so that students begin to get the idea that in Shakespeare, for instance, there's a lot of (frequently very interesting) life going on among the characters who aren't speaking. Anyway, I gave the two seminars, and was sitting in my office, jaded and irritable, wondering who to phone up and what excuse to offer, and also eyeing my typewriter and contemplating an attempt at *The Rector's Daughter*, when there was a knock on the door. A student, a girl, put her head in. I worked up one of those welcoming smiles that means, 'Don't move another inch.' She said, 'Oh, I don't want to disturb you, but I forgot to tell you earlier. Grahame McTavish sends his regards.' The hair on the back of my neck did what hair is reported to do on these occasions. 'Who?' 'Grahame McTavish. Don't you remember Grahame? He was in the drama seminar last year.' Upon which I remembered Grahame McTavish, a tall, limber, authoritative, and very English youth, with a powerful voice and strong bone structure.

The fact is that I've always had a problem remembering names, and connecting them to faces. I wonder who all the other names in the play belong to, and also what Grahame McTavish would have felt if I'd sent a message back saying that I couldn't accept his regards as I'd eliminated him a few days ago on the grounds that he's too coarse and farcical a figure, with too bogus a name, to be allowed to inhabit my refined fictional world.

9 December

I've thrown out all the previous versions, drafts, etc., of the play. I don't know if that's of interest to anyone but myself, but the fact is I had trouble lifting this dreadful accumulation of scenes, half-scenes, drafts. There were pages of the play that simply haven't changed very much and pages that I'd rejected, and scenes written pointlessly again and again because I was making no progress with them and kept thinking that if I wrote them through from the beginning they'd decide out of sheer boredom to end up somewhere differently. Anyway, there they all were, unliftable in a wastepaper basket. Although the wastepaper basket is actually an enormous wicker basket, not easily liftable in itself. Perhaps the rubbish men will refuse it. They're very choosy around here. What if I were to be confronted with a container holding all the ends of the cigarettes I'd smoked during the writing of the play? And another holding all the empty bottles?

I've pretty well decided to call the play *Partners*. And subtitle it 'Scenes from the Literary Life'.

I've been meditating on and off about something Harold said at the dinner after he'd just read the play. That I keep all my characters on a tight rein. I suppose that's one of the many differences between us. Harold can have a perfectly appropriate, or he makes it seem appropriate, monologue on, for example, the location of Bolsover Street (in *No Man's Land*) which is nevertheless apropos of nothing, and to which there may well be no further reference after no previous reference. I can't do that. My characters live within a precise, probably over-precise, world, and everything they say is in some way or another to do with it. There's scarcely a line in *The Rear Column* that doesn't arise from the practical problems of being marooned in the Congo. The same is true of this play. I must get into the habit of calling it *Partners*. The same is true of *Partners*. All of it is life in practice. The characters are mired in it. Harold's characters, though seemingly locked in habits and circumstances, always have an ultimate freedom from thisness or thatness which is likely to express itself in an aria of free-wheeling lunacy, sometimes comic, sometimes frightening, but never needing justification. Perhaps Charlie Peak, Professor of English at Queen Mary College, and a great admirer of Harold's, would like to add some notes to all this.

On the question of Queen Mary College. When I mentioned to some of my colleagues last Thursday that I had finished a new play, they immediately and adroitly changed the subject to something vastly more interesting, from their point of view.

12 December, 9 pm

Had lunch with Harold. The main issue was, of course, how to proceed with Michael. Or without him. Harold's view, which he came to over the meal, was that Michael had already signalled that he didn't want to produce the play, and that perhaps therefore we should let him off the hook by looking for another producer. This seems sensible, although depressing. I find it difficult to contemplate Michael not being involved in some way. We went on to consider alternatives. I should say that Harold, having just completed the film script of *Turtle Diary*, was in a state of exhilarated clear-headedness. My own head was stuffed with half-realized apprehensions, most of the exhilaration of having finished *Partners* having worn off. The main alternative was UBA (United British Artists), a consortium got together by the actor, Richard Johnson, with a board consisting entirely, apart from an accountant and/or lawyer, of actors – Glenda Jackson, John Hurt, Albert Finney, Maggie Smith, etc. – with the intention of making films and producing plays. As Harold had just accepted an invitation to join the board, and they were about to commission me to write the film script of *The Rector's Daughter*, we decided that Harold should show the play – offer it, really – to Richard Johnson. This has another advantage in that, given Harold's imminent connection with UBA, and my own imminent connection, Michael and I should be able to extricate ourselves from each other without distress to either side.

And yet. And yet. Beryl being out, I had a meal at a Chinese restaurant up in the village (Highgate). I have an odd relationship with the owner there. Years ago, when I went in with a friend for lunch, I asked him, quite politely, to turn the music either down or preferably off altogether. His response was to tell me to fuck off. Which I did, with appropriately dignified gestures and exclamations. Nevertheless, I've started going back there, and he's started treating me with great civility, now and then bringing to the table a free brandy. I've no idea why either of us behaved as we did, or are now behaving as we are. Except that I love Chinese food, and there isn't another Chinese restaurant for miles; and he needs as much custom as he can get. Perhaps that's the explanation.* As I sat brooding over my duck, I suddenly remembered that I hadn't reported to Judy Daish, who is agent to both Harold and myself, what we'd decided about UBA. I phoned her from the restaurant, got her at the office, and inevitably found myself unleashing all my worries about Michael. She was very calming, certain that we would end up with a producer who would do well by the play – 'and that's all that matters'. True. The problem for me is, after so many productions with Michael, it's no longer just business. Somewhere between personal and business, which is exactly the wrong spot, according to *The Godfather*.

But I'm not the only one in a stew about producers. Arnold Wesker phoned this morning to ask me about Ken Frankel, who directed the American production of *Quartermaine's Terms*, and is about to do Arnold's *Loveletters on Blue Paper* for the Hudson Guild in New York. Or was about to, Arnold having withdrawn the play when told that the Hudson Guild could pay him only a five hundred dollar fee, and no royalties. He's just received a letter from Ken Frankel telling him he's mad to withdraw the play, what matters is to give it an airing in a showcase, get along the critics, work for a transfer to another theatre, which will pay royalties on a (with luck) decent run. Arnold was sure I'd be on his side. Five hundred dollars is a miserable amount, after all. But I argued passionately for Ken Frankel's position. What matters in New York these days is not where you open but where you move to. I think I managed to change his mind. I hope so, as I know I'm right. I always know I'm right when deciding other people's destinies. Partly, I suppose, because I don't have to worry too much about the consequences. In my own case, the consequences being so serious, I worry continuously, and therefore usually make the wrong decision. Which brings me back to worrying about Michael Codron on the one hand, UBA on the other.

13 December

Michael back from Boston previews of *The Real Thing*. I told him that we'd decided to approach UBA. He sounded first surprised;

* But he still hasn't turned the music off.

then dignified; finally fed-up. It was agreed that he should have further discussions with Judy. I hung up feeling that I'd been a shit. I put the matter cogently but objectively to Beryl, pointing her carefully to the right conclusion, that it's really all Michael's fault for not having been more enthusiastic when he received the play. Beryl, however, let me down yet again by pointing out that all Michael had done was to agree with Harold that the play was uncommercial, and offer to do the best for it by going to Greenwich or Hammersmith or wherever, where we might well end up doing it anyway but without Michael, and what would be the advantage of *that*, she asked? In other words, she suggested that I was being impatient, and possibly even paranoid. She's possibly right, which seems to me even more unfair.

(There followed various conversations between Michael and Judy, Judy and Harold, Michael and me, Judy and me, Harold and me, the upshot of which was that (a) Michael felt the whole affair had become too muddied, and didn't want to be involved, and (b) that we shouldn't consider that the door between us was closed, as he'd like to read the play again, with a view to making an offer. Could we please get him a copy of the play before he went to New York for the opening of *The Real Thing*? In the meanwhile, between conversations with Michael, at a point when he appeared definitively to have withdrawn, Judy sent the play to Richard Johnson who promised to read it before the launching party for his newly founded company. I had been invited to the party. So, of course, had Harold. In fact, the party was being given on the day on which Harold was to become a member of the UBA board.)

Monday, 19 December

The UBA launch party, a lunchtime affair. I went along in a fairly smouldering state, not having heard a word from Richard Johnson, although Judy had left him numerous messages. I took my shoulder bag with me, with nothing in it except, I think, a handkerchief. I had an idea the bag would make me look distinctive – I might at least succeed in getting myself searched.* I wasn't searched at the

* The only time I've ever had my bag searched was in a seedy cinema below Leicester

launch although I'd packed the bag *en route* with a *Standard* and a few other newspapers to give it purpose and me an air of intent. It was being held in a restaurant off Wardour Street, new and in the American mode, with an upstairs, large and airy for ordinary lunches, and a downstairs, large and airless for UBA. The room was full of journalists, film directors, actors, theatre directors, and more journalists, a covey of whom were gathered around Harold, in black as usual. The journalists seemed to be in pinks or light blues, pastel, and crouching slightly as if they were taking pictures, though I didn't see any cameras. I think this was an illusion on my part, both the crouching and the colours, but that was the effect. Harold standing blackly upright in a little circle of crouching pastels. I ploughed my way shyly through to him, nudging the pastels out of the way and him into a corner. He asked me whether I'd spoken to Richard Johnson. I said I hadn't. He gestured to a circle of about nine people, in the midst of whom Richard Johnson was standing, fluently outlining his plans for UBA. 'Well,' Harold said, 'he loves the play. Bowled over by it. Mentioned it at the board meeting this morning.' We collected some champagne from a passing tray, talked a little longer, separated.

On my way towards Richard Johnson, who was now outlining his plans to about four journalists, I bumped into David Jones, who will, I hope, be directing *The Rector's Daughter* if the script gets written, the money raised, the film made. But all the time I was keeping a track on Richard Johnson who was now down to two journalists. I left David Jones and went up to him. His eye, I might say, completely failed to take me in. Perhaps because it was a trifle bleary. Or perhaps because, in spite of being six feet *and* sporting a blue shoulder bag, I don't cut much visual ice. I waited until the two journalists were down to one, a humble-looking grey-haired woman with a squint, who's probably ruined more reputations than I've had hot dinners, then scooped up another glass of champagne and interposed myself between them. He outlined some of his plans for UBA before taking in that I wasn't one of the journalists, but one of his plans. I told him I gathered he'd read *Partners*, and so got him into our talk.

Square. The Irish-looking chap who went in ahead of me, who was carrying several carrier bags and had a brown paper parcel tucked under his arm, didn't have anything searched.

He began promisingly by being immensely enthusiastic, describing it as wonderful, terrific, wonderful, moving, tragic, funny, just what UBA needed, a new play to announce at the launch, before extending the same sentence into a couple of provisos, the first of these being that *Partners* would have to be read by all the other members of the board: John Hurt, Maggie Smith, Glenda Jackson, Diana Rigg, Albert Finney, Uncle Tom Cobblers and all, which struck me as preposterous because what actor wants to read a play in which there is no conceivable part for him- or herself. But he was adamant, his sentence running on well above my protests, that this protocol would have to be observed, not, *not* that it mattered what they thought because the actors almost certainly wouldn't get around to it, why should they bother with a play they couldn't possibly be in, but on the other hand, *the other hand*, did I know that Harold wouldn't be free to do the play until the autumn, he had a previous commitment? I said I wasn't sure that that was the case. It depended rather, didn't it, on whether the film he was currently discussing with Joe Losey actually happened or not. If it didn't happen then Harold would want to do it in the spring, wouldn't he? 'But one should assume the autumn, shouldn't we?' Richard Johnson asked firmly. I should admit here, confidentially, that Richard Johnson, in the conversation so far, was striking off a very good impersonation of a chap who is keen on champagne, with a lot of it to hand. I wasn't altogether sober myself, being now on my fourth or fifth glass with an empty stomach waiting to receive it. He reverted briefly to the play, still finding it wonderful, terrific, wonderful, and then moved on to the question of how much I was going to be paid by UBA for *The Rector's Daughter* (my doing of which he'd apparently announced to the press), and his feeling that Judy (my agent) ought perhaps to discuss the matter with him yet again. He mentioned this in terms that clearly indicated a downgrading of what I'd been offered so far, which was nothing, as far as I knew. So the rest of the conversation was not to do with *Partners*, but to do with how much less money than the money he hadn't so far offered me he could get me to do *The Rector's Daughter* for. He then clutched my shoulder firmly, business satisfactorily concluded, from which, in retrospect, I deduce that he wasn't at all drunk; just practising producing, and went off to outline his plans for UBA to a cluster of journalists who had probably innocently thought their day's work was done, and that they could get down to the champagne and canapés at last.

I rocked about on uncertain feet, watching the board being photographed: Finney, Glenda Jackson, Harold, Richard Johnson, Tom Cobbler, and an enigma I took to be the solicitor and/or accountant. Taken individually they were pretty glamorous. But forced by the press photographers into a homogeneous group, they suddenly looked like a gang of corrupt prep-school teachers. Group photography is like group therapy, it exposes the worst in people, even if it isn't there. Harold detached himself as rapidly as he could, and told me to stop worrying. Richard Johnson wanted very much to do the play. We'd meet soon with Judy to discuss the next move.

Having thought about the above for several hours, I have come to realize that all my sourness really stems from Richard Johnson's forcing me to come to his party to find out what he thought about my play, instead of phoning when he said he would. Surely people understand that when one hands them a script, one expects them to read it within minutes, and comment on it both profoundly and favourably for weeks afterwards.

21 December

This afternoon I went to Harold's studio, where he and Judy had already had a long talk. Harold began by telling me that the projected film with Joe Losey was off for the foreseeable future, and that he therefore wanted to get on with *Partners* as soon as possible. Judy then said that she'd informed Richard Johnson of Harold's changed schedule and that Richard Johnson was aghast, UBA being committed to other projects until late summer. Nevertheless he was sure he could raise the money for a spring production,* and would phone in at four o'clock to confirm that he had.

We mulled over the situation and came firmly to the following conclusion: that we would wait for Richard Johnson's call. We did. It didn't come. Judy tried to contact him. He wasn't to be found. An hour and a half after he was supposed to call, we turned back to the Michael Codron question. I put the case for going ahead with Michael fairly passionately, my heart always having been in it. We

* From a Greek producer of his acquaintance. Of everybody's acquaintance, in fact.

agreed to send the script around to him immediately. I phoned Michael to tell him it was on its way. He'd left for New York half an hour before. We mulled. And mulled. It suddenly struck Judy that as we all really wanted the play to be done outside the West End, and that as the Lyric, Hammersmith, was our first choice, why didn't we settle that part of it, at least? Especially as she knew the theatre was available during the weeks that Harold was now free to rehearse in. If the Lyric wanted to do it, we could turn to Michael Codron, to UBA, or to a third producer, whom we could invite to participate in the subsequent West End production. We agreed that Judy should send a script around to Peter James, the artistic director of the Lyric, Hammersmith.

What this means, I now realize, is that owing to the muddle of the last few weeks we have somehow contrived to have the play on offer to three managements at the same time – to Michael, to UBA, and to the Lyric. This doesn't seem to me an altogether distinguished moral position.

The other matter we discussed was the designer. Actually, there wasn't much discussion because every play of mine that Harold's directed has been designed by Eileen Diss, with whom we both feel comfortable, mainly because she's a superb designer, and also a kindly and intelligent woman. Also she's beautiful. I can't see what other qualifications a designer needs, when it comes down to it. So we agreed to send the play to Eileen, Harold having already checked on her availability.

When I got home, I thought about the design. There are two sets; Stuart's rooms in Cambridge, then Stuart's office in London (which becomes Martin's office), then, in the Epilogue, Stuart's rooms in Cambridge again. The transitions from Cambridge to London, then back to Cambridge, have got to be effected very quickly, as they both come mid-act. That seems to me the major technical consideration. But there's a gap of years between the other scenes, when the set doesn't change, though time (a lot of it) goes by. I'm quite proud of the way in which I've worked this out, arranging the characters so that the ones who start a scene are always off before the end of the previous scene, giving them time to change, put on moustaches, wigs, whatever. Tonight, flicking through the play, I noticed that in one scene I've left a character (Nick) on stage, though he initiates the next scene, which takes place years later, thus giving him no time offstage to change costume, and to age. I've had to do some rewriting, getting him off earlier, while keeping the other characters on stage. I hope it works. It seems to me a more serious matter, at least right now, than who is to produce the play.

I have another little problem. I'm meant to be writing a film script of *The Rector's Daughter*, which I'm failing to write because I'm talking into a tape and worrying about *Partners*, and its future.

23 December

11 am

Judy sent a copy of *Partners* to Peter James at the Lyric, Hammersmith. He is going to phone her back at 5 pm to let her know whether he wants to do it.

5.30 pm

I've just phoned Judy to find out whether Peter James has phoned her. He hasn't. These people and their attitudes to people who write plays seem to me beyond belief.

7 pm

Judy still hasn't phoned me, from which I deduce that Peter James still hasn't phoned her. You'd think he could at least phone her to apologize for not being able to phone her.

8 pm

Judy phoned to say that Peter James had just phoned to say that he wants to do the play. Furthermore, that he wants the Lyric to produce it subsequently in the West End. Apparently they (who?) have just set up an investment company. *Partners* will be their first commercial venture. Thus at a stroke we have not only our theatre, but our long-term producer. Terrific. No more problems. Except that the play is still on offer to Michael and UBA.

25 December

Harold phoned to exchange Christmas whatsits. He goes to New York on Tuesday to have a look at Ken Frankel's production of

Old Times. We arranged that I should go around to his studio tomorrow to get on with casting. He's very pleased about the Lyric. He's already discussed dates with Peter James. The play will open some time in June, rehearsals therefore in May, if that's all right with me. It is.

(This was where we ended up – at the Lyric, Hammersmith, with the management of the Lyric as producers. But it wasn't, of course, quite the end of the matter. I phoned Michael when he got back from New York, where he'd gone for the first night of Michael Frayn's *Noises Off.* He sounded very glum about his successes – *The Real Thing* as well as *Noises Off* being the two biggest hits for years, with lashings of money all around. When I asked him why he was glum, he said it was because he kept having to go to New York. I told him we'd decided to shack up with the Lyric, and that they didn't want another producer involved. He said that he was sure that the Lyric was the right theatre for the play, was glad that Peter James had finally taken the step into producing, and wished us well. He also said that if we *did* need a producer, to let him know. So that was nice. Richard Johnson, however, who had only got around to phoning Judy days after his four o'clock deadline, knew only that we'd decided to send the play to the Lyric (which he also thought the right theatre to start from) but not that the management had set up its own production company and wanted to produce the play themselves. He had spent an intensely active Christmas, raising the money to produce the play, then phoned Judy up to announce triumphantly that UBA was ready to go ahead – first at the Lyric, then on to the West End. Inevitably, there was a lot of trouble between Judy, Richard Johnson and the Lyric, accusations and counter-accusations on the telephone, and dignified summaries in letters, until all the parties concerned realized that nobody meant to deceive anybody, and Richard Johnson withdrew gracefully. I don't go into any of this in detail because it was tedious to report into the machine as it was happening; was tedious and expensive to have transcribed; was tedious to read when transcribed; and would be tedious to edit into a coherent narrative, which it would still be tedious to read. My own feeling, though, which persisted throughout the subsequent weeks and through to the end of the production, was that we'd got off, through nobody's fault, to a poisoned start. And that in our beginnings are our ends. Or some such.)

28 December

Beryl and I went to a party at Martin and Judith Bax's, just down the road, an annual Christmas event. Martin is a paediatrician, a novelist, and the editor of the literary magazine *Ambit*. One of his advisers on *Ambit* is Irving Wardle, theatre critic of *The Times*. We met up at the party, as we annually do, and had a perfectly pleasant conversation, as we annually have. At least until about one in the morning, when overcome by drink, I suppose, I rounded on him about a play I'd seen some months ago. It concerns a young man going blind from diabetes. He takes back to his house a girl who is completely blind, in order to examine her blindness in close-up. It turns out that she too wants to examine him in close-up too, and asks him therefore to undress. He does. She strokes him gently, sightlessly, all over, until she comes to his penis, which she fondles. On the evening we saw it, his penis continued to dangle limply when fondled, but I can't, of course, speak for its behaviour on other evenings. It might have done any number of things, and it's clearly unreasonable to expect a consistent performance from a fondled penis when it might well have all kinds of business offstage. Anyway, on the night we saw it, it hung there, not only lazily and unflatteringly, but against the run of the plot, as we had been led to understand that both these young people, the blind girl and the boy-going-blind, were strongly attracted to each other. There was, however, a complication in the form of another girl, the young man's established girlfriend, who, while able to see, had her own serious disabilities, among them a foul temper, and a pretty scathing attitude to sex. One couldn't work out why, even when going blind, a normal chap would want her in the same room as himself. The fact of the matter is that I didn't care for this play very much and certainly nothing like as much as Irving did, but instead of commenting lightly on our difference of opinion, and passing on to another subject, or better still, exchanging good-nights and slipping away, I insisted on conducting him through my memory of his review, challenging virtually every sentence in it. Irving defended himself with obstinate reasonableness and stubborn courtesy, until able to slip away himself, leaving behind him the very image, I suspect, of a drunken, envious and spiteful play-wright. In *The Times* this morning, in his round-up of the year's theatre, he singled the play out – in a piece he must of course have written before the party – for special commendations. I decided to phone him up to continue our debate in a different spirit, relaxed, sober and confiding, but fortunately he wasn't in. Or had decided against answering the telephone.

We're off to dinner tonight with friends who are going to introduce us to a Greenham Common woman.*

3 January

I'm going to Paris later today, to hole up in a hotel and take a crack at a first draft of *The Rector's Daughter*. Harold has just phoned from New York, where he's been working hard on the production of *Old Times*, to wish us a happy New Year and to discuss possible casting. I'm looking forward to Paris, no telephone calls except crucial ones, with lots of work, punctuated by food, wine and films.

10 January

Filthy time in Paris. My typewriter broke before I left. I had to take a pen and an exercise book. For four days I sat staring dolefully down at the exercise book, my pen held in an awkward posture in my hand, my hand sensing it was back at school, unable to write. The last three days were spent writhing from gastric flu, or possibly from too much champagne on an empty stomach. The only bright spot was the appearance of Peter James, artistic director of the Lyric Theatre, Hammersmith, who was holidaying with his wife. We had a celebration lunch, a convivial occasion. His wife is Irish and an actress, very charming. Peter James has long grey hair, a beard, a gentle, solicitous voice, an easy manner, likes wine, good food. Reminds me of someone. Out of the New Testament? Or the sixties? Is it a trick of memory, or was he wearing a cape and sandals? Not sandals, surely, in Paris in January. Anyway, doesn't look at all like one's idea of a producer (i.e. Michael Codron) but could correspond to one's idea of the artistic director of a theatre in Hammersmith, I suppose. He said that the reason the Lyric had decided to go into West End productions was that they were tired

---

* She wasn't. Merely a woman who'd met a Greenham Common woman.

of trying out plays for other managements, who transferred them if they were successful and made a great deal of money, while the Lyric, who paid for the original production, ended up making very little. It was time, he said, that the Lyric forced its way into the real commercial world. So here, raising his glass, to *Partners*, their first venture.

13 Friday

Had lunch with Ian Hamilton, to whom I mentioned that various people, Harold, Michael Codron among them – hadn't been too taken with *Partners* as a title. He said he wasn't either. We discussed alternatives in a desultory sort of way until he suggested, out of nothing, *The Common Pursuit*, which with all its Cambridge associations, and Leavis* associations, of 'the common pursuit of true judgement', on the one hand, and its simple human associations, or the common pursuit of money, fame, sex, happiness, survival on the other, struck an immediate chord. He went on to talk about his days as literary editor, first of the small but influential *The Review*, and then the plushier version, which involved him in negotiations with the Arts Council, who first graciously set him up with money, and then righteously cast him down by withdrawing promises of more. I told him that I'd recently seen on television the author of one of the articles in *The Review* I'd most admired. He was quipping smartly away on a variety of irrelevant topics. His eyes were shiny with self-satisfaction, though the shine might have been from the studio lights, come to think of it. I suppose, given the way the world goes, it isn't necessarily depressing or wrong that a man who once wrote interestingly about literature and life should end up parading himself on television, as a kind of intellectual clown, but the history there, the professional and personal history, is one of the things *The Common Pursuit* is intended to be about. Ian and I reflected rather astringently on the old contributor's wasted promise, before moving on to a relaxed and tolerant discussion of our own lives, their strange reversals. Ian is recently remarried, to an Egyptian writer. He mentioned that she

* Two essays in the back of this book give some account of my relationship with, and feelings about, Dr Leavis.

was pregnant, which made him very happy. This was one of the reversals we were talking about, as for the last ten years he's been pretty miserable.

When I got home, I phoned Harold and offered him *The Common Pursuit* as a title. He thinks it's appropriate. As does Beryl, to whom I offered it, in lieu of supper and a bit of cosseting, when she came home tired and hungry from teaching. I've now got to stop thinking of the play as *Partners* and start thinking of it as *The Common Pursuit*.

16 January

Harold's written a new play, *One for the Road*. It's a crisp and brutal study of an interrogator/torturer going about his business in an unnamed country. (South Africa? Turkey? Albania? Almost anywhere in South America today. And probably anywhere else tomorrow.) The chap's name is Nicholas, and we see him having professional chats with three of his victims – a hideously tortured dissident; the dissident's wife who has been subjected to all kinds of brutality, including gang rape, to which she will be further subjected; and their eight-year-old son whom Nicholas finally has put to death, a fact he slips to the father in the last line or two of the play. Its running time is about half an hour, I'd guess, which is pretty short in terms of time, but quite long enough in terms of subject. What I like best about it is the ghastly richness of Harold's monster, the seemingly unmotivated switches of mood from bantering playfulness to self-righteous rage followed by a joke that he genuinely wants to share with whichever victim is immediately in his presence.* In fact, it's a study in the absolute power of someone who's gone beyond absolute corruption on to complete freedom of spirit. Which is also complete vacancy. Nicholas isn't simply good at his job, but was positively born to it. I suppose in some ways Nicholas is a relation of Max, Davis, Goldberg and McCann. He'd also find congenial company in Dickens's world – Fagin, Dennis the hangman, Bounderby, the murdering Chuzzlewit.

---

* Exactly like one of my teachers at prep school, now I come to think of it, although unlike Harold's monster he did the torturing as well as the interrogating. An all-rounder, in other words. I still dream of meeting up with him one day, especially if he's become enfeebled by time.

But then Harold's always been a very English writer, rather than the enigmatic European intellectual (Beckett, Kafka, etc.) that academics and critics would like to turn him into. Like Dickens, he can make one laugh in panic.

Harold himself, of course, loves laughter in the theatre, especially when it's provoked by his own plays. The cathedral reverence with which they're sometimes received (thanks mainly to the industrious spade-work of English departments and literary journals) must be exasperating. I remember being told to stop laughing during the first run of *The Homecoming* by a member of an audience (it was at the RSC) that looked as if it were composed entirely of British Council pamphlet writers far too busy, I suppose, working out the diagrammatic patterns of the territorial imperative, or making mental jottings of the symbols, myths, paradigms emblems, to catch the life going on on the stage. That was the first Pinter I'd seen, having been put off his previous stuff by the language of the reviews (the favourable ones, I mean) but Beryl insisted that she'd had a *terrific* time at *The Caretaker*. When I booked the tickets, I told the box office that I was accompanying an elderly relative with a game leg, could we have two on the aisle, please, and reminded Beryl that if by any unlikely chance we stuck it through the first act, we were to treat the interval as the first polite opportunity for returning us to the streets. The highest tribute I can pay the evening is that, we spent the interval in the theatre bar, listening quite good-humouredly to the guttural decodings going on all about us.*

* The trouble with the RSC, I suspect, is not that the company has a house style (though at its worst, it has, and I don't mean the tendency of the actors to curl up in your lap both metaphorically and sometimes actually both before – when they do it actually, and during, when they do it, thank God, only metaphorically – the performance; or the inability of their stars to speak a single line without vocal curlicues, loops and other lingerings; or their determination to point either their faces or their buttocks – remembering even as I write this, the recent Hal delivering one of the great speeches with his back to the audience, sword or crown – I can't remember which – held aloft as his buttocks jiggled and jounced to what purpose I still can't grasp; or – but I'm temperamentally unsuited to comment fairly on the RSC at their worst, being the only person I know to have left after a mere three hours or so of *Nicholas Nickleby*, still shaking at the recollection of the actors who'd impeded my progress to my seat with insolent assurances that I was about to have a good time, thus guaranteeing that I didn't; I didn't like the play much either, thinking it would probably work better as a novel), but that the audience has a house style to match it, being the kind of people who admire, even encourage, the kind of thing outlined in the bracket above, which I inserted as an act of revenge on Bernard

I suppose, finding myself unexpectedly back at my first Pinter play after all these years, that this is an opportune moment to work in an account of my first meeting with him. It was at his then house in Regent's Park, to which Michael Codron, David Sutton and I had been invited after Michael had sent him the script of *Butley*, with the suggestion that he might like to direct it. We were taken up to his eyrie by, I believe – my memory's not at all clear on this – a housekeeper. Harold was lying on a *chaise-longue* in a black silk shirt (and other garments, like boots and trousers, etc.), a dandy at first glimpse, or something worse even. That was the only time I've seen Harold as if he were posing for the *Yellow Book*, the only time I've seen him stretched on a *chaise-longue*, indeed stretched anywhere.* Normally he stands or sits bolt-upright. The only other thing I remember from that first meeting, apart from the incisiveness with which he talked about the play, was his new car, a Mercedes Benz, which had just been delivered, and which fifteen years later he still drives. Michael and David stood on the pavement eyeing it with reverence as he pointed out its body tone, its sultry panelling, its classical this and that. To me, a non-driver, it was a car, if not exactly like any other, not significantly different. In the days when we owned a car (Beryl used to drive), I could never remember its make, let alone its licence number. In fact we have owned at various stages three cars. One was small; one was red; the last one was black. That's as far as I can go. So Harold's passion for his machine was quite foreign to me. The first subject about which we really began to talk (apart from the play itself) was cricket. I count the intensely companionable summer of 1970 in which we took *Butley* through rehearsals in London, previews in Oxford, and into the West End, as one of the happiest of my life. Harold insisted that I attend all the casting sessions, all the rehearsals, all the

---

Levin, whose name, I've just learned, has appeared above a review published in the *South China Morning Post* originally written by me and published in the London *Sunday Times*. (Actually I was quite happy to have the review attributed to Bernard Levin, as it was so severely mangled that it might have damaged my reputation in the China Seas.)

* Harold has disputed this version of our meeting – denying that he's ever stretched out full-length in black silk on a *chaise-longue*. I am inclined to believe him, though I am quite unable to understand why my memory has presented me with this image, so uncharacteristic except for the *colour* of the shirt, as to be virtually a contradiction.

previews, and so he released in me the obsessive, which I suspect from time to time he has had reason to regret.

(It was about this time, mid-January, that we began casting. We nailed our last actor on 19 May, three days before rehearsals began. Some of our difficulties arose because we'd decided to cast to the age of the characters in the last scene, when they are in their late thirties, early forties, rather than to the first scene and the Epilogue, when they are all in their twenties. Once our first actor a name actor, something of a star had accepted, we were stuck with his age group, and furthermore wanted actors of equivalent authority and reputation to balance against him, our feeling being that as *The Common Pursuit* is an *ensemble* piece, we wanted six names *ensemble*. If we had cast younger at the beginning, the question of a name would have been irrelevant. All the actors would have been equally unknown. Perhaps, in retrospect, we fell into the trap of casting for Hammersmith as if we were casting for the West End. I don't mean by this that I was dissatisfied with the actors we ended up with. Far from it. I'm only attempting to account for the endless difficulties and frustrations as the months dwindled to weeks, the weeks to days. But it was, as they say, invaluable experience.* For one thing, I had never been engaged in so much of the nitty-gritty of casting before. Among the things I had to learn was that agents love their actors to be offered parts almost as much as actors love being offered parts, even if there's really no question of the actors being free to do them. It presumably confirms, or even enhances, an actor's status to be able to say that he's turned a part down, especially when talking to the actor to whom the part is currently on offer. The phrase that tips the wink is *technically* available, which usually means that the contract for the part he really intends to do has been drawn up, is probably indeed in the post, but hasn't yet been actually signed. Sometimes, however, the phrase means what it ought to mean – that the actor has been offered a part that he's thinking about but hasn't yet committed himself to, or that he's *almost* certain to take his children by his first wife on holiday at last, or that he thinks he *ought* to spend more time at the bedside of his disabled mother. But on the other hand he really is technically

---

* Meaning, as it usually does, that I hope I never have to go through it again.

available to do your part and, if he finds it interesting enough, might drop the other part, the children, the disabled mother, and do it. Therefore one has to send scripts to all the 'technically available' on the off chance that both they and their agents have scruples in such matters.

I have spared everyone, including myself, the boredom of going through the whole process detail by detail, I've also included events not directly connected to casting, when they seem to be part of the texture of that fraught period. I begin by giving five examples of the kind of thing we encountered regularly. As a matter of fact, they are five actual cases, but as they occurred right at the beginning, I wasn't aware until I read through the transcript that they were models of numerous cases to come.

Actor One

(Wanted for Humphry.) His agent told us he would be available. We had a script sent around to him immediately, but still managed to hear, before it reached him, that he wouldn't be available, as he was planning to go out of town to star in a revival that he was also helping to produce, and of course expecting to transfer to the West End. If it didn't transfer he'd be available, but by then we'd either be on the brink of, or into, rehearsals.

Actor Two

(offered Stuart) was available, but in fact wasn't. He was desperate to get out of the play he was currently in in the West End, in order to do a major television film that was scheduled to start immediately. If he couldn't get out, he'd be free in May to do *The Common Pursuit*, which he liked. (He got out, the producer of the West End play taking an exasperatingly decent attitude to his plight.)

Actor Three

(for Nick) was, according to his agent, available. According to the actor, however – Harold, who knows him, phoned him up – he wasn't available, as he was going to be doing something big at the RSC. The agent then phoned to say that the actor was mistaken, he was available, could we send around a script? The script was sent. The agent then phoned to say that the actor wasn't available, as he was going to be doing something big at the RSC. (The second time the agent had got it right.) It's difficult to determine what exactly was going on, though there are two obvious possibilities: (1) That the agent genuinely thought a leading part in a new play might be a better career move than 'something big' at the RSC; (2) That he wanted another positive offer to use in his bargaining with the RSC. There are about nine other possibilities, less clear, that I'd better not examine here. As it turned out, it was all quite irrelevant as the actor felt that the part of Nick offered him too much time in the dressing room, not enough on stage.

Actor Four

(for Martin) might have been available if the film he was working on (he was on location) finished on time. As the film was being directed by someone who is famous for running over schedule, there was little chance that he'd be back in London when we needed him.

Actor Five

(for Peter, or for Nick.) This was a complicated and interminable piece of nonsense. The actor was on holiday in Los Angeles (Could this be true, one speculated? Would any sane man holiday in Los Angeles, and if not, did one want an insane one in the cast?) and sometimes could be traced, and sometimes not, by his agent, who sometimes phoned us back when he said he would, but usually didn't. On one occasion, David Porter, the casting director of the Lyric, was left 'holding' on the line while the agent took several other calls, and was still 'holding' on the line when the agent left his office, I can't remember whether for lunch, or for home in the evening. This sort of thing went on until we eventually gave up, my own suspicion being that the actor was in Hollywood to get a film, and didn't want to make a decision until he knew whether he'd got it; and of course not getting one film leads to staying on in California and not getting another, and another . . .

20 January

Peter James, who has had flu, telephoned Harold and confessed to being surprised that we were going ahead offering parts without clearing it with him first. On reflection, I suppose it is rather brazen of the author and director to be casting away without consulting the producer. So we agreed to meet Peter James, the artistic director; Robert Cogo-Fawcett, the administrative director; David Porter, the casting director, for lunch, and to go through our list with them, adding to it names generally agreed to be worth pursuing.

21 January

This morning I phoned up Irving Wardle to comment on his recent review of *Masterclass* or rather on the last sentence of his review, which said in effect that the play raises the question of whether a tyrannical society (i.e. the USSR) that takes music seriously is any worse than a free society (I suppose he means ours) which takes music as a mere entertainment. He was rather surprised by my call in the first place, and my tone, although I tried to keep it moderate, in the second. He was nevertheless courteous, *gallantly* courteous. I don't know myself quite why I phoned him, except that I vaguely believe that reviewers should now and then be called to account, even decent ones like Irving. And there *was* something chillingly bland in his rumination, especially as a last sentence. Irving was sure that he can't actually have meant that murder and repression were justified by a serious interest in music. Nor that a lack of serious interest in music was too high a price to pay for comparative political freedom. He was no longer sure what he did mean precisely, but explained that reviews had to be written on the wing, after all, and were subject to editorial cuts, and half-thoughts were converted by circumstance into emphatic statements, and so forth; and anyway he'd forgotten the review, having reviewed one or two things since, and didn't have it to hand. All of which, being excuses rather than arguments, seemed to me utterly reasonable. The conversation ended on a rather unsatisfactory exchange of good wishes up and down the line. Given our little fracas at Christmas over the blind play, I've obviously made it my aim to unmask myself to Irving as a dangerous paranoid, desperate to turn friendly encounters into conversational brawls, phoning up unexpectedly to engage in political debate. Should I extend this tactic to other reviewers, or reverse it, and start sending playful and affectionate postcards and notes to Irving, or would this unnerve him further? I hope he doesn't get anonymous phone calls, though. He'll certainly assume they're from me.

23 January

I went to Harold's for a drink, and then the two of us went on to the Lyric, to see Peter James, Robert Cogo-Fawcett and David Porter, who is also in charge of the Studio theatre, where *One for the Road* is to be produced a couple of months before *The Common Pursuit* opens in the main theatre. We did a tour of the Studio, a natty little place, capable of more versatility than most studios, and then went on to the main house. It's both lovely and anomalous, having been pulled down while a hideous urban complex, with a high-rise car park attached, was constructed, and then rebuilt exactly as it was, inside the complex. If you approach it from the tube, you pass an odd little patch of benches and bushes where winos, tramps and drug addicts sit in clusters, or lie full-length, semi-conscious. Then on around the concrete into a downstairs foyer, where you can buy your ticket for the show. On up the stairs into a large and comfortable modern bar and cafeteria, out of which, through sliding glass doors, you can step on to a terrace. There, on a fine day, you can eat your lunch, or drink your drinks, peering over the wall at the human debris below. Then, as the curtain is about to rise, you go up further stairs, through a corridor of offices, into a late Victorian auditorium that corresponds exactly to your sense of what a theatre should be, if you're my age or older, a theatre of one's childhood, cosy and elegant. Nobody who loves theatres, or the theatre, could possibly wish it any different, but the contradictions that surround it provoke questions about how seriously we take, and ought to take, theatre in a free society, which lays waste to our cities, and to so many human lives, and compensates with little pockets of luxury and nostalgia here and there. Perhaps I should get on the blower to Irving and ask him what he makes of all this.

After our tour of the two theatres, the five of us went to an Italian restaurant down the road, and discussed casting. We confirmed that we were all agreed on the actors to whom the play had been sent, that offers should be made in the cases where we hadn't yet made offers, and then went on to consider other names. The lunch passed pleasantly, with wine and quite a few jokes, and there was a point when looking affectionately around the table I took in an astonishing fact. Two astonishing facts. Five chaps, all working in the theatre, all heterosexual, all smoking. The odds against that combination these days must be pretty high. Even outside the theatre. By the time we'd finished lunch we had compiled a list of two and even three names for each part, on the understanding that if our first choices turned us down, we'd move straight on to offer the part to the next choice, and so forth.

After lunch, Harold and I had a very peculiar return journey to Holland Park, being rejected by one taxi driver after another, I think on grounds of appearance. I suspect that I looked like Harold's minder, as he was very smartly dressed in a black raincoat and a sort of semi-suit and always walks very stiffly and upright, like a key figure in the Mafia or a prosperous undertaker. While I was in a sloppy raincoat, with my blue shoulder bag which I suppose might well look as if it contains a knife and knuckle-dusters – my whole effect being seedy and rough. Anyway, the taxis kept passing us by except one that stopped, then refused point-blank to take us to Holland Park or even to explain why, the driver just whisking himself off with a mumble. It was hideously cold, as well, late January weather all right. We got one in the end, but it was an unpleasant business. I always seem to have a lot of trouble with taxis. Probably my most disagreeable experience was after a Test match at Lord's. I saw one on the other side of the road, and signalled him. He saw me, signalled back, stopped, gestured me over. Whereupon a youngish, city-dressed member of the MCC, who had witnessed all this – I'd seen him witnessing it – climbed in. I ran across the road, across the fronts of cars and buses, flung myself at the door and wrenched it open. The MCC bounder was reclining in the corner, one hand resting meditatively on his member's tie, a uniquely disgusting tie, I always think, of red and yellow stripes. I gestured him out. He shook his head. I appealed to the taxi driver, who agreed that he'd stopped for me but otherwise wanted to 'stay out of it'. I returned to the bounder, who was now smirking defiantly. I turned back to the driver. The bounder closed the door. The driver drove off. Whereupon another taxi drew up beside me, and a face full of sympathy and outrage bent through the window. 'I saw all that,' it said. 'I thought it was very bad. Very bad indeed. Gives cabs a bad name, that sort of thing does. Now where do you want to go, Guv?' I said I wanted to go to Highgate. 'Highgate? Sorry, that's right out of my way,' he said, and drove off.

3 February

I have had a thought as I sit here, swooning softly from too much Scotch, that the best solution to the problem of the first scene change, when we go from Stuart's rooms in Cambridge to Stuart's office in London, is a revolve. All the people who are waiting for Stuart in his rooms would be carried off to the Wagner Humphry puts on the gramophone, as simultaneously Stuart, seven years later, seated at his desk, is revolved on. Then when we come to the set change from the last scene of the play to the Epilogue, the reverse would happen: Stuart, sitting at what is now Martin's desk to read Humphry's posthumous poems, would revolve off and all the people waiting for Stuart some fifteen years before would revolve on in the positions we'd left them in, the gramophone still playing Wagner of course.

4 February

I put the possibility of the revolve to Harold over lunch. He was very keen on it, and suggested I put it to Eileen Diss when we meet her on Friday. We then discussed casting, which is becoming increasingly complicated, as Harold is going to direct *One for the Road* at the Studio three weeks earlier than was originally planned. The fact is we're still nowhere on the casting, still waiting to hear from some agents, having been turned down by others. Now that [Actor One] is out for Humphry, we've decided to offer the part to Ian Charleson who lives just around the corner from the Lyric, and who will therefore receive a script in an hour or two. We're going to offer the part of Nick to Jack Shepherd,* who is currently at the

---

* For some reason I haven't followed the offer to Jack Shepherd up in the transcripts, but as I recall, he decided to stay at the National where he continued to give a remarkable performance in *Glengarry Glen Ross*.

National. We're waiting to hear from Ian Ogilvy for the part of Martin, but are currently at a loss about Peter as when we do make contact with [Actor Four's] agent, he claims he can't make contact with him in Los Angeles, and we're still wondering what to do about Jenny Agutter, who is also in Los Angeles, and would apparently like to do the part of Marigold, but only in Hammersmith, not in the West End, because she doesn't want to commit herself to a long run. We haven't really got a clue about Stuart, although we think Ian Charleson could also be a possible Stuart. Perhaps we ought to offer him both parts, let him decide. Of course, as everybody keeps saying, we have masses of time. Yes, but what is disconcerting is that we have offered the parts around a bit, and so far no takers.

6 February

Met Eileen and Harold at the Lyric. Eileen had brought along a design which she scrapped when I put forward my proposition about the revolve. The only problem she could see was that our two sets would be rather small, but she felt that the speed and visual effect of the changes would compensate for this. One of the things I found interesting about her discarded design was that she had faithfully reproduced redundant details that I had failed to eliminate in my last draft. In earlier drafts it was crucial that you should be able to see into the bedroom in Stuart's room in Cambridge, so in describing the set I'd made a point of the 'door opening on to the bedroom'. Later I'd cut all the action and dialogue involving the bedroom, but had forgotten to cut the stage direction. There, nevertheless, in Eileen's design, was the bedroom, brilliantly worked into the structure of the set. An example of the power of the written word.

A finer example comes to mind. Last year, at around Easter, I went to Germany to see a production of *Quartermaine's Terms*. I sat listlessly through the last dress rehearsal, keeping my eyes mildly averted from a large, florid, and totally bald Quartermaine, not because he was bad, but because I have my own image of Quartermaine, to which he certainly didn't conform. As we reached the end of the play I prepared a few routine compliments, as my getaway to an early lunch. In the last scene, however, I was appalled to discover that a character, an accident-prone North Country man, who was meant to turn up in a neck-brace was bending his head easily this way and that, while a middle-aged spinster, who in the script was meant to be sitting hunched over a cigarette, was instead sitting bolt-upright, locked in a neck-brace. I assumed German symbolism here, all right, this peculiar reversal of situations. When the director came up to me, I said smoothly that I had much enjoyed his production, but did find it odd, a trifle odd, that Melanie, not Mr Meadle, was wearing the neck-brace. Why? 'But that's what you have written,' he said. 'Nonsense,' I explained calmly. He handed me the English version of the text, and indeed it *was* written that Melanie was wearing the neck-brace, not Meadle. A typing error that I'd missed; a printing error that the editor had missed – but there it was. 'So it is *Meadle* who wears the neck-brace, good God!' he said. 'Good God! Of course. *That* makes sense! And to think – three days we spent in rehearsal talking about why Melanie is wearing a neck- brace, finally we worked it out that it was guilt from killing her mother' (she had) 'and so she'd possibly thrown herself down the stairs, like she'd thrown her mother down the stairs. You see?' I asked him why he hadn't phoned me, for clarification, and saved himself three days. 'But so it is written,' he said, pointing to the page again. I observed lightly that no harm had been done, all we had to do was to transfer the neck-brace from his Melanie to his Meadle, and then noticed that my German agent was looking rather drawn. 'So no need for any of us to worry, is there?' I added, making it clear that I didn't hold her responsible, even though she'd attended all the dress rehearsals. 'No,' she said. 'Well, you see it just happens that well – in the production at Vienna also Melanie has been wearing the neck-brace.' The production in Vienna had been running for three months. 'It's in the script, you see. It's written in the script.' At such moments, I feel almost Godlike. Supposing I had written, 'Melanie in a neck-brace and naked. Meadle in a tweed skirt, blouse.' It might, of course, mean the director's losing five or six days of rehearsal to work out why, but that's his problem. 'So I have written.'

8 February

The hot news today is that Ian Charleson has said 'no' to both Humphry and Stuart. The precise message passed on by his agent was, 'Ian Charleson says no.' Harold and I are both rather wounded by this, as we cast him for the student in *Otherwise Engaged* and so tend to think of ourselves as the johnnies that gave the laddy his first real break (though probably people were queuing up to give it to him). We felt we deserved a more emollient message or even a little personal note or card. If he didn't like the play he didn't have to say so, there being so many formulae: 'Not quite right for me at this stage . . .' etc. In fact, the more we went into it together, the more wounded we became.

9 February

Clive Francis, offered Humphry, has asked to read the script again. This always worries me. But perhaps he just wants to check my grammar. Clive is one of my favourite actors, having been a superb Troup in the original production of *The Rear Column*, and in the television version; and a very funny Meadle in the touring production of *Quartermaine's Terms*. So I can look forward to a 'Clive Francis says no' tomorrow or the next day. I attribute my increasing bitterness to the exhaustion of maintaining confidence in a play that so far every actor except Ian Ogilvy has turned down.* It's true that several have been highly complimentary, but then they could afford to be, being safely engaged in something else.

10 February

Late last night, stewing in Scotch and rancour, and feeling I'd played out the Wardle connection for a while, I wrote Ian Charleson a note that struck a perfect balance between affronted vanity and moralizing self-righteousness. I concluded, I believe, by *nevertheless* wishing him well in his career. I posted this five

---

* It's not clear in the transcripts exactly when Ian Ogilvy accepted the part of Martin, mainly because his name is entangled in conversations I had with Harold about Alan Bates (my fervent recommendation) as the lead in *One for the Road*. But I've recorded a conversation in which Harold announces 'good news' that I took to be Alan Bates's agreeing to play Nicholas, but on further scrutiny of the transcript, and closer listening to the tapes, might have been Ian Ogilvy agreeing to play Martin. Anyway, whenever it was, it was self-evidently before 9 February.

minutes after sealing and stamping it. I brook no delay in these matters, aiming for the maximum amount of time for regret.*

12 February

Three more actors have said no to offers of Stuart, Nick, Marigold. Although they produced widely different reasons, I begin to suspect there is something more behind it. Could it be that they have started reading the scripts they're sent, instead of just counting the lines, as I've always hoped they do?

14 February

Clive Francis has said yes to the part of Humphry. Why? What's the matter with him?

15 February, Wednesday

I went up to Cambridge with Eileen Diss to look at various rooms in Trinity that might serve as models for Stuart's rooms. Of all the places in the world I hate going to, I hate going to Cambridge most. I was there for nine years, and almost all my memories are in some way associated with the train, sliding along the longest, I believe, platform in England, or the United Kingdom or even Europe, I can never remember which, either carrying me from loneliness to a sour love affair in London, or depositing me back from the sour love affair to loneliness in Cambridge. I seem to recall a train that left at about six in the morning, on Sundays, and arrived in London around lunchtime – which must be memory being true to the experience, but playing fast and loose with the facts as usual – and thinking, after a few hours without breakfast, the dust from the seats in my nose, and the heating on (so it was surely summer), my head aching, my tongue parched, that I'd at last found the perfect

---

* Ian Charleson replied in due course, a charming if slightly puzzled letter in which he explained that he left all professional communications to his agent, in order to avoid embarrassment. This strikes me as a sensible policy, that others might do well to adopt. He also wrote glowingly of our past association, ending with salutes to Harold, etc. I bore up well before such good manners, good sense and good feeling, and may in due course forgive him for them.

expression of all that was worst about my Cambridge life, my London life, appropriately achieved midway between the two. About the only time I've been back in the last twenty years was to see a production of one of my plays, which I'm happy to report provided me with a thoroughly shaming evening in the theatre. So I dreaded my trip up, even with Eileen.*

It therefore turned out to be exceptionally pleasant, perhaps because I'd managed to pick up a bottle of champagne at Liverpool Street station. Eileen and I knocked it daintily off, in paper cups, the last swallow going down as we began the long slide along the longest platform. We met a young don who showed us over various rooms. Eileen took photographs, asked questions, made notes, until we found exactly the room I'd remembered in Great Court, which a friend of mine had occupied about a quarter of a century ago, and which I'd inhabited, imaginatively or in memory, when writing the first scene and the Epilogue of *The Common Pursuit*. It was eerily unchanged, except that the main room, the sitting room, seemed to be shared by a young man and a young woman, who allowed us to roam about with a courtesy that went against the grain, my natural inclination, which I don't like to have thwarted, being to find today's twenty-year-olds either unruly hopheads or cold-eyed sharks – after either my blood or my job. When Eileen had finished with the room, the three of us went to a pub that used to be called the Baron of Beef but is now, I think, called something else (but why?). On the way I saw posters advertising the touring production of *Butley*, which is coming to the Cambridge Arts Theatre in a few weeks. This rather pleased me. Over lunch, we talked vivaciously about a book on tragedy that the young don is writing (why?) and then, only moments (I'm convinced) before something was going to go wrong, as for example glimpsing, or even worse, being glimpsed by, some long-forgotten figure from my past, I hustled Eileen back to the station, and on to the train. So *that* was all right.

6 March

Beryl and I went to see Donald Sinden, but most particularly Clive Francis in *School for Scandal* at the Duke of York's. Enjoyed lumps

* There is a piece on my Cambridge days on page 214.

of it very much, the men mostly. We had a little trouble with the older ladies, who were in fact rather older ladies than the text suggests they should be, and clearly had difficulty remembering their lines. One of them dealt with this by substituting her own when she couldn't recall Sheridan's. All right if you're not Sheridan, or don't know the play, or don't mind the spectacle of other actors standing anxiously about wondering whether their own lines, to which hers sometimes led and sometimes didn't, would make sense. But there was an air of confident good humour on the stage that mostly got across the footlights and was shared by the audience. Clive Francis was, I'm relieved to report, in total command, effortlessly funny, effortlessly holding his silences to the second, and often triumphantly beyond. Donald Sinden boomed richly away, postured ripely away, and was delighted in by the audience, whose delight he delighted in. Who can resist Sheridan, when he's done half decently?

Afterwards we went around to see Clive. John McCallum, with whom he was sharing a dressing room, was getting out of his stage togs, and into his life togs, when we entered. He carried off having to pad about in pants and vest with sympathetic stateliness. Clive, on the other hand, was changing rapidly as he was having dinner with Sinden. He did say, though, as he unmade his face, that when he read *The Common Pursuit* the first time, he felt he didn't like any of the characters at all, and that Polly James, the actress with whom he has lived for many years, felt much the same. This, in one of Harold's phrases, 'stopped me dead in my tracks'. Could it be, I pondered to Beryl over dinner afterwards, that actors had been turning us down not only because none of the parts was a star part but also because they don't like the characters? Of course, I find this incomprehensible. Nevertheless I decided to pass Clive's comment on to Harold, with the recommendation that in future we ask actors to whom we offer parts either not to read the play at all, or to read it, as Clive has done, at least twice.

9 March

Been turned down by two more actors, one of whom was invited to play Stuart, one of whom invited to play Nick. Usual reasons given. On the one hand, a previous engagement; on the other, not exactly what he wants to do at the moment. There was compensation in the form of a letter from a very old friend, to whom I'd sent a copy of the play a month or two ago. He'd finally found time to read it, though had very little to say about it. He attributes his general lack of response to slowness of wit, absent-mindedness, an overall unfamiliarity with theatrical texts. I suppose he means his slowness of wit, etc., but it's possible he means mine. I've just checked. He means his. I find this quite reasonable, as he's a university lecturer. I wish, though, that he'd stumbled into one compliment. I could do with support from any source at the moment. Meanwhile, I wait for comment from another friend, mutual to the above and to myself, also a university lecturer, who has been unable to read the play yet as he's been laid up in bed with a damaged ankle.

13 March

No movement on casting. Harold is deep in rehearsals of *One for the Road*.

21 March

Last Wednesday I saw a preview – the last preview, in fact – of *One for the Road*. It's a concussive twenty-five minutes. Harold's direction is impeccable, every movement of the actors informed with meaning, not a detail left loose, not a gesture haphazard or lacking in eloquence. I wonder though, my reaction to the play on the page being what it was, whether the director hasn't slightly straitjacketed the writer. The terrifying, sometimes exhilarating, lunacy of the torturer has been subdued into a calculating sadism. We don't want to share the life of *this* creature, watching him from as far away as we can get, hypnotized, as if expecting to be his next victims. A man who has complete power must surely love his power now and then, just as now and then it fills him with despair. On the page he himself doesn't seem to know what he's going to feel next, and therefore what he's going to say next. On the stage he seems to be working to a plan, almost a habit, of repression. Not born to his job, in fact, merely practised in it. Alan (Bates), who I had thought a natural for the part in his easy extravagance, his charm, his gift for flirting dangerously with the audience, gives the most restrained and consequently the most violent and hateful performance of his career. This is clearly what both he and Harold intended, or came to during rehearsals, and perhaps they're right. Certainly some of the resulting visual patterns are extremely disturbing – in the scene with the wife/mother actually erotic – as if Harold had found formal means of signalling as director what he's otherwise shied away from in the writer. And of course the difference between reading on the page and expressing on the stage is emphasized in this case by the fact that the victims scarcely speak. When I read *One for the Road*, I entered quite cheerfully into the torturer's world. But we can't simply revel in this moral monster, if we're also forced to *look at* the man he's had tortured, the woman he's had violated, their child whose murder he announces in the last line of the play. So when it comes to it, perhaps Harold's channelling of Nicholas's malevolent exuberance into merely lethal efficiency was the only possible solution. Anyway, I came out of the Studio as if I'd been violated myself. I had a brief drink with Harold at the bar, and noticed that Harold has set himself and others a social problem. He can hardly stand at the bar as if in celebration of a work achieved, given the intended effect of the work. And friends can hardly present themselves to him with grins of congratulations, slaps on the back and so forth. (Though I can't recall ever seeing anyone slap Harold on the back.) Mainly the procession was a glum one, respectful, anguished, as if at a funeral, although loosening into humdrum cheerfulness with a drink or two, nevertheless careful not to dishonour the horror of the event. I also wondered, as this is lunchtime theatre, when precisely the audience prefer to take their lunch. Before or after (I exclude the possibility of during) the show.

24 March

The reviews for *One for the Road* were mainly excellent, although I thought they concentrated too much on what they saw as the political statement of the piece. I can see that they were unlikely to emphasize its value as sheer entertainment, but I'm not sure what kind of political statement the play amounts to. It should hardly come as a surprise that Harold is (a) against torture, (b) against totalitarian regimes. What he's making is surely a demand. Look at this – this is what goes on, daily, in this country and that. Look, and see what it really means to be in the power of such people.

26 March

We've just been turned down by an actor for Stuart. That's not quite accurate. He is prepared to do the play at the Lyric, but not to go on with it into the West End, his point being that he's a star, and when he goes into the West End he wants to go as a star, not as a member of a company piece. I would have found this honesty refreshing if anything could refresh me at the moment, apart from a positive piece of casting. Robert Cogo-Fawcett, Harold and I (in Harold's studio) began to go through further names, not of what one might loosely (or even tightly) call stars, but of actors not familiar to us, of whom we've heard good things. It will mean meeting them, and reading them, perhaps several times. There is nothing wrong with that – it can be very exciting – but we've now been at it for months, time is getting short, Harold is off to New York any day for the American première of *One for the Road*, and I'm off to San Francisco shortly after that for a production of *Quartermaine's Terms*.

After the meeting, I went to see a rehearsal of a touring production of *Butley* at a church hall off Holborn, where, as it turns out, there is also a badminton club. I found out about the badminton club because, true to my current form, I arrived at the hall a few minutes after the *Butley* company had left, to make room for the badminton players. I went home, tried to work on *The Rector's Daughter*, while glaring at the telephone, waiting for news.

30 March

A last casting session with Harold, before he goes to New York. We met at our usual restaurant in Hammersmith, for lunch.* An odd lunch, an odd afternoon. For one thing, I *felt* odd, having a slight touch of flu, I think. We were mostly in reminiscent vein, talking of everything except the matter to hand, but finally came around to our new list for Stuart, deciding that the play should be sent to five or six actors, with a covering note to their agents making it clear that we're not making an offer and that we will have to see and

---

* Usual while we were working in Hammersmith, I mean. Our usual usual restaurant is in Soho.

probably read those that are interested. We then went to the theatre, arriving just as the cast of *One for the Road* was emerging into the bar. The actors, having now played the piece often enough to adjust their lives to horror at midday, are beginning to relax. In fact Alan looked quite jovial after twenty-five minutes of concentrated sadism, and Jenny Quayle looked very pretty and lively after having had quite a lot of the sadism concentrated on her. This seems to me healthy, the experience of the play not being one that one would want them to live with for a minute longer than is necessary. But Harold, who had had a fairly convivial lunch, found himself nevertheless in the situation I described earlier, having to find an appropriate manner when accosted by shell-shocked, distressed and respectful friends. When they'd cleared off, we suddenly found ourselves developing a small party, all tension released, as if the need to celebrate the success of *One for the Road* as a play had taken us unawares. I was in no state to drink much, so of course did, and finally left feeling distinctly woozy. I picked up a copy of the *Spectator* in the underground. In it I came across a review which compares *One for the Road* with 'a great rendition of *King Lear*', thus simultaneously missing the point of both plays, the one being about the triumph of innocence over evil, the other being about almost exactly the opposite. Reassuring, though, that sometimes the reviewers' little errors go in the playwright's favour. After a brief discussion with Beryl, when I got home, about my condition, which I attributed in a shaking voice to flu, to bed.

1 April

Where I remained most of yesterday.

2 April

One of the actors to whom *The Common Pursuit* was sent, with a covering letter saying this didn't constitute an offer, phoned up the Lyric to say he was very excited, and was this an offer? On having the meaning of the letter explained to him, he said he'd phone back in the afternoon. Which he did, to say that on rereading the play he'd found himself less excited by it, and didn't want to be considered. Another actor phoned to say that he didn't really think the play was for him, really, as he didn't like it. How invigorating, I mendaciously cried, that at last *someone* has had the honesty . . . Another actor we thought was out of the running as he was in a West End play is back in the running as the play he's in is about to close early, though he doesn't know it yet. Judy, who represents the playwright concerned, passed the information on to us. The actor has been sent *The Common Pursuit* but not for Stuart, for Peter. It would be nice to get Peter fixed, but the problem of Stuart is the crucial one.*

11 April

Lunch with Harold, just back from New York. He was in good form, pleased with the production over there, which had been directed by Alan Schneider, an old friend and colleague, who directed not only the first of Harold's plays to be done in the States, but also many of the early Beckett plays.†

But he (Harold) was worried about his health. He has been advised to cut down on his drinking and smoking and I suppose all the things on which you have to cut down if you're not to cut down on life. After lunch we went to the Lyric to see two possible Stuarts. One of them has just finished in a long series on television. He gave an extremely accomplished and intelligent reading, but worried me by closely resembling Ian Ogilvy, looking almost like a brother – not really a good idea. The other fellow – the Lyric is very keen on him – is immensely attractive. Extraordinary eyes, bluish violet; and very intelligent, I thought, in discussing the play (i.e. he liked it). But I detected something odd in his speech, especially in his reading. He sounded precious. *Slightly* precious. I decided that perhaps he was queer, but discovered afterwards from Harold that in fact he's South African. Then we saw a girl whose name escapes me.‡ She was very nervous, I think, arriving like a wounded bird, fluttering and gasping

* I don't know what happened with the actor to whom we offered Peter. I haven't followed it up on the tapes, so assume that he said no but that in my concern over Stuart I didn't take much notice.
† While we were rehearsing *The Common Pursuit*, Schneider came over to London to cast a play he was going to direct for the Hampstead Theatre Club. He was run over on the Finchley Road, when crossing back to the theatre after posting a card to Beckett. He died a few days later, in hospital.
‡ It was Nina Thomas, who was in fact to play the part.

and struggling for breath, and gave a first reading that had a strong charge of the Dorothy Tutins about it – interesting, idiosyncratic and highly wrought, but (as she wasn't Dorothy Tutin) not completely convincing. Harold then took her through the scene, as reassuring and clinical as a doctor. No, as one's best idea of a doctor, mainly derived from old films. She read again, very much more naturally, and yet with an idiosyncrasy (not this time mannered or imitative) that lifted my spirits. I still feel, though I haven't looked at the part and its problems for ages, that the Marigold I've written needs special help from the actress: someone who's so *particular* that we don't notice how general, how functional my Marigold is. Of course I hope that my rewriting has given/found *some* particularity, but . . .

Harold, by the way, read all the other parts, as he's going to have to do through auditions. His instinctive grasp of where the conversational stress should fall was immensely helpful, I think, to our three actors, whom he constantly and gently nudged into a more considered response. It was invaluable for me, too – hearing my lines spoken for the first time, getting a whiff of almost forgotten intentions. In fact, Harold's reading reminded me of the enormous advantages of having a director who is also a playwright who is also an actor.*

After the Marigold audition, we went up to the Lyric offices and compared reactions. The general feeling is that we have a Stuart in the violetish-blue-eyed actor, and a potential Marigold in the Dorothy Tutinish actress (although we intend to see a few other Marigolds). I'm still worried, though, about violetish-blue's accent, which, though not queer, merely South African, still seems to me prissy. A prissy Stuart isn't on the cards, at least not on my cards. Tomorrow we see another little crop of Stuarts, the best of them an actor called – called something French, Huguenot, I suppose, who was in *The Jewel in the Crown*, which I didn't see, but was much

---

* The first time I attended auditions, about twenty years ago, my eyes were fixed on the reader, not on the actors we had come to see. At the end of the session, I couldn't remember a single one of the candidates clearly, though I couldn't forget the reader, who had dominated the stage with uninhibited confidence. I would have cast him on the spot, even though Alec Guinness was already contracted to the part. Fortunately, the director, John Dexter, was looking in the other direction, at the actors we were there to audition. Furthermore, he took notes. In the end we did well, casting Simon Ward.

admired by everyone, including Beryl, who once called me in to admire an actor with a French, or Huguenot-sounding name. I remember that I thought he looked and sounded pretty good, without at all remembering what he looked like, the way he spoke.*

12 April

The actor whose name I couldn't remember from *The Jewel in the Crown* is Nicholas Le Prevost. He's very intelligent and attractive, saturnine, about thirty-seven, I'd guess. He was sporting a number of militant left badges on his shirt, but was otherwise both shy and composed, his eyes alert for professional complications. We took him up to the second floor lobby of the theatre for his audition, had scarcely got into a preliminary conversational skirmish when Harold, seeing David Porter trekking up from the bar to his office, rose abruptly and went over to him. All Harold wanted to know was whether there was a quiet room we could use instead of the lobby, but it looked — Harold gravely muttering, David Porter nodding and whispering — as if something prime-ministerial were taking place. Nicholas Le Prevost continued talking to me about his early education — he seems to have had a bad time at schools, or to have given his schools a bad time — but his eyes kept rolling towards Harold and the casting director, David Porter. We were taken off to a quiet room a few flights up or down (at the Lyric up often leads to down, down to up) and Nicholas Le Prevost launched

* Beryl has a sharp eye for the coming actor. When Michael Codron, Harold and I were casting the part of Jameson in *The Rear Column*, she insisted that we go to see the RSC production of an eighteenth-century comedy called *Wild Oats*, written by an Irishman called O'Keefe. (I've since heard that the Inland Revenue tried to make contact with O'Keefe, with a view to getting a share of his royalties. I suppose an income tax inspector passed the theatre one day, saw O'Keefe's name on the hoarding, long queues at the box office, and struck like lightning, two centuries late.) Beryl wanted us to see Jeremy Irons, a young actor who was playing the second lead with the authority and glamour of a chap playing the starring role. As we were after glamour and authority in Jameson, we cast him forthwith. Although *The Rear Column* had only a brief run, Jeremy Irons won awards and critical praise for his Jameson, which led to his being auditioned for, and getting, the main part in *The French Lieutenant's Woman* on Harold's recommendation (he wrote the script) which led to his getting the main part in the film of *Betrayal* (a scrupulous version of Harold's play) which led to his getting the main part in the Broadway production of *The Real Thing*, more praise, Tony awards, etc. So from Jeremy Irons to Beryl a magnum of champagne at least, please, to share with her husband.

himself into the reading proper. I felt almost at once that he was the chap for me, but had to acknowledge that he was also a trifle low-key, beginning quietly, and sliding from there down the scale until at the end he was picking out a few syllables for articulation, with noisy little smiles between. When he left, Harold made it plain that he was the man for him too – a bit hard on the violetish-blue-eyed South African, but there we are. We went up, or down, to the bar, bumped inevitably into David Porter, gave our verdict. After Porter had agreed to set about contracting Le Prevost, and had gone up to the office to do so, Harold and I noticed Le Prevost out on the terrace, standing with a friend, gazing compassionately down on the derelicts in the patch of shrubs and benches beneath. We went over to him and offered him the part, which he promptly accepted. So we have a Stuart, unless of course Le Prevost's agent phones tomorrow with a rebuff, or Le Prevost decides to reject the play for political reasons. Assuming he's fixed, all we need now is a Nick, a Peter, a Marigold.

15 April

This afternoon, a Sunday, I went to Harold's studio to see an actress for Marigold, recommended to me by someone who's directed her in South Africa. She gave an interesting reading but was too old. She wasn't unattractively too old, she simply had the presence, the style, the movements, the body of an attractive woman in her middle-to-late thirties, who would therefore work well in the last scene, but would seem an imposter in the first scene, and in the Epilogue, when she has to be twenty-one or twenty-two at the most. Lesser actresses of the same age might be able to move convincingly from twenty to their late thirties, but she couldn't – nature having chosen to develop her in a strictly linear fashion, month by month, year on year, a perfect product, a classical example, at each stage, of growth, and change. I'm probably making my point even less urbanely than Harold did, who, when she had finished, and after passing her a few deserved compliments, found himself saying, 'Look here, I think it's better to be honest. I mean, let's face it, the thing is that you have a very attractive, no doubt are, unquestionably, a very attractive woman. Mature woman. You are a mature woman. But the part does call for somebody who can be nineteen or twenty and there is no doubt whatever, in my mind, that however – um – striking – uh – attractive you are, you are nevertheless too mature for that sort of part.' And looked at me for confirmation. Which I gave. She accepted all this – two blundering men bent on honesty – with as much grace as anyone could muster under the circumstances, and left. What was awful was that we both really did think she was (a) talented and (b) attractive, but between us must have given her the impression that we thought she was (a) over the hill as an actress and (b) over the hill as a woman. Harold and I drank a glass of champagne, to make it up to her, while acknowledging the fact that we still haven't cast Marigold (at least officially. But we talked enthusiastically again of Nina Thomas) and we haven't cast Peter, and we haven't cast Nick. In two days I go to San Francisco, for two weeks.

3 May

I'm back from San Francisco. I would prefer not to go into my experiences there in detail, except to say that at the end the production seemed to me OK although nobody in San Francisco seemed anxious to go to it.* It's a hick town, is my belief, except in sexual matters, where it has been making medical history for a decade or so. There was one small incident I'd rather leave unrecorded, but recording it may help me to make it unremembered. I was peeing in the men's lavatory late in the interval during the last preview. From the booth beside me came the sounds of somebody also peeing. The bell rang audibly for the second act. We were the only two still at it. There was the sound of the main lavatory door opening, an elderly woman's voice calling out: 'Henry, Henry, are you all right!' Silence from the next booth. 'Henry! You there!' A non-committal moan from the next booth. 'Well, are you all right, Henry?' A brief pause this time, then, 'I'm all right, I'm all right, but I'm not going back in the theatre, you and Maureen go back in the theatre, but I'm not going back in the theatre.' There was the sound of the main door closing. Complete

---

* See footnote on page 21 for the review of *Quartermaine's Terms* by the Most Influential Critic in San Francisco.

silence from the next booth as I went back in the theatre. But then I had no choice, while old Henry had a night of San Francisco at his feet. Or over them, I strongly hoped. Which brings me to an important question. Why do lavatories in the States, men's anyway, have such a big gap between the floor and the door, and such a quick cut-off on top, so that not only can you see a chap's feet and even ankles if you glance down, but if he's tall enough, also his face if you glance up?

But the fact is, this *is* 3 May, I'm back from San Francisco, and we still haven't got a Peter or a Nick. While I've been away we've had a number of top-class refusals for both parts, one, for Nick, by an actor who, after he'd enthusiastically accepted, explained that actually he'd morally committed himself to something else which he'd hoped wouldn't happen, but was after all and against the odds now about to happen. I can't be bothered to go into the reasons for the other refusals for Nick. Or for Peter, come to that.

10 May

We saw three actors for Peter. One of them was Simon Williams, whom we saw last. My observations about him were as follows:

Simon Williams had the edge. He brought a great deal of instinctive wit to the reading, and is also an extremely attractive and sympathetic man. One sensed an understanding of the deep daftness in the character, most importantly of Peter's habit of meaningless sexual conquest that would one day ambush him into causing pain to others without teaching him a single lesson about himself.* This Peter would always survive in the affection of his friends among whom, I trusted, would be the audience. He is, quite simply, very likeable. So let's hope that his agent doesn't, etc. . . .†

We decided to consider the two other actors who'd auditioned for Peter as possible Nicks tomorrow, then went upstairs to look at rough drafts of the poster. The designer is a glamorous Argentinian Czech or Pole – half Czech/Pole, half Argentinian – called Carlos Sapochnik. Most of the images he'd worked on were strikingly

---

* I mean here no reflection on the actor's private life, only a compliment to his professional understanding of the part.
† We offered him the part. He accepted on the spot. His agent didn't etc. . . .

inappropriate. There was one extraordinary vista of tree stumps in a desert, another of a withered but full-grown tree with a half-human skeleton lying beside it. They were all powerful, one particularly so: a man-baby erupting from a typewriter as if being born from it, his barely formed fingers aiming down towards the keys. We sensed a future in that image, if only we could find some way of making it – I don't mean to sound perverse – more cheerful. We suggested that he might make the head an adult head, a literary intellectual's head, or the conventional view of same – glasses, balding, undeveloped – which might give it at least an air of comedy. He agreed to have a go, and to come back on Friday with further versions. So by Friday we should be on our way with cast and poster. The set is almost designed. We go into action – well, into rehearsals – in eleven days' time. On Monday week.

11 May

Today we saw the two actors we'd transferred from Peter to Nick. The first, for whom I'd had high hopes, gave a perfectly accomplished reading, but there was something in him, a lack of warmth, that made his Nick seem an already beaten fellow, operating from the cunning of one who has had a very bad time throughout his school career and has learnt how to cringe and grin in order to win tolerance, if not respect. A craven Nick, in fact, while Nick has always seemed to me the reverse of craven – impertinent, deceitful, vulgar but always sure of affection.

The other actor, whom I knew from a touring production of one of my plays, began by saying he was very bad in auditions (having proved quite the opposite the day before, when he'd read for Peter) then turned to me and said the only part he'd ever got through auditions was the one I'd offered him, and he wasn't quite sure what it was he'd done that had led me to give him the part. I said I'd given him the part because, out of the ten or so people who'd read for it, he struck me as by far and away the best. This surprised him, he said, as he was so bad at auditions. Harold then said something to the effect that he couldn't be *so bad* at auditions, could he, or we wouldn't have asked him back for another one after yesterday's, would we? The actor supposed, doubtfully, that we wouldn't. But he couldn't understand it, given how badly he'd read for Peter. Yes, well anyway, Harold said, let's come to the case in point – Nick. What did he think of Nick? Meaning, really, we'll have a few preliminary words about the part, and then on with the reading. What did he think of Nick, the actor repeated. Well, for one thing – and like a man methodically plaiting a noose with which he intends to hang himself, he told us what he thought about Nick, exposing Nick's insecurities, probing and then condemning Nick's morals, finding a soupçon of compassion for Nick's all-round unlikeability – all this with the confident air of a social worker analysing a particularly maladjusted case. Of course he wasn't confident at all. I think he'd merely hoped for a short intermission before taking the plunge into reading. The delay generated its own momentum, unfortunately backwards, further and further away from what he was there for. Harold became increasingly impatient, his questions, polite to begin with, got increasingly austere and consequently increasingly devastating; and the more devastating his questions became, the more desperately fluent the actor became in answering them, at one point correcting me in some observation I made in defence of poor old Nick. By the end, when the actor had finally closed the file on Nick and put him back on the shelf, a dead issue, Harold was convinced that he didn't want to direct him. We parted awkwardly, the actor having achieved what he'd set out to achieve, which was not to read at all. But he'd only achieved it in the end by having Harold not wanting him to read, either. A muddle of unfortunate feelings, responses, things taking the wrong turn. I blame myself really. I know the actor better than Harold does, could sense therefore why he hurried so eagerly into a trap of his own making, and should have found some effective way of intervening. What interventions I managed fuelled him on to disaster. The upshot of it is that we still haven't got a Nick, which is a consolation all round, I suppose, especially with a whole nine days to go before the first rehearsal.

13 May

We looked at new versions of the poster. Instead of a desperate baby collapsing out of the typewriter on to the keyboard, the artist, encouraged to buoyancy and uplift, now offers us an exhilarated martyr surging out of the keyboard, skywards. He's still naked, still looks like a baby, a large, rugged baby. What is interesting, from our point of view, anyway, is that bits of the typewriter are flying about, from the strain of delivery. Hardly surprising, given what is being delivered. I wondered tentatively if we couldn't keep the exploding typewriter, but instead of the powerful rocket of a baby, have a pair of hands playing across the keyboard, very composed hands, in complete control, writing calmly, the typewriter exploding to the touch. Carlos took this up, did a quick sketch, and it looked OK. Perhaps that's the poster we'll end up with.*

15 May

Yesterday an urgent summons from Harold to report to the Lyric, where he was to meet an actor who would, he thought, make a perfect Nick. Harold had worked with him before, and had admired him. The actor had also played Hamlet here and there (mainly in Scandinavia, I think) abroad. And he was a bit of a name. Why hadn't we thought of him before? He'd received the play last night, had read it during the early hours and phoned up first thing in the morning to say that he loved Nick, the best part in the play, he thought. Harold arranged for us to see him at five this evening. Well, actually five thirty. I got the time wrong, but by a series of remarkable coincidences, to do with taxis arriving early for once, I arrived at five. I was sloping around the corner of the cafeteria with my coffee when I encountered Harold, who had just spotted our actor seated at a far table. He took me across to him. The actor was much as I had always imagined Nick. He had a lot of hair springing curlily from his scalp (still has, I imagine), his eyes bulged with innocence and wit, a neat little interrogative face and a thin, long frame − perfect, a perfect Nick, albeit with a Scots accent. But then why not a Scots Nick? We wanted him to do it, he wanted to do it, handshakes all round, the bargain sealed. Then he produced from his pocket a puckered envelope on which were written certain dates. It transpired that he'd also been engaged by the BBC to do a film in Norfolk. He assured us that this would be no problem. The dates on which he was scheduled to film allowed

* It was. The hands, though, were less composed than I'd imagined, looking more like claws, sinister. But the image was very striking.

him to get back in good time for our rehearsals. The only difficulty was that one of the dates conflicted with our last preview. But again this was no problem, because he would see to it that the BBC got him back from Norfolk in time to appear on the stage. My heart, I must confess, began to sink. There was a kind of Scots cunning mixed into his general air of Scots ingenuousness that indicated that he was a little too much like Nick in life to be likely to appear as Nick on the stage. When he went on to say that if the BBC objected he would simply walk out on the film because he didn't care whether he worked for the BBC again, as after all what did the BBC have to offer but poor money, bad parts and long hours in rubbish, my heart sank further. This seemed exactly like the kind of thing a chap says when there's an agent waiting behind him to invalidate it an hour later. So I felt pretty gloomy about it though I shook him warmly by the hand and invited him to a drink, which he accepted. Time passed merrily enough until Harold and David Porter (casting director) offered to go up to Porter's office together and phone the actor's agent, whereupon the actor tossed what was left in his glass down his throat, and as Harold and Porter went up the upstairs to Porter's office, sped down the downstairs to the exit, calling out that he'd just remembered he had to collect his daughter, or anyway somebody's daughter, from school. Whereupon my heart sank well below the plumb-line. In fact, as Harold and Porter were unable to get through to the agent, the actor could have downed his drink at leisure. Harold, Porter and I stayed at the bar and had a few more celebration drinks. There was a general euphoria, induced in Harold and Porter by the assumption that, at the very last moment, we'd caught an ideal Nick; induced in me almost entirely by the drink.

The next day Harold phoned me at Queen Mary to tell me that the deal had fallen through. The actor had, in fact, signed a contract for the BBC for the whole of the film production, which went well into our rehearsal period, then beyond it into our preview period and our opening. None of his days was free.*

---

* In spite of his behaviour, I bear him no grudge. I have borne a grudge against only two out of the hundred or so actors I have had dealings with; one of them because he did pratfalls and slow burns and double, even triple, takes in a part calling for the normal human responses ('But that's what I do. *That's* what they've come to see'); and the other, because he announced that he was leaving the production early (and

Six days before rehearsals I went up to Harold's to consider actors for Nick. It was too late to read anyone. We had to come up with somebody we all knew, or that some of us knew. David Porter and Robert Cogo-Fawcett were also in attendance. We went through name after name, touching tentatively on one whose work Harold knew very well, and I knew slightly, that we had considered at the very beginning for Stuart and for Martin, but not previously for Nick. This was Robert East. We went through the other names – I can't recall them now – and found ourselves reverting to Robert East. According to David Porter, Robert East was acting as company manager to a Ray Cooney Theatre of Comedy show at the Criterion, but there was a strong chance that he could get out of it in time to join us for rehearsals, if not on the first day, then very soon after. We tried to get hold of him on the telephone, but the line was engaged, and remained engaged until I left, and was still engaged when I got home and telephoned Harold. Beryl and I went up to the Chinese restaurant. When we got back there was a message from Ben (our son), saying that Robert East had received the play and was now reading it. My heart didn't actually rise at this. I went to bed wondering about Robert East's contract with Ray Cooney, whether he hadn't signed himself up for a year or two, for instance. The next morning, Harold phoned to say that Robert East wanted to do the part, and that he was available. He'd given up his job as company manager at the Criterion the previous Saturday because he was desperate to get back to acting, and had been waiting by the telephone for offers.

17 May

So that, at last, is that. Nicholas Le Prevost is playing Stuart. Ian Ogilvy is playing Martin. Clive Francis is playing Humphry. Simon Williams is playing Peter. Robert East is playing Nick. Nina

---

therefore in the lurch) as he found it rather hot on stage, and couldn't stand the dreadful drip in his dressing room – I think he meant the one from the tap. I have made no effort to discover how many actors I have worked with bear a grudge against me, being unable to think of any reason that they should.

Thomas is playing Marigold.* Harold is directing. The set has been designed by Eileen Diss, costumes will be designed by her friend, Liz Waller. The lighting man at the Lyric Theatre, whose name I will no doubt discover, will be doing the lighting, and the sound man at the Lyric Theatre will be doing the sound. The show is being produced by Peter James, Robert Cogo-Fawcett and David Porter of the Lyric Theatre. We began casting four months ago, and finished it today, four days before rehearsals begin. At least I hope we've finished it.

(We had. The four-day period between casting Bob East and beginning rehearsals was a period of deep tranquillity, disturbed only by flashes of intense panic, dread, etc., at the prospect of going into the production proper. I haven't covered the next five weeks day by day, but, as with the casting, have selected and condensed, reporting on incidents outside the rehearsal room as well as in it.

One of the things that struck me, when reading through this section of the transcripts, was not how much I recorded but, given its bulk, how much I managed to omit of the pleasure that the rehearsals gave. The reason for this, I suppose, is that my nature is of a worrying and fretful kind, and so each evening I came back and brooded aloud about what was worrying and fretting me, rather than describing what had given me satisfaction. The result is that I don't at any moment make clear my admiration for the actors and the director, although I feel pretty sure that those most concerned were fully aware of it at the time. I also fail to describe in general terms Harold's working method. But then his method, unclouded by theories and principles, amounts merely to the bringing of his concentration to every part of the play. In fact Harold demystified the whole directing process for me years ago. For example, previous directors had tended to keep me out of rehearsals while they were doing something called 'blocking' – 'No point your coming in yet, why not wait until I've finished the blocking' and later, 'You might as well take a day or two off, I want to concentrate on reblocking Act One.' And later Act Two. And sometimes, if I made a tentative reservation about where an actor was standing – or, indeed, a

* I have no record on the tape as to when we decided to offer Marigold officially to Nina Thomas, but it must have been weeks, if not months, earlier. We'd really cast her during her audition, which is why – along with all the hassles over the other casting – we saw so few Marigolds.

tentative reservation about almost anything on the stage – 'But if I change that, it'll mean reblocking the *whole* scene.' I therefore assumed that 'blocking' was a mysterious, virtually ungraspable activity, at least to such laymen as playwrights – until I at last saw Harold actually at it. Whereupon I immediately understood that 'blocking' is simply discovering where the actors should stand, when they should move, where they should sit, to the maximum dramatic effect while appearing natural. Apart from a few technicalities – for example, making sure that characters don't actually stand in front of each other (this is called 'masking') and can be seen from all parts of the theatre (this is called 'paying attention to the sightlines') and don't 'upstage' each other, i.e. aren't so arranged on the stage that one actor engages the audience's attention when you actually want the other or both noticed – there is nothing to 'blocking' except the usual application of common sense. When I initially told Harold that I didn't really understand about 'blocking' he looked at me in bewilderment, and said: 'But that's the easiest part of the whole business. And you can always change it if it doesn't feel right.' Harold starts rehearsals by blocking rapidly right the way through the play, then goes back to the beginning, and works through the play again more slowly, examining the lines in relation to the moves as his understanding of a scene deepens, adjusting the moves accordingly. For example the first time around he might think a scene relaxed and playful, and so have the actors sitting in relaxed, if not playful, postures. Later, on uncovering various tensions in the scene, he might think it more effective to keep them on their feet. And so forth. There were various moments in our rehearsals when the blocking became of the utmost importance – one, which I've reported, when Harold unblocked and reblocked a couple of scenes not only for immediate dramatic purposes, but to release the actors in a way that affected their total performances. But even this was a *practical* response to a growing sense that the actors had become slightly inhibited in their characters because inhibited physically, and not an example of specialized or privileged 'directorial insight'. In other words, anyone possessed of the requisite powers of concentration, instinctive sympathy with actors, and a natural dash of authority would have done the same, and can therefore direct a play.)

21 May

First day of rehearsals. I arrived at Turnham Green underground station – a long trip from Highgate – and walked along Chiswick High Road to the Ballet Rambert studios. Although I was nearly half an hour early, I saw Harold standing on the pavement in front of the Ballet Rambert, looking composed and powerful in black. We were the first to arrive apart from the stage management, who provided us with cups of coffee. Harold went upstairs to the rehearsal room to look at the model of the set. I sat in the green room attempting to look like Harold, composed and powerful, though in pink and blue, as the actors appeared in dribs and drabs. I took it upon myself to make introductions, thus bringing together with gestures and 'Do-you-know-each-others?' Simon Williams and Ian Ogilvy, who had not only arrived together, but were old friends. I then attempted to introduce Liz Waller, the dress designer, to the stage management, then remembered that I still hadn't quite got the names of the stage management, so ended up introducing Liz Waller to herself. At about that point I gave up, hoping that somebody would start introducing me to somebody. When all the actors had turned up, and we'd sat around for a bit drinking coffee and making meaningless conversation, Harold came down from the set, gave calm greetings, and led us back up to look at the model. It was extremely convincing. Models always are. We all muttered appreciation as Eileen showed us how the revolve worked, how bits of dressing and furniture could be moved off for the unrevolved set changes. We bent over it, crouching and gesticulating, stepping backwards for perspective and forwards for detail, but we all really knew that it was a formality – something to be gone through before getting to the reading which was the main, in fact the only, real business of the morning.

It began when we'd all sat down at a long table, Harold rearranging people a little, so that the actors were together. I sat at the far end, my script on my lap, my pen in my fingers, as if I were myself 'Doc' Simon, already called in to add some one-liners and frisk up the text. I can't bear to look at the actors at read-throughs, partly because I'm convinced that my face is bright red from embarrassment.

Harold began by making a pronouncement about not wishing to

make any pronouncements. Looking forward very much to the weeks of rehearsal ahead, exploring, discovering the text, ·feeling sure we would all enjoy it enormously, 'Simon, is there anything you'd like to say?' Redface, without looking up, shook his head and gobbled a few negatives. Pause. Then Redface gobbled, 'Looking forward to it very much.'

Harold went through the changes we'd made to the text. The only important one was to rename Hubert Parkin the offstage poet who accompanies Stuart through the play. It had occurred to me that as Parkin rhymes with Larkin and Hubert contains the same number of syllables as Philip, there might be imbeciles abroad who'd insist on confusing Hubert Parkin with Philip Larkin. I've always admired the sadness, wit and impeccable formality of Larkin's poetry, and as Parkin's life in the play is a long, sordid decline, I wouldn't want to give even imbeciles the opportunity for confusion. They'll doubtless make their own. I wonder what sort of poetry Parkin wrote, though. It would have to have *some* of the classical virtues of Larkin's to please Stuart. We spent some time in a parlour game, looking for a new name for Parkin, until somebody – I can't remember who, as I was still keeping my head lowered – suggested Stout. We all tested it. Stout, Hubert Stout. And accepted it. But none of the changes, not even that one, was really essential. Harold went through them only so that the actors could sit writing in and crossing out, to create the illusion that they were taking part in a routine process of which the read-through was merely the last mundane step.

But a read-through is never mundane. For my part, I find it almost impossible to listen consciously. Wherever I turn, however much I attempt to block my ears by thinking of pleasant matters like cricket and sex and the first glass of wine, or the later first Scotch, of the day, every word somehow gets through. The actors get through, too.

On the whole the actors were OK. Ian Ogilvy seems to have a sure-footed sense of the possibilities of Martin. Bob East was pretty bold with Nick, although I suspect he'd slightly overprepared his reading, especially his last scene, in which he seemed to be dying hideously at the age of about ninety, instead of struggling for breath at the age of about thirty-eight. Simon Williams, clearly besieged by nerves, was a great deal less spontaneous and witty as Peter than he'd been in his audition. (Why wasn't he besieged by nerves then, too?) Nicholas Le Prevost's Stuart was certainly intelligent, certainly serious, but consistently dour and therefore dull, which was valuable as it showed the danger of the part. We'll have to avoid making him the play's 'meaningful' centre, and concentrate on keeping him as simply another (I hope, attractive and vivacious) character. Nina Thomas gave us a charming and individual Marigold. Her brief is to make up for the deficiencies in my writing, but I don't think we need tell her that. Clive Francis was vivid – he's never less than vivid – but turned Humphry into a posturing Cambridge queen, which seems to me not only wrong, but almost perfectly wrong. Humphry, as we eventually discover, is homosexual. But he is also always resolutely normal, the most down-to-earth character in the play. The scene in which his death is announced was ghastly, by the way, full of sickly reverence and low-toned melancholy, whereas I'd intended it to be, if not light, then at least matter of fact. But that was valuable too, as it reminded one of the obvious trap: of playing the play for laughs in the funny bits and seriously in the serious bits. We'll have to make sure that the funny and the serious are simply played naturally, leaving the audience to find out for themselves which is which. If the play is about anything, it's about the way things go on – 'old life itself' as Stuart says, just before his wife-to-be announces her abortion.

What worries me most, though, is me. My work. I found myself hating bits of the play quite a lot. For instance, a long stretch at the beginning of Act One, Scene Two that seemed to me very lumpish, and an interminable patch in Act Two of lifeless exposition. There are also embarrassing lines scattered everywhere, some sounding facetious, and some brutal.

In fact, all in all, I was pretty depressed. Of course, post-coital depression is common to all read-throughs. The actors are convinced that the director and producer are already recasting; the playwright is convinced that as soon as the actors get home they'll be on the blower to their agents, demanding to be got out of this; the director is convinced that the playwright is blaming him for landing the play with a dud cast, while at the same time thinking that the actors are blaming him for landing them with a dud play. Of course, I may have got all this wrong. It's possible that every other playwright swells with pride when he hears his play being read for the first time, that the actors in my own plays are dazed by their good fortune in having such plum parts, with such fine lines, in such a powerful, funny and moving piece, and that the director is gloating over his good fortune in having such a play, such a cast, to enhance his name with. The fact is, *I'm* always depressed after a read-through and certainly am so now.

We finished much earlier than Harold and I had expected. Does that mean the play is too short? Will we have to stretch it out with heavy pauses, long and complicated moves, numerous curtain calls? Today, at least, we solved the problem by stopping when we'd got to the end and going down the road to an Italian restaurant for lunch. Peter James, who'd strolled with us but didn't intend to stay for more than a quick drink, very sweetly ordered some champagne. I was the actual host, very lordly in my ordering, and felt distinctly shifty when the bill came and Peter James, who never quite got around to leaving, insisted on paying for all the other wine, too. It wasn't a particularly cheerful occasion, too much was drunk too quickly as a way of obliterating the memory of the read-through, and what conversation there was came from conscious attempts not to talk about what was most on everybody's mind. Yet the meal dragged itself on and on. It took over three hours to get back on the pavement, stomachs full of food we hadn't really enjoyed, heads swimming with wine we hadn't really wanted. Everything seeming, to me anyway, unreal and a little unpleasant. As if I'd banqueted my way through one depression into another.

Harold and I went to a coffee house in Holland Park and swapped our impressions. Harold was particularly disconcerted by Clive Francis's Cambridge queen, and determined to correct it immediately. I touched on the question of Nick Le Prevost's glumness, on my worries about the text. Encapsulated, the conversation would seem very brief, but of course we kept returning to the same points, or peering at dim but disconcerting memories through the haze of our indigestion.

We separated at about six, which left me with three hours to kill before meeting Beryl for dinner in the West End. She was coming on from a party at the college where she teaches. I thought of taking my depression off to a cinema, but found myself, will-less, going home in the hope that I might catch her before she left. The tube was packed. Everybody seemed to get out at my station (Highgate) so I was jammed against the escalator rail going up. The only person on the escalator coming down was my wife. She came towards me, then went past me, completely unaware of my gesturings and callings out, intent on her own business. Rather alarming. And now I'm off to meet her for dinner, having spent most of the time since I got home dictating this into the machine.

22 May

Second day of rehearsal. We spent the morning discussing costumes. Liz Waller had brought along various magazines from the sixties, Ian Ogilvy an album full of photographs of himself and his friends from the early sixties to the end of the decade. I loathed the sixties while they were going on, and loathe them in retrospect. Whenever I come across photographs of myself taken then, I always assume that I was an anachronism, somebody whose spiritual home was in the fifties who had got born too late, or in the seventies, who had got born too early. My hair is short, I'm in cords, pullovers, big black shoes. Around me, invisible in the pictures, are the real sixties people, in flared jeans, beads, kaftans, mini-skirts, etc. So it was rather a shock to see from Ian Ogilvy's collection that the young actor of the time was really just a sprucer version of myself – hair shortish, pullovers, etc., though with something snappier on his feet, like suede. What surprised me most was the prevalence of ties, not only in Ian Ogilvy's album, but in Liz Waller's magazines.* Liz Waller tends to believe that people dress to a dominant trait in their character, which I suppose makes sense on the stage as it assists in instant recognition, but I am never entirely convinced. Lazy men can be fussy dressers, unhygienic men dress neatly. Furthermore, I believe that people's attitudes to their dress change considerably in

---

* In my day as an undergraduate (when the people in the play were also up), virtually everyone wore a tie, because we had to wear a gown for lectures, supervisions, going to hall, going into town in the evening. Wearing a gown meant wearing a tie. Of course, there were quite a few smartie-boots and fops who were prepared to change from their polo-necks to shirts when gown occasions came up, and I did, I suddenly remember, go in for polo-necks myself, out of which I didn't bother to change when going to town in the evenings, solving the problem posed by the gown–tie statute by not wearing a gown either. I was mortified at never being stopped by the proctor or his bulldogs (university policemen) who used to tour the streets looking for sartorial infringements. Evidently, I didn't look like a member of the university.

the course of their lives. Some start off by being indifferent to what they wear, but pay more and more attention to their clothes as they get older. Others worry about the way they present themselves to the world when they're young, but as life closes in, take less trouble. Peter, for example, might be a bit of a peacock during the first scene when he wants to attract the young ladies. But in the scene before the Epilogue, when he is in his late thirties, and has to deal with two wives, lots of children, making do on a limited salary while desperately hacking out books he doesn't want to write that he knows nobody wants to read, he might give the impression of having dressed with indecent haste in the clothes nearest to hand. In fact, now I come to think of it, I'm not sure philandering and peacockery inevitably go together. A crumpled undergraduate could be just as obsessed with women, just as successful with them. The danger of dressing the actors to a dominant character trait is that we make them stereotypes. I suspect that none of the people in *The Common Pursuit* is interested in clothes except possibly Nick and Marigold. Anyway, who knows what immediate events, what subterranean history, makes people dress as they do on this date or that?

We talked about clothes all morning, Liz Waller seeing all the characters in terms of types and fashion, I arguing for unguessable-at haphazardness, Harold listening, commenting, reserving judgement. Then we had a brisk lunch, and began the rehearsal proper, not in the Ballet Rambert room, as we had all assumed, but on the stage at the Lyric, the Ballet Rambert having let out their rehearsal room to somebody else for the afternoon. Whether this was our muddle or theirs, I don't know. From tomorrow on we're back at the Ballet Rambert. But this afternoon, on the stage of the theatre in which we will finally present the play, we began our rehearsals. Harold worked his way through the first scene in Stuart's rooms in Cambridge, blocking the moves rapidly, and then got rather jammed in the long second scene, in Stuart's office in London, when it suddenly became clear that the furniture was badly positioned. One chair, set upstage, almost against the back wall, completely altered the focus. When Martin (Ian Ogilvy) sat in it, I was unable to look at anyone else. And yet Martin was meant to be shyly and diffidently on the outer fringes. Because of his position, he became majestically shy and diffident, all the other life in the room somehow sucked towards him. This accidental other (which is what I presumably meant when I called it strangulated) – and got on with the business to hand. But if he was being frustrated by his need for a cigarette, *and* frustrated by Bob East's tenacity over a detail of phrasing, he'd have had to keep a doubly strong hold over his impatience to avoid a doubly powerful explosion. Which he did, visibly. Although the sight of so much visible patience didn't unnerve Bob East. This surprised me until I realized much later that the discussion/argument wasn't over a detail at all, at least from Bob East's point of view. Given his line of reasoning, he must see Nick as someone who would instinctively sneer at Martin. Whereas Harold and I, given our line of reasoning, must (I know we do) see him as a high-spirited and likeable show-off. Certainly not a sneerer. Bob East's fight was for something fundamental to his understanding of the character of Nick, although I don't think he himself fully realized it at the time. Certainly I didn't, nor did Harold, but it explains why, I suppose, we all sensed that something more crucial was at stake than the position of a comma and a full stop. I must remember to raise this with Harold tomorrow, the implication for the whole play of a sneering rather than a light-winged Nick.

To come back to Harold's struggle with smoking. I probably make things more difficult, being a chain-smoker. In previous rehearsals, we've chain-smoked together. This time, he chews away at his nicotine gum, with the smoke of my cigarettes leaking reminiscently up his nostrils, down into his lungs. On top of that he used to *use* his cigarettes in rehearsals, taking one deliberately out of the black box (Sobranies) putting it in his mouth, lighting it with a swift gesture, inhaling it deeply, as often as not walking a few paces away to take the cigarette out, study it, put it back in his mouth, inhale. It was a pantomime, an enactment of thought, he was making it clear to everyone that he was thinking, making it clear to himself that he had taken the time to think. Now, without a cigarette to resort to, he finds a lacuna between a question and its answer, which he can only fill with a baffled silence, which leads to further silence and further bafflement as the need to answer looms larger and larger, the people waiting for his answer no doubt seeming to do likewise. He hasn't yet found an alternative ritual to accompany thought, and I doubt if he'll find it in his chewing gum. You can't do much more with chewing gum than put it in your mouth and chew it. At least not without disgusting everybody.

One last thought. All the actors and our one actress are extremely attractive. People will enjoy looking at them. But can I take credit for that?

23 May

We are back at the Ballet Rambert, which is a relief. Yesterday, sitting in the stalls watching rehearsals going on, I suddenly realized how many days and days and further days of my life have now been spent sitting in the stalls of theatres in the dark, convinced that the sun is shining outside. Whether it is or not, there I am, with an ashtray full of cigarette stubs beside me, attempting to control my impatience and irritation at the slow progress we're making, while actually aware that my impatience and irritation are unjustified because there is usually enough time in which we can patiently and without irritation sort out the problems. When I was about to direct (my first experience of directing) one of my own plays, I asked Harold what to be most on the guard against, in myself. He thought for less than a second, then said: 'Your impatience.' When it came to it I found it much easier to be patient as a director running rehearsals than as a playwright attendant on them. It seemed to me quite obvious that the director and the actors have to find their own routes.* It's no good the playwright saying continuously, 'Well, actually what I meant here, heard here, saw here, was this. Now, you know, just cut the crap and get on with it.' But then of course I didn't have a nuisance of a playwright lurking at my shoulder, nagging away, which Harold has. Six straight weeks of *me* ahead, and *no smoking*. Poor Sod.

There's no point in making further excuses for my behaviour, so I might as well just cut the crap and get on with it. For instance, after

* Two sudden memories should modify this boast. One, that during rehearsals I had a severe bout of flu, and then mysteriously damaged a nerve in my leg, which meant that for the next nine months I limped about with dropped toes. I've never been ill when present merely as the playwright. Two, that I adopted such a free and easy attitude to the text that at one point the actors ganged up and demanded that I show more respect for the playwright (i.e. myself).

'A plump and pampered playwright, with a glass of white wine in front of me fairly early in the morning...' A photograph that didn't appear in *Time Out*

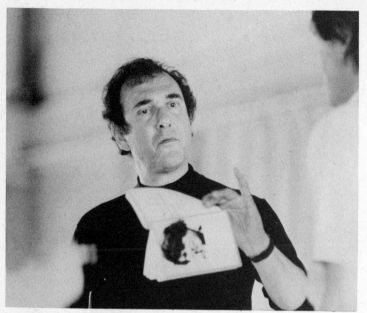

Harold Pinter with the playwright between his fingers

Harold Pinter with Ian Ogilvy and Nicholas Le Prevost discussing the opening o
Act One, Scene Two

Rehearsing Act One, Scene Two
Above: Simon Williams (Peter) and Nicholas Le Prevost (Stuart)
Below: Clive Francis (Humphry) and Robert East (Nick)

Rehearsing Act One, Scene Two
Above: Clive Francis
(Humphry) and Nina Thomas
(Marigold)
Left: Clive Francis (Humphry)
with Ian Ogilvy (Martin)

a)

(b)

(c)

(d)

Ideas for the poster
(a) and (b) Carlos Sapochnik's first thoughts
(c) The revised version of (b)
(d) The final poster

The opening of the play: Nina
Thomas as Marigold and Nicholas
Le Prevost as Stuart

Act Two, Scene One: Clive Francis as
Humphry

Act Two, Scene One: Nina Thomas as Marigold and Ian Ogilvy as Martin

Act Two, Scene One
Above: Nicholas Le Prevost as Stuart
Below: Simon Williams as Peter

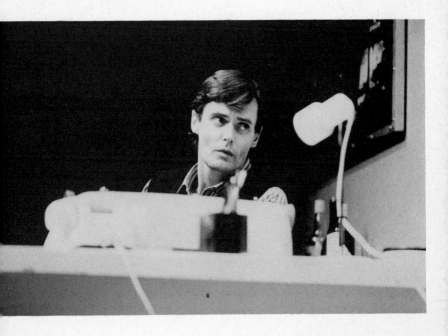

Act Two, Scene Two: Robert East as Nick with Ian Ogilvy as Martin and Nicholas Le Prevost as Stuart

The full cast in the Epilogue
Left to right: Ian Ogilvy as Martin, Simon Williams as Peter, Nina Thomas as Marigold, Robert East as Nick, Nicholas Le Prevost as Stuart and Clive Francis as Humphry

yesterday, I simply can't understand why Ian Ogilvy is *still* displaying an irony that amounts to effrontery in Martin. I meant him to be ingenuous, eager, diffident, on *everybody*'s side really, but most of all on Stuart's. What he ends up getting (like Stuart's wife) he gets by burrowing away from within, and today (as yesterday) we had a Martin who is foraging cynically from without. We see him *at it*. Nicholas Le Prevost's Stuart is doing what Ian Ogilvy's Martin should be doing, offering ingenuousness and a glum (though I don't want that from Martin, either) stumbling sweetness. Clive Francis is now some distance from his Cambridge queen, though, being me, I keep suspecting that any moment the queen will make a comeback.

But it was Bob East that perplexed me. By which I mean, drove me crazy. It's true that Nick has a smoker's cough that begins as something of an affectation in the first scene, and gets worse throughout the play, until in the last scene (before the Epilogue) he actually has emphysema, but Bob coughed, and he coughed, and Christ did he cough. My plays attract enough coughers in the audience. We don't need them on the stage too. I had a hideous vision of Bob East and the scattered coughers in the stalls (where they most like to sit, towards the front) going at it together, answering each other, developing each other's themes, capping each other in volume and meaning until the whole audience joined in, the dress circle, the circle, the gallery, led by Bob East in a mighty cough-along, the cathartic fulfilment of something latent in most evenings in the theatre. But even if we contain the effect, there are still technical problems caused by Bob East's coughing, particularly for the other actors, who risk having their lines drowned when speaking on cue, or may decide to meet the challenge by bellowing their lines above the cough, or, I suppose, hang about doing bits of business, therefore slowing down the action, etc., until he's finished his cough then quickly squeezing in their lines before he starts another one. And finally, of course, in the delicate, and melancholy and quite amusing (I hope) scene in which Humphry's death is announced, by which stage Nick has got his emphysema, there'll be no chance for the audience to indulge in a little tender grieving, if at the same time they are watching another character in what appears to be his hectic death throes. So what was Bob East up to?

When Harold drove me to Holland Park after the rehearsal* he asked me what I felt about Bob East's cough. I said it should be pared down, surely, to the bone, as a matter of fact, what had Bob been up to? 'Well,' Harold said, 'you wrote in quite a few coughs, you know. In the stage directions.' 'Yes, probably too many,' I agreed, 'and we certainly don't want them added to, do we?' So we agreed to eliminate any coughs written into the text, eliminate all Bob East's superfluous coughs, and start from scratch, finding out as we went along where the cough could be economically placed, with a proper reference to the context. 'The trouble is', Harold said, 'he's obviously given a lot of thought to the coughs. Worked hard on them. They're not inappropriate, in realistic terms. He might want to cling on to them.' Harold finally decided he'd better discuss the matter with Bob East privately, over lunch, I to attend to give authorial consent to the cutting of coughs from the script. Neither of us is looking forward to it very much, given the long public tussle over his 'in fact' as opposed to our 'in fact' only yesterday. I told Harold I was also worried by a feeling that Bob East was isolating himself from the company. All the other actors stayed in the rehearsal room even when not actually working themselves, to observe the way in which the characters and the play is developing – or at least changing. Bob East stayed downstairs all morning until summoned. I'd seen him there in the morning, when I'd had to make a series of panic-stricken telephone calls in an attempt to trace my son Ben, who'd failed, I'd been informed by his school just before I'd left home, to turn up to his first class at ten. I knew for a fact he'd left the house at eight, having bidden him farewell myself. As I'd dialled around London trying to track him down, entertaining the usual flood of parental images to do with tumbles in front of incoming tubes, fallings under buses, knives at Camden Town, etc., I'd been conscious of Bob East in the green room opposite, his head bent over the text, pencil in hand, and wondered – as I asked demented questions as to Ben's whereabouts†

* This became our evening ritual. First a drink in the pub, sometimes with members of the cast, sometimes just the two of us. Then the drive to Holland Park, where I either picked up a taxi to Highgate or if I felt up to it (i.e. no taxi available) got the tube home.
† I finally got him at a friend's, where he'd decided on the way to school that that was where he'd prefer to spend his morning. Which allowed me to relax into a paternal tantrum. I pointed out that his school – tutorial college, actually – was very expensive, charging almost by the minute for teaching him, even when he wasn't there to be taught. I expect that during this Bob East was observing *me*.

– why he wasn't upstairs with the others. I mentioned this to Harold who said he also wished that Bob would join the company in a post-rehearsal drink, it wasn't good for company morale when an actor kept himself apart. I took this up, raising *en passant* my view that Bob East misunderstood something fundamental about the nature of Nick. By the time we'd finished we were both dreading the lunch.

Later

Harold phoned to report that he'd gone through the text, and discovered that Bob East was coughing *only* where I'd specified in my stage directions* and we could hardly blame him for that, could we, especially as we'd made such a big deal of his slight deviation from the text only yesterday; that now he'd had time to think about it, Bob East was perfectly entitled to study his lines in the green room – every actor has his own way of working; and why should we insist that he has to have a drink with us when he lives such a long way from the rehearsal room, and has a wife and children to get back to, whose company he might actually find more congenial than ours. I see the point of everything Harold says, but I'm still worried about the lunch.

What is recorded in the transcripts of our first conversation about Bob East doesn't do proper justice to its tone, which I remember quite clearly. In fact, what I really succeeded in doing was to convince us both that Bob East would fight, and to the death, to hold on to every single cough he'd so far coughed; that we wouldn't be taking him out to lunch but cornering him in a restaurant in order to strip him of his coughs, every one of them, by force if necessary. We'd have to back each other up, guard our rear, make it plain to him that not only was he not to cough except under strict supervision, he was also not to learn his lines in the green room but participate fully in rehearsals and, furthermore, we'd like an explanation as to why he wasn't joining in the post-rehearsal drink, along with the rest of the boys. And the girl. The transcripts go on to show, however, that the lunch was in fact an extremely pleasant

---

* So *that*'s what he was up to. For the powerful effect of my usually irrelevant stage directions see page 64.

affair, with Bob East agreeing that I'd written in too many coughs, and that it would be best if he were to find out where they should come in rehearsal. This must have taken about five minutes. The rest of the meal was apparently spent in discussing cricket, allowing me to transfer my paranoia to the England selectors, with, I expect, special reference to Peter May, for not picking Mike Gatting as captain, and so possibly ruining David Gower's career.

I realize in retrospect that Harold's brief and uncharacteristic collaboration in my original spasm of paranoia about Bob East came, not from his not smoking, or at least not *only* from his not smoking, but also, probably more centrally, from his long relationship with Bob East. He has always had a high regard for his acting. His name had been on our very first casting list. And then Harold directed one of Bob East's plays at the Hampstead Theatre Club, a play full of interest, I thought, which nevertheless – perhaps I should really say therefore – most of the reviewers trampled over, wondering, as they've also done with my plays, why Harold wastes his time directing such stuff, etc. (The answer is, I suppose, that Harold likes directing, and such stuff is the stuff he likes to direct. Most people like doing things they do well. Also he gets paid for it, which I expect he also likes.) Harold also cast and directed him in a key role in the first production, *The Hothouse*, which Harold wrote at about the same time as *The Birthday Party*, decided to shelve, and recently rediscovered in a tea-chest or a suitcase and did a few years ago at the Hampstead Theatre Club. On top of this, for many summers he had captained Bob East in the Gaieties Cricket Club, of which Harold was the president and founding member, Bob East the leading batsman and star all-rounder. And now here they were back again in yet another relationship, Harold directing Bob East in a new play by an old colleague. Such a history would inevitably contain a number of downs, a number of ups, the most dramatic of both probably coming during their cricket-playing days, cricket after all being life, and plays only art, or aspiring that way. After so many different and complicated connections, they were bound to be particularly sensitive to each other's feelings, and to their own about each other.

As for my own part in the Bob East incident, I should like to announce here that I don't normally behave like a paid police informer, or perhaps more accurately the school sneak, even in rehearsals at their most fraught. I see now, of course, that this really very minor episode marked a significant phase in the growth of my almost pathological relationship with the production, which was unlike my pathological relationship with previous productions only in the degree of its intensity, and the never quiescent sense that something had gone wrong somewhere, probably long before we'd gone into rehearsals. I think it's worth pointing out, though, while I'm still amazed by it, that all the above excerpts come from my recording on 23 May, after only three days of rehearsal, and that while I seemed to know something of what was going on in myself, I seemed, as subsequent events establish, unable to learn from it. My impatience, which at times over the following weeks blossomed into full-fledged lunacy, was unflagging, but clearly without much of a memory.

24 May

I simply can't make out what Nina Thomas is up to. As soon as she enters a scene she stops and wonders aloud where she should move. Where an actor moves must depend, to some extent, on intention (and of course where other people happen to be, etc.) but the intention must be the character's. Not where the *actor* wants to go, but where the character, given his or her motives for entering the room, his or her relationship with the people in it, would naturally end up. Well, as a beginning, at least. But Nina Thomas is entering the room as Marigold, stopping, looking around, and saying, as Nina Thomas, 'Where should I go next? I feel I should sit down. Where do I make for? What is my plan here?' Plan. She did this three times, not going anywhere, not sitting anywhere, just brooding about it at the door, halting the momentum of the rehearsal, also making it impossible to answer her questions. If she'd gone somewhere, as Marigold, one might have answered her, but as she'd stopped being Marigold, and refused to go anywhere as Nina, her question had no meaning.*

* It probably had a meaning for Nina Thomas, who was probably indirectly asking a question about the other people in the room, or was anxious to discuss her attitude to them, or both. In other words, code for the usual message: Help me — which was in due course decoded.

25 May

At the end of rehearsal, Harold and I arranged to meet the actors in
the pub. We had to hang on for a while, to talk to the sound man
(although he looked more like a boy, a boy with a beard) who had
turned up unexpectedly. As there was nothing much to say at this
stage about music, or sound effects (what sound effects?), we spent
a pretty meaningless half an hour talking about having nothing yet
to talk about, then hastened to the pub. It was empty. We toured
around a few more pubs, looking for the actors, then returned to
the original one, where they still weren't. This was perplexing.
Pooter-like, I entertained the possibility that they'd deliberately
suggested one pub, while actually going to another in order to enjoy
a drink without the playwright and director spoiling it for them. Or
(again Pooter-like) I'd simply misunderstood the directions, and
had led Harold off to the wrong pub, and was now blaming the
actors for not being in it. Anyway, we left the main bar for
something called the Garden Bar, which turned out to be a
concreted patio at the back of the building. Perfectly pleasant until
the usual bloody awful music suddenly billowed out at us. We rose
tetchily and found a wine bar further down the street. We sat down
at a table and waited for the girl who was clearly meant to be
serving drinks to serve us with a drink. She had her back to us, and
was on the telephone, where she continued to be for the next ten
minutes or so, sometimes talking urgently, as if to her lover,
sometimes laughing intimately, as if to her lawyer (I'm trying to
avoid stereotypes here), but completely ignoring the only two
customers. As did the only other waitress, who came in and out
carrying baskets of bread and bowls of potatoes. When the girl on
the telephone finally hung up, she began a long conversation with
the bread and potatoes girl, during which she picked up a pad, put
it down again, picked up a pad, put it down again, picked up a pen,
frequently beginning to back towards us, once even beginning a
swivel that, if completed, would have brought us face to face at last.
This series of movements, always interrupted by a further exchange
with the bread and potatoes girl, at least suggested that the idea of
service was lingering somewhere in her mind. Nearly twenty
minutes must have elapsed before she got the pen and the pad in her
hands, and came to our table, a mere second or so after Harold had

risen to his feet, with a declamatory gesture and some words to the effect that he'd had enough of this, and taken himself to the door. Rising myself, I said that we'd been waiting an awfully long time for a drink, and she said (she was Australian), 'I was only on the telephone for a minute [a lie] and I couldn't help it.' (This was probably not so much a lie as a piece of irrelevant self-analysis.) Although I longed to continue our discussion, I was acutely aware of Harold, now out on the pavement and striding up and down past the windows. I tried to think of something crushing to finish her off with, failed, joined Harold outside. We both glared in at her through the window, then went off to Harold's car. Now the fact is we spent nearly twenty minutes in a wine bar, the only customers, with two waitresses in evidence, without getting a drink. That's not the point, of course – without *service*. No, that's not the point. The point is, was, without a drink. What was odd about it, though, is that we spent the whole of that time, except for the first two or three minutes when we talked about professional matters, watching closely, commenting on, and becoming increasingly incensed by the girl's behaviour. And I haven't the slightest idea, just a few hours later, of what she looked like.* Anyway, we drove back to Campden Hill Square, where we found Antonia, who had just returned from being honoured at a literary luncheon at Blackwell's. So we had our drink at last, several drinks as a matter of fact, and I described to Antonia (with pantomime) the effect Harold's not smoking had had on rehearsals so far. It was all very pleasant.

26 May, Saturday

It's 1.15 in the morning. I am dictating this while of unsound mind. When I got home, Beryl told me she'd found a house that she'd liked the look of up in the village. (We've been planning to move, off and on, for the last ten years.) At nine o'clock we went up to look it over, having phoned the owner beforehand to ask if we might. It's a delightful house, seventeenth century, with a nice garden, but not quite enough rooms for our purposes. When we'd made the three mandatory inspections, one in hope, one to confirm

---

* I have a suspicion, though, that she was plump. I have a history of altercations with plump girls.

it wouldn't quite work, one from courtesy, and had had a glass of wine and a gossip about military matters with the owner (he was a retired major), we'd been there well over an hour and it was time to go. Lucy, our fourteen-year-old daughter, had gone to the cinema with a friend from school; we didn't want her returning to an unaccountably empty house. The retired major, elderly with an unhealthy bald dome, led us to the hall, made a charming farewell speech, took out his key, with which he failed to unlock the door. He tried endlessly, it seemed, turning the key this way and that – failing to understand – didn't make sense – trouble was the windows were no good – double-glazed – wall around the garden about eight feet high – we could walk the gutter – jump – little dangerous – phone the police – really didn't understand. I managed to control my mounting panic with the help of cooling-down looks from Beryl, although becoming convinced that the retired major was a madman who'd locked us in on purpose. I phoned home, to leave a message for Lucy (now due back) but also to make sure he hadn't cut the wires. Finally, when he did something precisely like the somethings he'd been doing all the time, the key turned, the door opened, and we hurried home, to find the house empty. This was all right for a quarter of an hour, was slightly less all right after half an hour. At twelve o'clock, just as it began to rain, I went up the hill to stand at the bus stop. At half-past twelve, after a couple of buses had passed followed by no buses at all, I came home to find Lucy and friend sitting on the front step. They had been next door since a few minutes or so before we got back, we worked it out at, but as Lucy had forgotten her keys, they'd decided to watch television with our neighbours, confident that they'd hear our return, which was why Lucy hadn't bothered to slip a note through the letter-box to let us know where she was. (I provide this information for the benefit of those who fret about details, motives, so forth.) Beryl and I had a brief discussion with Lucy (but not her friend) on the subject of thoughtlessness, then I came in here to dictate this.

What disturbs me is not the little run of accidents that led to a spasm of parental terror, but the feeling that anything I embark on at the moment, even the simplest thing like looking at a house, is liable to go wrong. I suspect that my growing anxiety over Lucy somehow transmitted itself to the old major, who became therefore more and more incompetent. After all, he presumably lets himself fluently in and out all the time, otherwise a good part of his day would be spent crouched at the keyhole.

28 May

Rehearsals began for me at about three this morning, when I started out of sleep with the conviction that Nick Le Prevost had a lisp, and was concealing it from us. I'd suppose this was the product of a dream if I weren't a straight-down-the-line literal dreamer. I don't dream in symbols, i.e. a mysterious dish of over-boiled carrots, I dream that I'm impotent. More importantly, I don't dream of children's parties, I dream that I'm in the middle of rehearsals, the actors getting their characters wrong as usual, Harold chewing gum and staring urgently at nothing, I shaking with impatience. So I took the dream about Nick Le Prevost's lisp quite seriously because I took it to mean that he had a lisp and was deceiving us about having it. I've got nothing against Nick Le Prevost having a lisp, but I do think the chap who plays Stuart shouldn't have a lisp. Or a club-foot or a hunchback. At least without giving me a chance to rewrite the text.

I spent the morning going through a draft of *The Rector's Daughter* with David Jones, attempting to keep my mind off Nicholas Le Prevost's lisping his lines and getting away with it by pretending that he was still working out their meaning. By the time I got to the rehearsal room, I had formed a plan to watch Nick Le Prevost's lips like a hawk, and the moment I saw or heard the lisp, to alert Harold to it. He could take it from there.

But Nicholas Le Prevost fell into such a natural, easy, amusing account of Stuart that not only did my preoccupation with the possibility of his having a lisp vanish, a great deal of my other worries about him vanished with it. He was steely, ironic and funny. When he was watching Martin, and then Humphry, his stillness made him the most impressive figure in the room. He's also beginning to find a lot of fun in lines that he'd previously made sound gloomy. What's more, no lisp.

On the other hand, Clive Francis was camp again. I suggested to Harold over lunch that as Humphry's parents live in Exeter, we might encourage Clive to adopt a West Country accent, strong in the first scene and again in the Epilogue, but thinning out in the intervening scenes as he gets older. To root him in a background, in fact, and one, unlike Cambridge, with no tradition of queens. It seems to me difficult, though I've tried, to imagine a West Country queen. Though I suppose there are some, rolling about on tractors or running the Hardy museums.

During the afternoon, I made a few cuts and changes to the text, all of which pleased me, although I think I might just have overdone it. A terrible tendency of mine that Harold has to keep in check. Clive Francis rather wryly observed that the play was getting shorter and shorter. But there is nothing as irritating in a play as an unnecessary line, although no doubt many people will think almost every line in this play is unnecessary. But then, I should do my best for *them*, too, shouldn't I, by giving them, if not none, then as few as possible?

What cheered me up most was listening again to the passage where Nick tells Stuart that the Arts Council is going to refuse a grant to his magazine on the grounds that it's élitist. I observed to Harold, on the way back in the car, that the same charge would probably be made about the play. He agreed cheerfully. So, in a spirit of *je-m'en-fou*ism (fuck-'em-allism), we drove élitely back to Holland Park in Harold's Mercedes to a glass of our usual tipple, champagne.

Monday, 28 May

Day six. And a bloody awful day it's been, too. It's Whit Monday and we appeared to be the only people in London working, at least in confined spaces, like offices. We laboured steadily through Act One, Scene Two. Almost every line in it seemed to be written dead by me, delivered buried by the actors. Furthermore, the Cambridge queen was back again, posturing and drawling away. When he made a comment about the quality of the wine in Stuart's room, he didn't even bother to glance at the bottles, thus making himself not only a peacock, but a fraud. The thing about intelligence, surely, is that it can't demonstrate itself in a vacuum, it requires an object both to animate it and to fix on. But then, now I come to think of it, Clive has just come from *The School for Scandal*, so perhaps his problem is that he still hasn't shaken himself free from Joseph

Surface. Certainly his smirk when he tossed off perfectly simple lines as if they were French aphorisms belonged more to Surface, or Restoration Would-Wits, than to Humphry. Bob East's Nick was heavy-handed, by the way; Simon Williams was all charm and no rhythm; Nina Thomas, who a few days ago couldn't enter the room, is now either hovering at the door as if taking a curtain call, or racing in like a whippet. As these are all very good actors, the fault must be entirely mine. Either I've written a whole clutch of bad parts, or good parts that don't mesh. I don't know. But I do know the last moments of the scene don't work. They dribble away to nothing, to neither a situation in suspense, which is what I think I wanted, nor a situation concluded which would at least be something. The atmosphere at the Ballet Rambert after we'd finished a run of the scene was one of defeat. The actors left with direly cheerful goodnights, see-you-tomorrow-loves, dears, darlings, sloping off into the evening as quickly as they could. We went to Harold's car, drove to a pub off Holland Park and discussed the problem fitfully, with intervals of remote and exasperated silence. During rehearsal, my sensible impulse had been to leave Harold alone, and yet I'd kept rising to my feet, lumbering across the room, my finger half-raised interrogatively. There'd be a second between my proposal offered and my proposal considered, just a second's silence, during which Harold seemed to go through a physical transformation, his cheeks swelling, his jaw jutting, when I felt something quite different from either acceptance or rejection was about to take place. Then he'd discuss the proposal or point with a control that is more alarming, I think, than any actual outburst could be. Of course we've gone through this sort of thing together before although less perilously because he smoked, and one comes to take it as Pooter, or more likely his great descendant, A. J. Wentworth, might have said, 'in one's stride'. But we both acknowledged that it had been a miserable day, full of tensions and frustrations.

I wonder what there was about other professions that put me off them. Tonight I rather wish I'd been what my father was, a pathologist, especially as I feel I'm developing a cast of mind useful in the conducting of post-mortems; or as my mother was, a housewife, a breeder of children, a stately knock-about comedian who confined her most terrifying jokes to her family captives, pretending to me on an occasion when I brought her tea in bed – she always took an afternoon nap – that she was dead, lying half out of the bed, mouth open in a grimace, eyes fixed in vacancy. She didn't as much as twitch until I began to phone my father at his hospital. A few years later she announced firmly, with just the right hint of apology, to my younger brother who was about ten at the time that actually he was adopted. The best riposte to which, we worked out years later, would have been a cry of relief. I summon up these two shades not to comfort myself, but only to wish that their pooled genes had evolved me into a different line of work. God knows what I'll have to report tomorrow. I would tend to say that it can't get worse. Except that in my experience it can, and often does.

(Actually, it didn't. Harold talked to Clive Francis about adopting an accent, to give him a background and to avoid the generalized Cambridge queen. Between them, they settled on North Country. My own preference for West Country was partly because Clive had been North Country in the tour of *Quartermaine's Terms*. Nick Le Prevost, Bob East, Simon Williams and Nina Thomas all made, or at least so I felt, the right sort of progress over the next few days, although at this stage Ian Ogilvy still seemed to me to be contradicting the spirit of Martin by exposing the character's unconscious motives through his social manner. But much of my concern was with my own defects as playwright. I give a lengthy analysis of what I thought was weak about the ending of the first act, and what I did to change it, am pleased with the result, but go broodingly on:)

I've noticed that sometimes I've added a line because it seems like a good line, without sufficiently considering the effect it's going to have on lines further away. The other day, going through the proofs for the published text, I found myself writing into the speech in which Stuart compares himself to various noble animals in decline (a threatened lion, a tattered tiger) a concluding image of himself as a bankrupt rat. The next time the passage came up in rehearsal I stuck it in. It worked quite satisfyingly until I noticed this afternoon that the word 'bankrupt' turns up in two other places within a minute of dialogue. Then, at the beginning of Act Two, Martin says something about his secretary going into 'competition' with him as a publisher, and five or six lines later Martin refers to the 'competition' Nick is facing for his television job. These things are easy to sort out, but nevertheless make me feel a chump; and as if I had a tin ear when writing dialogue.

(There were also various things happening offstage, or behind the scenes, that Harold and I picked up accidentally as, for instance, when having a quick drink with the management.)

A row is going on between two of the actors about their respective billings. There is no problem about billing at the Lyric, where it is alphabetical, just as the pay is a flat rate all around. But if we move into the West End, i.e. into the free market, the billing and the money become endlessly negotiable. Unfortunately, these negotiations actually take place when the original contracts are being drawn up at the Lyric. Rather bizarre and a waste of time, though I have no doubt the agents enjoy it. The intelligent moment to begin West End negotiations would obviously be when and if we have a West End theatre. The size of the theatre would dictate how much the actors can be paid, and the likely run of the play and the actors' desire to go on doing their parts would bring real realism as opposed to agents' realism to the issue. The problem at the moment is that one of the actors was signed up so late that negotiations are still going on for West End money, billing, etc., even though he is now deep in rehearsals. He's probably entitled to better billing than one or two of the other actors (particularly one, he feels) whose billings have already been fixed. The odd thing about all this is that it is *personal*, not an agent's disagreement at all. The actor in question is determined to get the number two or three spot or whatever it is, the other actor determined not to relinquish it. The argument between them is being conducted entirely outside the rehearsal room. Inside, they are perfectly friendly, and I gather that there are actually no ill feelings, merely a genial determination on both sides to get their own way. I have no idea how it will turn out and if we don't move to the West End I will never know, I suppose, as at the Lyric, Simon Williams, for instance, victim of the alphabetical system, remains at the bottom of the poster, while Bob East, a beneficiary of it, remains at the top. It doesn't matter where

Nick Le Prevost and Ian Ogilvy are, because they're somewhere in the middle where you don't read names anyway.

30 May

A medium-sized confrontation between Harold and myself over the end of Scene One. At the moment, Humphry sharply interrupts a salacious conversation between Nick and Peter with a demand for some music. Nick says to Peter, 'I wouldn't resist him if I were you. He's got a rather powerful personality' and puts a record on the gramophone. This is exactly as written. The trouble is that when I wrote it* I visualized Humphry on the far side of the room, Nick by the gramophone. The present staging has Humphry sitting close to the gramophone, with Nick and Peter some way from it. Thus Nick's crossing the room to put the record on makes him look as if he's turning himself into Humphry's handmaiden. A day or so ago, I proposed to Harold that either we change the dialogue to justify Nick's cross; or that we change the staging, getting Nick closer to the gramophone, Humphry further from it. I didn't mind which although my inclination was to change the dialogue. Harold agreed. That, I thought, was that. Today, when Harold told the actors of the dialogue changes, really quite minor ones, they began to object. There are times when actors appear to have an anal retentiveness about any line, however inconsequential, that they are given in a play. Bob East (Nick) began to argue vehemently in defence of both his long cross and his lines, and Clive Francis (Humphry) joined in on the grounds, presumably, that he liked his sit and his lines. Harold began to see that there were arguments here that ought to be considered and discussed. I became increasingly impassioned, Harold increasingly resolute. At one point we were standing almost nose to nose, smiling grimly into each other's faces, insisting courteously on our own points of view. It ended with my saying that as far as I was concerned I had an extremely simple position on this one, I was convinced, *convinced* that we should change either the staging or the dialogue. And I was perfectly willing to change the dialogue. Harold said he would change the staging. Which he did. Humphry is now across on the

---

* For the context of this exchange see Appendix B, page 183.

other side of the room, Nick is close to the gramophone, and the whole scene is being played both as written and as I visualized it. But I now suspect that the dialogue is wrong in ways that won't be affected by the moves, and that it'll have to be changed anyway. I also suspect, from a rather cunning smile Harold gave me when he'd finished restaging, that he knows it too. But I think I'll leave that problem for a day or two. Or even a week or two.

1 June

The most dramatic moment came from Harold's wanting a line (at least for the purposes of rehearsal) that would make Martin's concern for Marigold and his feelings about the possibility of her having an abortion, explicit. As written, the scene goes as follows:

MARTIN: The money was a gift to the magazine. You know how much I want it to survive.

STUART: Yes I do. So do I. Want it to survive. But not as a subsidiary to something else, you see.

MARTIN: Does that include Marigold and the baby? Sorry, sorry, none of my business, but – well, it'll break her heart – (*The sound of footsteps, off, coming up the stairs.*)

HUMPHRY: (*Enters.*) What's going on, this room reeks of passion, in the famous phrase. What have you two been up to?

Harold's point was that the line, 'it'll break her heart –' is a dangling line, making it impossible for Martin to convey the real intensity of his concern for Marigold. I therefore suggested that Martin undangle his line, i.e. complete it, and that we then have a pause during which Martin and Stuart look at each other, a pause interrupted by Humphry's entrance. So what I proposed was that Martin simply say (what in fact he really means), 'It will break her heart if you don't let her have the child.' This gives to Martin a kind of moralizing passion which is perhaps more than I had originally intended, but which I think is justified by Martin's state (that is, his love for Marigold). Ian Ogilvy tried the line out. Nina Thomas, who was sitting in her usual chair, doing the *Telegraph* crossword puzzle, jerked her head up when she heard it, and scampered* forward: 'I've only just heard

---

* This is the word in the transcripts. It can't really be right (except possibly dramatically) as Nina is an elegant mover – not the scampering kind.

that line. I've never heard that line before.' (Which was not surprising as the line had never been said before.) 'And I think it's the most repellent line I've ever heard. I don't understand what it's doing in the play.' There, facing her, was Harold (emphatically CND) who had asked for the line; Ian Ogilvy (very much a gentleman of the old school – Eton) for whom the line had been asked; Nick Le Prevost (far left and a declared feminist) to whom the line was being said; Clive Francis (of no known political opinion, but always a gallant) who had interrupted the line; and I (undecided between Liberal and SDP) who had provided the line. Five men who think themselves well disposed towards women vied with each other in putting Nina Thomas down. She finally withdrew, with little gesticulations of despair and distress. We proceeded with the rehearsal.

Everything was going well until we got to the next scene with Marigold, who announces this time (Act Two, Scene One) that she's pregnant. We quickly found ourselves in an intricate conversation with Nina Thomas, who began by asking what kind of state she should be in, what was the condition of the two men in the room – the very matter we had in fact been discussing before she made her entrance. So there was no progress. Actually, there was regress. I suppose there are two problems for Nina: one, that she is the only female actor in the company; two, that she comes on at the end of scenes, which means she has to sit for hours waiting her turn, and when she finally gets it, is quite naturally keen to make the most of it. Something like this also happens to Bob East, who is playing Nick, and to Simon Williams, who is playing Peter, both of whom interrupt scenes rather than originate and control them, and therefore feel a need, again quite naturally, to question and challenge. But whereas the discussions with Bob East and Simon Williams tend to move us forward, those with Nina sometimes tend to move animatedly nowhere, so that a decision about a line or a move seems, when it comes, like male bullying. I am sure Nina feels just as trapped in this ghastly web as we do.* At one point there was a dialogue between Nina and the rest of us about her entrance (yet again) which was really a dialogue about men and their inability to understand anything at all about women, and vice versa. The most interesting

---

* One of the actors was rumoured to have said on the first day of rehearsal that things should go OK in this production as 'There are five men and only one woman.'

moment came when Ian Ogilvy tried to break the deadlock by offering to rearrange his text so that Nina would feel more 'comfortable' – her word, taken up by him – when she came in. In other words, he was offering to rewrite my play a fraction. At which point I claimed, no doubt incorrectly, that the lines seemed to me OK as they stood, thank you, Ian, etc. What touched me, or does now but didn't then, is that a chap who on the surface has so little in common with the current feminist line should have countered the implicit feminist arguments with a gallantry that couldn't have affected those arguments in the slightest, but might well have been detrimental, though no doubt only slightly, to the play. Harold resolved the situation by changing the subject, and then going straight from the first scene to the play's Epilogue.

I was ashamed to notice how badly written the Epilogue is, and how clumsily it hammers its points home. I put it to Harold as we left – people scurried off at six o'clock – that I seemed to have botched it yet again. We discussed various possible rewrites without coming to any conclusions and then drifted to the pub where we found the whole company having a drink. Sitting there, looking haunted and charming, was Nina Thomas. I felt it crucial that I should engage her in conversation. I pondered deeply and then asked her what she thought of Viv Richards's innings in the third one-day match. There was a short pause, then Nina said, I think, something to the effect that she hadn't seen it. Simon Williams, or it might have been Ian Ogilvy, had, however, and took up the subject of Viv Richards with tremendous confidence and style for the next hour or so. The conversation then flowed around Nina Thomas, marooned, thanks to my social deftness, silent on her stool.

Harold and I drove back. He was going on to play bridge with Antonia and friends. I raised points – odd how these things surface – this surfaces, that surfaces, one notices, forgets, then remembers. He had things, I had things. We talked until he dropped me off at Holland Park where I had a meal by myself, worked through the Epilogue, came home exhausted.

4 June

Thirteenth day of rehearsals. An apt number, I think. It's been an unsatisfactory day. No, that's not right. An inconclusive day. Harold went back to the second scene of the first act, a very long scene, I think the longest in the play, and drove through it. I noticed his noticing my noticing that Marigold arrived to announce her abortion in much the same way as she'd done the last time.* Harold and I looked across the rehearsal room at each other – I don't know whose darkness meeting whose brightness, in a perfect glance of great politeness – but it was one or the other way round. We went through to the end of the scene. However, nothing radical was accomplished except that I became increasingly convinced that as we've added quite a few lines to Peter at the end of the act, a few of his earlier lines should be cut. He should get from the news about the magazine being saved to phoning up his latest fuck as quickly as possible. Anything in between is a kind of indulgence. However short the lines are, they're *longueur* lines. But I decided not to mention this to Harold until I've spent some time with the text.

5 June

When it comes down to it, today was simply one of those days I'd remember only because I'm making a record of it. Just another day in which I sat in my chair, chain-smoking and sometimes concentrating and sometimes failing to concentrate, turning towards my *Standard*, rising to my feet and molesting Harold with an enquiry or a proposed alteration. One of the things I have realized about rehearsals over the years is that the memory of individual days recedes very rapidly, blurring into one long day, without definition, except for little dramas here and there which I can never place in any sensible chronology when trying to remember them. On the other hand, it was probably one of those days in which the actors made progress, almost unnoticeably. Or regressed, unnoticed.

So, at 12.30 in the morning on 6 June, now Wednesday, I wish

---

* In earlier rehearsals, we'd had a disagreement about the spirit in which Marigold enters after she has had the abortion. My view was that she would be chippier than usual as she'd want to conceal the fact of the abortion from Stuart and the other people in the room; Harold's view being that she would be unable to help showing something of the emotional and physical trauma of the abortion in the way she spoke, moved, etc. He finally came around to the chippier view when he realized that if the scene started on a sombre note, it really left itself nowhere to go and that there was also a danger that Marigold was (indirectly) letting the audience know that she'd had an abortion before we wanted them to know it.

myself some sort of sleep. That's really all I crave. But I think this exhaustion grows, a developing exhaustion of spirit that actually, in the days before we open, transforms itself into a kind of (I wish I'd stop saying 'a kind of' and 'a sort of', by the way)* feverish animation. So there we are. I hope I remember to buy a new tape.

Two days later we ran through the whole of Act One for the first time and therefore saw for the first time not snatches of performances, but what they amounted to in a whole stretch. This inevitably put one's previous reflections on the actors, the text, the direction into a different and larger perspective. I think it is true to say that the first complete run of an act is, for a playwright, a frightening prospect, taking its place somewhere between the read-through and the first run of the whole play.

The beginning of the play was strangely drab and I began actually to fester with self-resentment, wondering whether I haven't written some of the dreariest dialogue I've ever heard on the stage. The exchanges between Martin and Stuart were very low-key, boring *and* hurried. One of the reasons for this is that Ian Ogilvy has a tendency to push scenes along, perhaps because his last performance was in a farce. Secondly, it seems to me that Nick Le Prevost is still expressing certain passages of the play too seriously. He's an odd actor in that he suggests seriousness far better when he's being light and ironic than when he's being tortured and defeated.† It was glum in other words, the opening of Act One, Scene Two, and it wasn't helped by a slightly forced performance from Bob East, while Clive Francis seems to have invented for himself a rather strangely placed but invisible pocket just above his hip, into which he places his right hand. He then juts his right knee out. This makes him look like an Edwardian army officer, unrelaxed and posturing. But he's no longer posturing with his voice, and he's developing considerable charm, which can only be to the advantage of the production. On the other hand Nina Thomas was fine. Funny, individual and extremely touching. Overall, though, the problem that haunts me is to do with the dialogue. As always Harold and I had a talk about various things

* I've edited most of them out, I hope.
† Not odd at all. Most people, whether actors or not, are more likely to get themselves taken seriously when not struggling to seem serious.

afterwards, a rather strange talk as he didn't want to go to the pub we've been using because he finds the wine undrinkable. So we sat in his car for about half an hour, I smoking of course – chain-smoking – Harold not smoking. It struck me afterwards that it was the longest conversation we've ever had in which Harold had neither a glass nor a cigarette in his hand. But then I was partly distracted by his worry over the dullness of the exchanges between Martin and Stuart. He discussed it as if it were an acting problem. I couldn't bring myself to say what was most on my mind, that perhaps the real problem is that the passage is dully written. It was as if I'd got Martin to drop in on Stuart to ask him questions about his domestic life with the sole intention of providing the audience with information – information that they won't know they lack, and therefore won't particularly want. Could anything be more tedious in fact? Even Shakespeare tries to give a character a proper motive for launching into an interminable stretch of exposition except in *The Tempest*, of course, when the only conceivable reason I can find for Prospero telling Miranda his life story is to expose himself as a ruthless old bore. And a bully too, as he seems to kick or cuff her fairly regularly to keep her awake and listening. The thought that I couldn't do better than Shakespeare depressed me.

On the way home, though, it struck me that a long time ago, when I wrote the play, I understood perfectly what Martin is up to in questioning Stuart. He's in love with Marigold. He really wants – *needs* – to know whether she and Stuart are still living together. Therefore, he's in Stuart's office on his *own* behalf, not the audience's. I suppose I'd forgotten this because there's been a greater gap between the writing of *The Common Pursuit* and its production than I'm used to, and so I've lost touch with the intention behind some scenes and lines. This excuse isn't good enough. I've merely been stupid. When I got in, I telephoned Harold and explained. He grasped the point immediately, and I'm pleased to say, blames himself for having missed it.

What this experience underlines is that dialogue with no proper intention behind it, however deft and witty it may sound out of context, is undramatic. This is probably one of the most pedantic and boring things I've ever uttered. Or what is worse, it probably isn't. Nevertheless, I need to keep remembering it. Especially as I have a distinct tendency – in *The Common Pursuit* anyway – to over-explanatoriness, as if I can't bear the characters not to report on every event in minute detail. This sometimes makes them sound like a gang of adulterers practising their alibis on each other. 'Why', one feels like asking, 'are you telling me all this? Come on, what have you *really* been up to?' All they're up to, of course, is expressing my literal-mindedness. With this literally in mind, I've spent the rest of the evening going through the text. I rewrote a passage between Stuart and Martin, the little scene in which they discuss whether Peter has gone to the Arts Council to try and get the magazine a grant, or whether he's really holed up in a hotel, having it off with a girl. The trouble with the writing here wasn't that it was over-literal, but that it was imprecise, thus making the two men appear incapable of marshalling simple thoughts coherently. Not too good, when they're meant to have razor-sharp intellects. I think I've got that right. At least it moves cleanly now. Then I settled down to a little cutting, all over the first act, a snip-snip here, a snip-snip there, a judicious and loving gardener, keeping the foliage in trim, is how I'd like to see myself, though Harold will probably see me as an old-fashioned barber, administering a short back-and-sides. I'll probably just show him the rewrite tomorrow, and indicate *possible* cuts, leaving it to him to listen in rehearsal and decide later.

8 June

I showed Harold the rewrite before he started the rehearsal, and he decided to put in. Then he explained to Ian Ogilvy and Nicholas Le Prevost the real reason behind Martin's questioning of Stuart. Or at least tried to. He scarcely got beyond the first sentence before they were enthusiastically denouncing themselves for not having seen the point a long time ago.

Harold then assembled the whole company and talked about his feeling that nothing in this play should seem to be struggled for, that the characters were friends who had known each other for a long time, and that what therefore distinguished their relationship should be freedom and naturalness, except at very precisely observed moments. But what made those moments shocking was that they happened in a general atmosphere of tolerance, no, more than tolerance, of mutual acceptance. Therefore it was crucial that the actors should never feel physically at odds with a scene, and he'd become fairly sure, over the last few days, that he'd pushed them here and there into inhibiting positions. They had to *feel* free to move, even when they didn't want to. So he'd decided to start again from the top of the play, going through it scene by scene, opening it out, making it as fluid as possible.* He wanted to encourage them to occupy the rooms in their own particular way – especially in the first two scenes, when the characters were young and likely to roam about a room, sit wherever they felt inclined, lie on the floor in the middle of a conversation, etc. So the morning was spent with Harold reblocking the play, or more accurately, with a collaborative reblocking, Harold letting the actors move as they felt inclined, guiding them rather than directing them into positions. I thought it was invaluable, the scenes he got through becoming both more comfortable and more expansive, the rooms seeming to be inhabited at last by friends who had conversations rather than by actors who spoke lines to each other.

We lunched at the small Italian restaurant where we'd gone after the read-through. We both felt buoyant, as if his liberating the actors had liberated us, as well. Furthermore I was ravenous, having had an early breakfast. I studied the menu with the obsessiveness with which I normally study only my own scripts, and after considering *pollo* done this way, veal done that, scampi and even pasta, which I normally can't eat, finding it technically too complicated, selected a steak, chips, a green salad. Harold had chicken. We shared a bottle of wine. We gossiped and anecdoted and laughed our way through the meal, not once discussing the morning's rehearsal, nor the afternoon's to come. I mention this only because it was so clearly an interlude, badly needed by both of us, instinctively seized. There aren't many of them in rehearsals. At least not of my plays.

11 June

It's nearly midnight, the end of the eleventh day of rehearsal – can that be right? We seem to have been at it for much longer.† I got to

---

* This is the episode I refer to when discussing blocking on pages 85–6.
† We had. In fact, it was the end of the fifteenth day. Although every working day was reported into the tape machine, I'd still managed to get the arithmetic wrong, mainly because I often forgot to give the date. But I didn't discover the mistake until much later. (See footnote on page 136.)

rehearsals late, as I'd spent the morning on *The Rector's Daughter*, and was already tired when I arrived. I came in at a point that had been worrying me – when Stuart discovers that Martin (his best friend) has been having an affair with Marigold, and is responsible for her pregnancy, which she has just announced. Originally I'd written a long exchange between Stuart and Martin, but I got rid of it a week or so ago, though I left in Stuart's speech because Nick Le Prevost (Stuart) was keen on it. I have come increasingly to loathe this speech, full of passionate hatred for Martin, for Marigold, for the baby to come, mainly because Stuart seems to get to his feelings too quickly, too precisely, and too emphatically. In my experience it doesn't happen like that. In moments of crisis we never know quite what our feelings are, we fumble towards them, get them wrong, go off at tangents, possibly worry about our grammar. (A friend of mine told me that when he heard his father was dying, his first thought was, 'Bugger, that means I'll miss the football tonight.' He was deeply fond of his father, too, fonder even than of football.) Altogether, I felt it would be much more interesting if we were to leave Stuart floundering for his response, especially as Nick (Bob East), who has been entering on cue just as Stuart finishes his speech, would now have to enter just before Stuart can begin it, thus preventing him from making it at all. I suggested this to Harold. He agreed to try it. It seemed to work. And that was my only contribution to the day. I sat back, inert, while Harold went back to the beginning of the scene and worked through it again. Then he ran it.

(It was painful to come across, in the transcripts, the following description of what Harold ran, and I was of course tempted to censor it, not for what I say about the actors, but for what I reveal about myself. Nevertheless, it seems too central to the truth of the experience to omit. I have kept it in virtually as spoken. As no subsequent rehearsal had anything like this effect on me, I can only assume that I was either hallucinating when I saw it, or hallucinating later, when I reported it into the machine. I don't discount both possibilities, but incline to the latter. I think possibly I had reached a point where fatigue, obsession, the dark premonitions that I've mentioned earlier, and probably alcohol, combined to produce a late-night poison that I discharged into the tape recorder, having nowhere else to discharge it. If I hadn't had to keep my diary going, I'd probably have had a few more drinks, dozed through some television and gone to bed, the memory, or rather the distorted memory, obliterated. I trust at least that that night the actors slept well, as I'm sure they deserved to. On the other hand, they may all have been sitting in their rooms at two in the morning, speaking into tape machines their views of the author's, and the director's and each other's performances. Harold might have been at it too, for all I know. Anyway, this period was for me, I've discovered – thanks to this diary – almost the nadir. The nadir itself was to come very shortly.)

We moved into the theatre today, where we'll remain until we open. For the moment, of course, we're rehearsing on the set of a different play, *Black Ball Game*, which is currently in performance. This probably disorientated the cast. They've been working for two weeks in an extremely comfortable rehearsal room and now found themselves on stage, in the right space, with the right furniture, but in the wrong room. The setting of *Black Ball Game* is a conference hall in a tacky modern hotel. Also the stage, at least for *Black Ball Game*, has a slight rake. Either that or I was slightly drunk, or tired, or both. Anyway, the run of the scene seemed to me bizarre. For one thing, I had the distinct impression that the actors were either speeding downstage towards me, or labouring upstage away from me. When they came towards me they seemed, at the very last second, to be pulling up, braking in fact, their bodies inclining sharply forwards, then stiffening upright; then turning awkwardly around and clambering back up to the higher reaches of the room. I attribute this to the rake. If there was a rake. And, as I say, the actors seemed disorientated. Although this didn't explain everything about their performances.

Humphry, for instance. A lot of the time he was to be found absolutely centre stage. He stood with his back to the desk, absolutely dead centre, looking as if he were back in *The Rear Column*. In *The Rear Column*, the characters are meant to take up stage-centre positions. In *The Common Pursuit*, the characters should always be slightly to the side of things, there is never quite a centre there. And yet there was Clive, where I was sure he'd never been before, absolutely and immobilely stage-centre throughout most of the scene. Until, that is, Simon Williams knocked him over. I always look forward to this moment, but for once it didn't work. There was a gap of about six inches between Simon Williams's fist and Clive Francis's jaw, though Clive Francis went down like a ninepin, whatever a ninepin is, whereupon one's eyes went straight to Ian Ogilvy, sitting at the far side of the room at the other desk, in fact lying prone over the desk, I think to suggest embarrassment at the fracas between Humphry and Peter, but of course looking as if he too had been felled by Humphry's blow, although in his case from a distance of about twenty feet.

Humphry went off, Peter went off, Stuart (alias Nick Le Prevost) trudged on, slowly, exhaustedly, leaning against the rake, if there was a rake, at an angle that suggested German Expressionist cinema. One of the melancholy madmen from *The Cabinet of Doctor Caligari*, for instance. His ensuing exchanges with Martin weren't helped by the fact that when he sat down in his tip-back chair, his face disappeared from view behind the desk, so one occasionally believed that Martin was quite alone in the room, either talking to himself or projecting his voice behind the desk. Enter Marigold, giving a double impersonation, now as a saint undergoing a minor martyrdom, now as a silent-movie comedienne, her eyes rolling, her mouth working, her words inaudible. After her, Bob East, snarling and laughing at his own jokes, not laughing because they've taken him by surprise, as people often are by their own jokes, but sneeringly, as if to make it clear that he'd heard his own jokes before, and still didn't find them funny.

After the run Harold and I went back to Campden Hill Square in the evening sunlight, and had a drink. I felt exhausted and depressed, but nevertheless sat analysing the run with Harold, who seemed to think it ropey and strained, but then the actors were tired after a long day, however lots of good things emerging, etc. I didn't have much to say, as I could tell that our experiences for once completely failed to coincide. I came home, had dinner, recorded this.

12 June

Most of today's work was spent on the Humphry death scene, and for most of the day the cast was lively. Harold had reminded them that they weren't there to mourn Humphry, but to deal with his funeral arrangements, and that this didn't preclude the jokiness of old friends gathered together. Section by section it went well, neither frivolous nor gloomy, all the characters to the point and relaxed with each other, and so, section by section, it seemed to be on its way to being touching, making no palpable claim on our emotions, etc. But when Harold ran the whole scene, it settled immediately into pathos. First Bob East, who had been saying, 'Hey, what about "Fear no more the heat of the sun?" ' – the first line of the scene – in the spirit of one coming up with a bright suggestion for something that could be recited at the funeral, now said it with heavy melancholy, as if old Humphry's corpse were stretched there at his feet, and he was about to deliver the dirge itself, right over it. Which was what the whole scene then became, a dirge, not only making a palpable claim, but sending in the bailiffs too. When it finished Harold reminded them of what he'd reminded them of before the run, then set them to it once more. Bob East tried to get the scene off more lightly, but didn't quite succeed, Simon Williams picked it up a little, Ian Ogilvy pushed it along. We seemed to be on the right tracks, then Nick Le Prevost entered, knotted in gloom. Told of Humphry's death he'd previously asked, quite briskly, 'Was it suicide?' (After all, he *knows* all about Humphry's homosexuality and growing death-wish.) What he gave us this time was: 'Was it – (*long pause*) – *suicide*?' and from there downhill all the way, right to the graveyard in fact. So. Having worked hard throughout the day in one direction, we nevertheless observed the cast, who had themselves worked hard and enthusiastically in the same direction, taking a completely opposite one when we did the run. Perhaps they're afraid of being thought irreverent, of being casual about the death of a friend. Or perhaps, quite practically, they haven't adjusted to the different time schemes. On stage Humphry has to go from live to dead in a matter of minutes; in life there would be a few days in between, time to think about the matter, discuss it over the telephone, etc., before meeting to work out the details for his funeral. I don't know.

After the rehearsal we all went to the bar. There was conversation, not very much and rather tense, about the day's work. Gradually everybody relaxed into a discussion about the armaments situation, the probabilities of a nuclear war within a decade or so, or even a month or two. It struck me that this was a far more serious matter than the murder of poor old Humphry, and yet we were pretty animated, anxious all of us to chip in with our little bits, our prognostications, snippets from reports we'd read in the papers, and in the middle of it I wished I could have videoed it, and played it back afterwards, saying: 'Look, this is how people really talk when they're talking about serious matters. How friends and colleagues do, anyway. So when it comes to Humphry . . .' Which, now I make the point, suggests to me that to some people there are more important things than the death of Humphry or even the death of the world, and that's how to get a scene in a play right. Which in turn leads me to reflect that that's precisely the point of the scene. All the characters are *talking* about Humphry's death, but are also *thinking* about various matters in their own lives. They're not ashamed of that, they acknowledge it in themselves and each other. Which leads me to the yet further reflection, which, being about life, 'old life itself' backed up by a quotation or two from Kant, I can't bear to impart. Too tired.

13 June

The day when I believe I reached my nadir. The crucial section comes virtually verbatim. Towards the end of it some of my sentences became jumbled, but I think I've transcribed them accurately. I offer it up without excuse, having exhausted my stock excuses of nicotine poisoning, alcohol poisoning, fatigue, paranoia, premonitions. I trust, however, it has a clinical value.

Eighteenth day of rehearsal. An unattractive day. A desperate day. A humiliating day. But let me be calm. Beginning at the beginning.

We spent the morning running through Act One. Most of the things I didn't like seemed to me my fault. For instance, I thought that the end of Scene One went badly because I'd underwritten Peter, giving him only a few heavily signalling lines with which to establish his identity. Then the end of the scene, when Humphry puts a Wagner record on, was formal and plonking. The rest of the act had moments of intelligence and intensity, also moments of wit, until we got to the recently rewritten passage between Stuart and Martin, about whether Peter has gone to the Arts Council or is having it off with a girl. Nick Le Prevost forgot his new lines and he wasn't helped by a sudden banging overhead just as he came up to them, as if somebody was doing something radical either to the theatre or just outside it. Anyway, *something* made the whole rewritten passage seem very thin. Actually, what it really seemed was rewritten. I hope it was just the banging. I was relieved when we stopped for lunch, I wanted to get away from the banging, the rehearsal, the thought of rewriting rewrites, and when Harold went off to have lunch with Judy (our agent), I went off to the Italian restaurant, where I rewrote the rewrites. I felt awful.

We met again at just after two, plodded through the first scene. In fact that was as far as we were to go during the course of the afternoon. We considered passages at the very beginning of the scene, the middle of the scene and the end of the scene that weren't quite forceful or rich enough, or weren't quite explicit enough, etc. Then we partially incorporated my newly rewritten passage and stopped at six o'clock and went to the bar as usual. At least Clive Francis, Nick Le Prevost, Ian Ogilvy, Harold and myself did. After a time, Harold went off and talked to a plump girl* in a long dress who kept showing him things. I couldn't make out what they were doing as I was having quite an engaging conversation with Nick Le Prevost about films and politics, the usual kind of conversation that one has with Nick Le Prevost. Then Harold suddenly appeared before me and said, 'Simon, would you come over here?' So I plodded after him to this plump girl, who was looking down at some pictures. Harold said, 'The thing is about the programme. The fact is that we can't fit all the pictures – there is going to be photographs of all the actors and so forth, thing. And, one of the actors comes out badly, only once in a cluster of other actors, and he really ought to be in the programme on his own, too. So I just wondered whether we could cut you out of the photographs of rehearsals in the programme. Do you mind if we cut you out and leave the rest in?' The rest being himself and the other actors. And I must say, the old gorge did its usual thing. It rose rapidly like a barometer in a fevered mouth, just shot up. I immediately thought how extraordinary that the one person to be cut out of the sequence of photographs to do with production was the author, who had been present at every day of rehearsals. But as I didn't really know

* Exactly. See footnote on page 103.

this plump girl and felt that somehow pride, pride, pride was important, I got the old bile back down the old gorge and said, 'I don't care what the fuck you do, that's fine with me.' Harold said contentedly, 'I knew you wouldn't mind.'

But of course, from that moment on, the whole matter began to ferment, the whole matter being, from my point of view, that the person who was responsible for the whole evening, i.e. the author, who had been present at every day of rehearsals, could simply be cut out of the pictures, so that present in the photographs of the rehearsal proceedings would be all the actors and, at various times in various photographs, the director, but under no circumstances the author, because an actor needed to appear twice. The actor appears twice, the author not at all. We had a very strained quarter of an hour in the bar after this, strain coming from Harold's sensing that I was angry about something, but having no clue as to what it was, and my feeling inhibited because we were surrounded by the actors. Robert Cogo-Fawcett, the director of the theatre, was also present. So it was difficult to say, 'Harold, look, the real problem is . . .' So I couldn't. We then went down to get a taxi that Harold had ordered – a minicab actually. In the minicab it was again impossible to be absolutely clear about my feelings because the minicab driver had no partition between himself and us. So that everything I would be saying to Harold I would be saying to the driver too. We discussed various aspects of the performances, and I suggested to him that one of our problems was that Nick, having recently done a very successful television series, was still acting to the camera rather than acting on stage. That he didn't really look at the people he was speaking to because he was in the habit of thinking that the camera would pick them up and they would subsequently be spliced into the sequence. This actually was a slightly tetchy conversation because Harold misunderstood me. When I said Nick, he thought I meant Nick the character, when I meant in fact Nick Le Prevost, the actor. So he was trying to make all this criticism correspond in some way to Bob East instead of Nick Le Prevost, and when we'd actually unravelled our misunderstanding, our being rather like two Mr Pooters in transit together, it was time for me to get out. I was seething all the way to Highgate, and when I got home, I phoned him up and put it to him that when it came to it, I really did object to being cut out of the photographs in the programme. It was actually properly of the nursery.

He began by being very calmly surprised by my objection and then, infected by my sense of grievance, became increasingly aggrieved himself. One of the things he said was, 'All I want to do is to get the play on. I don't give a damn whether I'm photographed in the programme or not' and then went on to say that, anyway, he felt fairly strongly that the only photograph in which I appeared was one in which he was also present and he hated the shot of himself, so he didn't particularly want that to be published in the programme. And so it went, ending with his announcing that, under the circumstances he thought the best thing was for him to get himself out of the programme altogether, kick out both of us. *Both* of us was his solution. Which I sort of vaguely conceded to at the time, but I think I don't when it comes to it.

As a matter of fact, this is vanity. Of course it is. I realize it is. But, on the other hand, I do actually feel very passionately that the play was written by me, I am the author, I have been present every day, and yet the only people who are going to appear in the programme are the actors and the director, with the author, the only begetter, not visible. If I were a member of the audience, I would say, but where is the author? What role did he have to play in all this? Didn't he come in to rehearsals? Why not? Actually if I were a member of the audience I wouldn't say anything. I probably wouldn't even note the author's absence. Harold said, 'But don't you see, I mean it's a matter of no consequence, it's only for the actors that it's important.' His boiling reasonableness against my mean spiritedness made for a very unattractive, I think, telephone conversation, which ended virtually with our hanging up on each other. It's not a very satisfactory state of affairs because I do actually agree with him that the most important thing is to get the play on. Certainly that is the most important thing. I have, myself, no objections at all to getting the play on. I want it to get on. I also want it to get on at its very best. I also actually want to be acknowledged as the author which is what the whole fuss really comes down to. But instead, what seems to matter is that a particular actor should have two photographs of himself rather than the author allowed to exist at all. I don't know. I would like to say it's a matter of principle. I think in a way that it might actually be a matter of principle. I feel the kind of anger that generally comes to me when I'm quite sure that something is a matter of principle. But, on the other hand, I do have to acknowledge that finally it might just be a matter of vanity. Goodnight.*

So tomorrow I hope that I shall be talking in a very different tone. I actually do think it is all piffling, but crucial. It is like life. This is life. The awful thing about life is that it is so frequently a matter of egos on issues that are in themselves trivial. Anyway, that's all for tonight. Goodnight.

14 June

Nineteenth day of rehearsals. Nine pm. The day began by my pondering the situation re the photograph and diagnosing more lucidly, in a morning condition and sober, my paranoia. I decided to phone Harold and say we should forget entirely any discussions about the programme, because we really had to get on. I felt like saying, let's not quarrel about *that* because there are far more important things to quarrel about, but I actually said that we had more important things to worry about, and went on to propose some additional dialogue in the first scene, which we discussed on the telephone. It was a fairly short conversation, as I had to get to the theatre to be interviewed by some fellow from *Time Out*. He arrived twenty minutes late, which was infuriating. With the rehearsals about to begin, with new dialogue to be given to the actors, I was going to be stuck with *Time Out*. So I became very surly. In other words, last night's or this morning's paranoia was still there all right. When he was fifteen minutes late, I decided that I'd give him five more minutes and then just piss off, to hell with him. I was not simply merely angry at the inconvenience, but bridling that I'd been kept waiting, which I suppose again is my vanity. Really, you know, I think in the course of the production of

---

* Many weeks later, after the opening, I explained coolly to Harold that the reason I'd become so frenzied over the photographs was that I wanted one for this diary. He saw my point at once, but a little later wondered why I'd become so panicked – 'After all, you could always get the photographer to develop some more from the negatives.' I conceded that that was true, but further explained – I forget precisely what. All I know is that there were a few brief moments when I felt that I'd salvaged my dignity.

a play, so many of the vices and the weaknesses, anyway the most unattractive aspects of one's character, are constantly being exposed. But I really did bridle. I felt offended that I should be kept waiting by a journalist from *Time Out*, though of course I told myself that I was offended because I should be busily concerning myself with the new dialogue at rehearsals. Anyway, he arrived, looking earnest and ascetic, with a kind of spoor of fringe magazine clinging to him, and I felt that I looked like a plump and pampered playwright, with a glass of white wine in front of me fairly early in the morning, and a cigarette to my lips already.* The PR lady brought me another glass of white wine as she introduced us, and to him of course brought an orange juice.

The conversation mostly centred on the question of my fashion-ableness and the nature of a well-made play. I said that many years ago I had read in the newspapers that I was a fashionable playwright, which I knew meant that from that moment on I had ceased to be fashionable, and would therefore have trouble continuing to be a playwright. I went on to defend the well-made play, along the lines that playwrights have an obligation to make their plays well in a way that a man who manufactures chairs or cars or sweets or writes sonnets or whatever has an obligation to do his work well. Anyone who does *anything* has an obligation to do it as well as possible, to make it as well as possible. I've never understood the sneer about the well-made play, and consider that although one might *fail* to make it well, one had an obligation at least always to *try*. We then discussed things like shape and harmony, etc. He was perfectly pleasant. He had a small recording device with him that I was very sure would fail to pick up almost everything I said. And indeed when he played it back what we mainly got was the clatter of tea cups and the occasional cough from the canteen, underneath which ran almost inaudibly a disgruntled whisper, which I identified as my voice, and an agreeable but slightly detached voice, much clearer than mine, which was his. It was quite a decent interview as interviews go, and he seemed actually to like my work. He said that he read *Butley* regularly, every – it can't be, this must be some kind of fantasy of mine that he said every month. I think he must have said every six

* Actually, I'm not Jewish or American.

months. It will be very interesting to see what actually turns up in *Time Out*.*

Anyway, that having been done, I cantered off to rehearsal just managing to arrive as the new lines of dialogue for Peter were being considered. There was tension between Harold and myself for the first hour or so, as a consequence of the photographs-in-the-programme business, but we eventually got back to our usual routine. Then we did a run of Act Two. We weren't, by the way, in the theatre – there was a matinee today – but in an unused bar above a peculiar pub called the Clarendon, an Edwardian mausoleum. Initially, I went into the pub itself by mistake. There were three Irish drunks leaning against each other in a dark, cavernous room, like something out of an O'Neill play. I moved out of there pretty rapidly because I felt that, although the three drunks were incapable of assaulting me, the barman looked up to it, and willing. I found my way around the corner and upstairs to the rehearsal. The room itself, though good for rehearsing, was surrounded by several enormous bars which had obviously not been used for decades. There were beer taps, obsolescent beer taps, high ceilings, an air of dusty and sad majesty about the whole place.

We ran Act Two. I felt pretty good about it until we got to one of the bits I'd most enjoyed writing, when Stuart describes (to Martin) how Martina, his clumsy cat (given to him by Martin, of course) attempted to jump from the kitchen counter to the fridge, missed it and ricocheted off to the floor. It is a long speech, full of details about Martina, the way she moves, speculations on her character, etc. I found myself thinking, what the hell is this speech doing here? It comes when the play is moving dramatically and crisply (I hope) forward and suddenly there is this long, complicated aria, with the proper logical and emotional reasons for it simply not established.

We broke rehearsals off at about six, and Harold and I then spent twenty minutes trying to get a taxi. At Hammersmith, they've actually refined the art, the taxi drivers, of manoeuvering their way past you with their 'For Hire' signs up. They were swinging rapidly across to the other side of the road, bending their heads lower over their wheels. But we finally made it back to Campden Hill Square,

---

* Nothing turned up in *Time Out* – though the interview was announced in two different issues, I believe.

where we looked at the last stages of the Test Match, talked a bit about cricket, then went over to Harold's studio house, where we looked at the Martina speech. I made suggestions about cutting lines here and there, Harold suggested alternative and further cuts. Then I said, 'Frankly, I've now got terrible doubts about this whole section of the play anyway.' And he said, 'Yes, let's consider the value of the speech as a whole. It seems to hold up the action. Instead of fiddling around and cutting little bits here and little bits there,' he said, 'why don't we go the whole hog and find out what would happen if we cut it altogether?' My first response was one of shock, because, as I've said, I still remember my pleasure in the writing of the speech. Then I suddenly realized that nevertheless he was absolutely right. When we cut the whole speech, an enormous cut, we saw that it didn't create any real textual problems, just a few cuts in the next scene and some shifted dialogue. The whole section still made sense, which reinforced our feelings that the speech was irrelevant.

The next question was how to approach the actor (Nick Le Prevost) on this. We were both slightly apprehensive about breaking the news. In my experience, actors are loath to drop speeches and there is always something about a large cut that creates unease even in the actors who aren't involved. They start to wonder when their turn for the chop is coming up. Harold said he would make a short announcement to the effect that there would be a moratorium on cuts (unless of course we thought they were needed). I suggested he should phone Nick Le Prevost straight away. Harold said, no, on the whole he wanted tomorrow's run-through to be undisturbed by such dramas as cuts. We could cut on Saturday or get together and look at it again over the weekend and make sure we were sure about it before cutting it on Monday. On such occasions, Harold invariably counsels patience while I cannot bear to hear any speech in rehearsals or run-throughs after I've found it redundant.

15 June

Twentieth day of rehearsals. Harold phoned this morning at 9.30 to say that he had changed his mind. He thought that we should meet Nick Le Prevost, whose speech it was, and Ian Ogilvy, to whom the speech was addressed, at lunchtime, after he'd given the actors notes taken from yesterday's run-through of Act Two, but before the run-through of the whole play. The first real run-through. This was slightly complicating as I had deliberately planned a leisurely morning. I had to be interviewed by someone from the *Times Higher Educational Supplement*, and after that I'd anticipated a rather splendid and solitary lunch with a book, a steak and chips, and a bottle of wine at the restaurant down the road from the theatre, before going back for what is always the major ordeal, the third major ordeal. The first ordeal with a new play is the read-through. The second ordeal is the first run-through of the first act. The third, the run-through of the whole play. I thought that the more comatose I could be, the better it would be for my psyche, nerves, whatever. But Harold was determined to get the cut over with. He expected trouble, as indeed did I, and with every good reason because, as I've said, my experience of actors when confronted with a large cut is one of anxiety and argument, a desperate determination to keep in this line, that line, 'what about that line? and this line always seemed to me the best line in the play', and so forth until one actually finds oneself with almost the whole section back again, with perhaps a quarter of a line missing.* I said, OK, it seemed to me that under the circumstances I'd better cancel the lady from the *Times Higher Educational Supplement*. I didn't mention my feelings about having also to cancel my lunch.

I phoned up one of the directors of the Lyric Theatre, David Porter, at his home (I can never get anyone at the theatre itself before eleven in the morning), and said would he please ask the PR lady to cancel the interview with the lady from the *Times Higher Educational Supplement* because I had to be in rehearsal. I arrived at quarter to eleven, had coffee with Harold, proceeded to rehearsals. We were there for an hour when I suddenly thought that I had better make sure that the *Times Higher Educational Supplement* lady had been properly and courteously put off. I plodded down to the bar to discover one of the public relations girls looking rather fraught. The *Times Higher Educational Supplement*

---

* My favourite: 'To tell you the truth, I only took the part because of this speech' from an actress who had plenty of speeches. As she made them all sound, to my prejudiced ear, exactly the same, it didn't seem to me to matter much which she said and which she didn't – except, of course, where it affected the other actors.

lady had turned up in spite of attempts to warn her off, and although she wasn't there at the moment – she had just gone off to the lavatory – she was upset because she hadn't been given any reason for the cancellation, apart from the fact that I didn't want to give the interview. I swelled up and burst out explosively just as the *Times Higher Educational Supplement* lady came back, forcing me to conjure on to my face a grin of welcome and apology. I explained that there had been a misunderstanding, but that it might be possible after all to do a brief interview. I scurried back to the rehearsal, told Harold I would have to give the interview after all, then scurried back again to the *Times Higher Educational Supplement* lady for the interview which was, as these things always are, amazingly tedious, enlivened only by losses of control on my part – when, for example, she informed me that a critic had pronounced the moral of my plays to be that education and intelligence were absolutely worthless, as they didn't help you to cope with the messiness of life, which led me into a harangue against the critic, on the grounds – I believe – that his own life (what I knew of it) was disordered beyond belief, as was his writing, in which there wasn't a shred of evidence to suggest that he had even a passing acquaintance with intelligence or education. I went on to say that it didn't seem to me the function of plays, mine or anyone else's, to help people cope with the messiness of life – my prime example here being Tolstoy, my point being that *writing Anna Karenina* didn't teach Tolstoy how to cope with anything, least of all himself. He was not only a mess himself, but the main messiness in the lives of quite a few others – i.e. his wife, his children, his friends. So did *she*, the *Times Higher Educational Supplement* lady, or rather the critic that she'd adduced, really think that *reading Anna Karenina* was going to reduce human messiness? Actually, I have an idea I spoke loudly as well as angrily, and that my frequent use of the words 'mess' and 'messiness' must have given the impression to coffee drinkers in the foyer that I was upbraiding the *THES* lady for her personal habits. For the rest, it was mainly routine question and answer (apart from another outburst, on the recent architectural barbarities of Cambridge). When we'd finished I scurried back to the theatre.*

* In fact the interview that came out in the *THES* is the only one I've ever given that accurately reported everything I said, and showed me a self I recognized (with the temper left out). A doff of the hat to the lady from the *THES*.

Harold had just finished, and was organizing lunch with Nick Le Prevost and Ian Ogilvy to disclose the news of the cut. I particularly dreaded Nick's response because, though he has been consistently intelligent and clear-minded and therefore very helpful about the text, he has also been resolute about lines that he doesn't think ought to go. And the Martina section is a very long one. We sat down at a table, ordered some wine, talked intensely on a number of subjects unrelated to our main concern – life, family life, art, some show that Ian Ogilvy had seen, the fact that Nick had the squitters and was constantly running to the lavatory, which I attributed to a chemical-free vegan's dinner he'd had the night before; that he attributed to a sandwich bar he'd visited when we were rehearsing at the Clarendon the day before. Finally Harold worked his way into a little speech about our moving towards clarification of the text – hadn't *quite* arrived there yet – this, he hoped, was to be the last major revision – 'Now.' He cleared his throat. Harold always clears his throat on such occasions. 'Now I'll turn you over to Simon, who will discuss the cut that we are all gathered here to discuss.' I said, 'Gentlemen, we are here to discuss an execution' which I hoped was sufficiently facetious to pave the way to a warm and friendly conversation about killing off the cat, though really knowing that however warm and friendly the conversation might be, there were difficulties ahead. I was therefore slightly *bouleversé* to discover that the two actors not only accepted the cut, but welcomed it with rapacious eagerness.

My only objection to the passage was that it held up the dramatic drive of the scene. But it turned out that Nick Le Prevost hated the passage because he found it extremely difficult to do – it came, he asserted, in the wrong place. Whereupon Harold said, 'Yes, it's whimsical, isn't it?' He went on to say that when he'd first read the play, he had had serious reservations about Martina and had hinted as much to me. If he had, I must say I'd forgotten it.* Then Ian Ogilvy said that he hated sitting through the speech because it had never seemed relevant, and he didn't know what expression he was meant to assume. It was really rather extraordinary. The two actors and the director competed with each other in slanging the speech

---

* Checking through the transcripts, I confess that Harold was telling the truth. He'd made the point at our first L'Epicure dinner in fact. (See page 33).

that I had only been apprehensive about cutting for the actors' sake. Furthermore, their vocabulary was distinctly wounding – the word 'silly' crossed someone's lips at some point. So, far from having a tough battle to get the speech out, I was faced with an unflatteringly comprehensive victory.* I read out the few lines that were needed to make the cut work. They wrote them down and with the matter settled, we all had lunch. After which, we rehearsed the cut, then got ready for our first run-through.

Harold sat on the left of the stalls, I sat on the right, several rows behind him, feeling both sick and fatalistic. Did we or did we not have a play? If we did, what sort of play was it? A good one? A bad one? A run-of-the-mill one? The first act was OK, I thought. In fact, more than OK. What delighted me most was that all the work done on the text over the previous three weeks hadn't made the play worse, it had actually improved it. Harold was equally delighted. We agreed that the second act was bound to be a bit of a disaster, especially with the large Martina cut coming up, but settled down to it with almost complacent gloominess. But the second act was also OK. In fact, more than OK. So the whole play was OK, more than OK. Of course, not all the surplus fat has been cut off. There is lots more to be done. But, for me, the important thing is that the text is right, and once the text is right, other things begin to fall rapidly into place. Which means that the weeks of working in the dark, changing lines, making cuts, fretting about the performances, but all in bits and pieces, not really knowing what the effect would be when everything was seen in relation to everything else, hadn't been wasted. We'd been working our way towards finding the play, and now we'd got it.†

Everyone had a cup of tea, not saying much. Nobody ever seems to say much after a run-through. Harold gave a few notes, then ran out of steam. I think he was emotionally exhausted and also wanted to think about a number of things before commenting on them. We went upstairs to the canteen and had another cup of tea while waiting for the wig lady. Simon Williams, who has made so many

---

* For the full (and in my view much maligned) Martina speech, see Appendix C, page 184.
† Actually we hadn't. When casting for the American production I found myself re-writing the whole play – not for any American audience, but because I was dissatisfied with it.

happy contributions,* came over to the bar, to which we had now removed ourselves, and said that the chief pleasure of the run-through for the actors was that they had all found themselves *quite* liking the play again, after having gone off it for a long time. When I looked slightly surprised, Clive Francis said, 'Oh, don't take it as an insult. It's a compliment really. Because that's the truth. Let's speak the truth.' Which seemed to me more Humphry's voice than Clive's. On these occasions, I suspect I prefer Clive's to Humphry's, the truth being something I like to keep at bay until I'm ready to face up to it by myself, alone with a drink.

The wig lady eventually arrived, extremely late as a matter of fact, and held court at a table. On being asked whether she knew the play, she said, 'Oh, yes, of course I do.' On being asked whether she'd read it, she admitted that she hadn't. 'At least, not all the way through.' But somebody had obviously given her its gist because she talked confidently about its time span, then did some measurements of Bob East's head, Bob East being nominated for a wig, then did some more on Nina Thomas's head, Nina requiring virtually a wig per scene.

Harold and I drove back to Notting Hill Gate, talking of various things, some good, some that needed attention, in the production. What we both felt, as we admitted to each other, was that whatever the public future of the play might be, we were on our way to realizing our own understanding of it. It was a nice little journey. We stopped to look at a house in Addison Road where Joe Losey had once shot a film. A strange house of Victorian lavatorial architecture, with lots of green and purple glazing outside, of the kind that you expect to find inside. I got off at Notting Hill Gate and came home, had dinner with Beryl, and dictated this. I still feel pretty good, though knowing that tomorrow I will probably be back to my usual desperation. I hope to God it will be desperation and not despair. But then tomorrow is Saturday. There will be a brief rehearsal in the morning (the first time on a Saturday), and then I will take myself off to Lord's. So everything should be all right. At least tomorrow.

* Two others I still remember: one when he said, 'I think I can help the dialogue out here a bit if I do –', accompanied by a gesture, presumably intended to support the dialogue by distracting attention from it; the other when he said, 'I think I can take the curse off this scene if I do –' – I can't remember again what he did to take the curse off the scene, or whether he succeeded.

From now on rehearsals took on a different tempo. With a week to go before previews,* Harold called a run-through every day, not all of them as gratifying as the first one. Indeed, the very next one, on the following Monday, I describe as seeming to take place 'under water, muffled, blurred, frantic and drowning', but only, I think, because our expectations had been raised and we (I, anyway) became impatient if progress, *visible* progress, wasn't being made from day to day. I continued to do work on the script, at one point, about two days before we opened, presenting Harold, whom I'd tracked down to a restaurant where he was lunching with Judy, with a newly rewritten scene that I wanted him to incorporate that afternoon. He folded my pages (I had only the one copy) and slipped them into his briefcase, commenting that we should wait and see, his own view being that it would probably work as well, but no better, than the scene I'd been trying to replace it with, which the actors had now been rehearsing for nearly five weeks. The scene as it was only embarrassed me, he said, because I knew it was coming. But an audience, happening on it for the first time, might be surprised, even – which was what we wanted – shocked. Then there was a tussle with Clive Francis. He became remote for a day or two, evidently pondering something, then put to Harold that he felt that the North Country accent he'd adopted to get away from the Cambridge queen had served its purpose, he'd now like to abandon it. I suppose he disliked the idea of continuing to employ what had after all been a ruse, now that he was in command of the real Humphry. I sympathized with him, though I'd become fond of the accent, and Harold, who'd also become fond of it, encouraged him to stay with it on the grounds that it had long since ceased to be a ruse, had been integrated into the part, was a fascinating reminder of Humphry's background. But the general movement I believed at the time (and still believe) was forward, the actors increasingly at ease, the text increasingly refined, Harold in full control (although not always of me – I conclude one entry halfway through the week with the hope that 'Beryl will drug my food, or even knock me out

* It was the day after the first run-through, Saturday, that I discovered I'd mislaid a week in memory (see footnote on page 118), having gone back at the end of a week and started it again numerically. I've always had a good sense of watch time, a lousy one of calendar time, which presumably means something, i.e. living for the minute, not for the future?

with a hammer, anything for the sake of a rest from myself. And for her sake too. And the children's. And Harold's. And Hazel's.').*

19 June

Yet another exhausting day, perhaps the most exhausting so far because of the heat. The air conditioning isn't on in the theatre although, perversely it seems to me, they've taken the roof off, or anyway somehow opened it, so that there is a constant whistling of wind. But what wind? No discernible wind down below, just its whistle to disturb the actors, but no change in temperature to cool them. Just whistle and heat. This isn't flaming June, but sultry, resentful, punitive June.

We began in the morning with a dress display, all the actors turning up in their costumes, vanishing to change them, reappearing. There was one moment when Stuart and Peter both stood on stage, shoulder to shoulder, in ties of similar design; one blue with a red stripe down it; the other red with a white stripe down it. The effect was to make them look like members, brothers and members, of the Artillery Club, or old boys of a minor public school. Apart from such details, Liz has done well, as far as one can judge when a parade of clothes is bound to be an intrusion, an intrusion nevertheless crucial to the success of the play. The only reward for meticulous attention to costumes is that they *aren't* noticed by the audience.

Then the music. We listened to Bach, specified for the beginning, and to Wagner, specified at other points in the play. The choice of Bach was fairly simple, but with the Wagner we found ourselves listening several times to a passage from *Parsifal*. It would have been apropos, if I hadn't used *Parsifal* in a previous play of mine, *Otherwise Engaged*. In the afternoon we did a run-through. The Bach we'd chosen, when amplified, killed the opening dialogue, making Stuart and Marigold seem as if they were miming their emotions, as in a silent movie, but without benefit of sub-titles.

After rehearsals we went to the multi-storey car park to collect Harold's car. He was saying, 'I don't know if you've noticed one thing about my approach to the actors . . .' Then he stopped. He stared with intelligent vacancy at a completely empty spot in the lot

* Hazel is my dog. See p. 28.

and said, 'Oh, my God!' After checking a couple of levels above us and the level below us, we went down to the car park gates where Harold reported that his car had been stolen. I was interested in the contrast between my response, which was merely one of irritation at not getting to the tube station as quickly as I'd hoped, and his. Because I don't drive, I have no interest in cars at all. I see them merely as taxis that people who drive have to keep in the garage, as opposed to taxis that fail to come when people who don't drive phone them up. But Harold's Mercedes is some seventeen, I think it is, years old.* In fact the same car that he had shown me shortly after its delivery the first time I met him. It had meant absolutely nothing at all to me then. Simply a gleaming and expensive-looking car of no particular denomination, that he was clearly very proud of. But between its purchase and its theft, it has become an antique or vintage car, to be even more cherished. All I've vaguely noticed, although I've been driven in it many times, is that it has a rather elegant, wooden dashboard, and smells of leather. So I had to make an imaginative leap to grasp what Harold must have felt about his car – much as I felt about my fountain pen (which I loved for seventeen years), I supposed, when burglars stole it from my desk about six months ago. I made a puny effort at such a leap, then left him dealing with the prospect of the police, and got a taxi – it took hours to draw one to me – and came home, where, after dinner, Beryl pointed out my stars (Patrick Walker in the *Standard*. I'm a Libran): 'Sometimes it is necessary to be cruel to be kind, especially if you now instinctively feel you are spending too much time trying to get *someone else* to get to grips with a particular problem.' I'm sure he's right, but which particular 'someone else' does he mean?

20 June

The day began with Harold phoning to ask me if I was going to the Dramatists' Guild dinner on 6 July. Well, it actually began with Harold phoning and getting Beryl. Before handing him over, she asked him about the car. He skated over that with an intimation that everything had turned out all right, and requested in a deep and husky voice to be passed over to me as quickly as possible, implying

* See page 56.

that there was serious business to talk about. The serious business was whether I was going to the Dramatists' Guild dinner on 6 July. I said I was, then of course asked about the car. He said, 'Yes, well – uh – very odd thing. Rather embarrassing actually is that – well – the fact of the matter is – well, it is slightly embarrassing' – he made a sound somewhere between a cough and a laugh – 'I didn't park it in the car park at all. I actually parked it on the road. In fact I was walking away with the chap at the gate to report the theft to the police. I suddenly smote my forehead because I suddenly remembered that I'd actually parked it in the street. And there the car was. I saw it there actually.' So that was that.

The afternoon period of rehearsal was particularly difficult, at least for me. We seemed to go through an interminable stretch when either the moves seemed to expose the dialogue (do I mean by this, didn't sufficiently obscure its inadequacies?) or the dialogue seemed to expose the moves (by which I suppose I mean, sometimes made them seem irrelevant or over-precise). I was at my fussiest, quite unable to prevent myself interrupting with suggestion after suggestion, and so stretching and stretching Harold's patience. Every time I got up to make a point, I would be conscious of Harold's fingers rapping on the stage. (He stood in the front row of the stalls; I sat beside him.) It must have been exasperating for him to feel that a scene had been properly dealt with, and then the clatter of the seat going back as I stood up, stammering slightly. I know that he knows that I always assume a stammer before trying to wriggle my way into a point which he knows also, knowing me very well, I am determined to make.

The day was partly redeemed at the bar after rehearsals. Simon Williams (of course) said that he was doing a charity show fairly soon, and that he did think on the whole that, as actors weren't paid for charity shows, they really should be allowed to choose their own material. After all, he said, when you're paid, you expect to do any crap, making a kind of gesture towards me, as the author of the crap he was currently being paid to do.

21 June

Twenty-fourth day of rehearsal. Always so difficult to get the day into perspective. In fact, about the only thing I really remember, apart from waiting interminably at Harold's for a taxi that never arrived, is the bizarre fracas over the cold beef. Why? Anyway, what happened was this. Before going back to the Clarendon to rehearse (there was a matinée in the theatre) we had our lunch in the Lyric self-service restaurant. Harold, who has a particular passion for the beef there – as indeed have I, because it's very good – was told very sweetly, but quite firmly, by the girl behind the counter that he couldn't have any beef because 'the staff', she said, 'isn't allowed to have beef'. Harold said, 'What!' She said, 'The staff isn't allowed to have beef, I'm afraid, the staff isn't allowed.' 'What do you mean?' Harold said. 'Well, it's just that the staff isn't allowed to have beef.' Whereupon Harold became extremely angry and demanded further explanation, e.g. 'What do you mean? what are you talking about?' etc., until everyone in the queue had become very attentive. When he'd finished, the girl behind the counter said, 'You see, it means if – um – you have the beef, you'll have to pay the *proper* price for it.' Whereupon Harold, when he had emerged from his state of shock, said that he 'would *indeed* pay, he would *indeed* pay' the proper price for the cold beef and, on paying the full price, was allowed to pass with his platter piled, less high than I suspect he would have liked, with cold beef. There was an altercation, which I slightly missed as I was behind him in the queue to do with some girl with a foreign accent reprimanding him for something.

Anyway, we sat down at the table. Various people passed by, functionaries of the theatre. Harold called one or two of them over to register a complaint about the incident, his point being that it was acutely embarrassing to be treated as if he were one of the winos that hang out just below us in Hammersmith. Come in off the streets, so to speak, in the hope of a cheap, or even free, platter of cold beef. While this was going on the actors came in, and seeing us engaged in a series of important-looking conferences, began to settle down at tables with glasses of wine, coffee, etc. Harold, noticing this and suddenly realizing that we were on our way to being late for rehearsals, broke off and said, 'I think we should go over immediately, don't you, to set the example.' So forth we went to the Clarendon, Harold leading the way, Nick Le Prevost and I trudging behind him, the other actors fanning out behind us, down Hammersmith Broadway, through the traffic and the dreary heat of this summer, up the stairs of the old Clarendon, into the rehearsal room, where it was at least cool.

I suppose I thought the run-through was OK but I'm not sure I can tell any more.

22 June

The twenty-fifth day of rehearsal. I'll try not to preface it with 'Another exhausting day.' We were back in the Clarendon with a run-through at 10.30, which I contrived to miss because what with this and that – a late dinner and a few drinks when I got home – I was so tired from the previous day, tired and sluggish, that I actually felt unable to propel myself towards my duty.

I got there in time to have lunch with Harold, who said that it had been very much a ten-thirty-in-the-morning kind of run-through; there was a great deal of struggling, over-compensation, etc. There was also a problem with Nick Le Prevost in that, having got rid of all the gloom, he had begun to get a trifle cute. I began to argue that I would rather cute than gloomy, then remembered that, as I hadn't seen the run-through, I was hardly in a position to debate the matter. It was a very long lunch break because the actors needed time to recuperate. Nick Le Prevost ordered a bottle of wine for everyone, and then found nobody prepared to drink it with him because it was warm. He clearly drank a bit too much himself, and then drank a little too much of a small bottle or two he ordered for himself subsequently.* He became a bit strange. On the way to the Clarendon, he was extremely impassioned on the question of the reselection process for Labour MPs, who, he said, were now more representative of the people that had elected them. Well, I said, they were certainly representative of the views of the minority that could be bothered to turn out for constituency meetings, but not necessarily of the thousands of people who had far better things to do with their lives than attend them. He took this up very vigorously, and then launched into a hectic sermon about my apparent unwillingness to do anything to change the world, a flaw of mine that he clearly took quite personally. By the time we got to rehearsal, he had

* This, I hope I need hardly say, was not only a rare occurrence, it was unique.

become almost belligerent. Nevertheless, the rehearsal proceeded amicably until Marigold's outburst in Act One* – the moment when she turns on Humphry and says, 'You don't always know everything.' Harold said that he thought that there was something wrong with the way in which the other characters reacted to this; they took it too comfortably. Whereupon Nick stood up and said he wanted to dispute the way the scene had been directed. He thought it was wrong. Harold said, yes, that's precisely why he wanted to look at the scene again, because it was wrong. But Nick, unaware that they were in perfect harmony, went on building up his case. In no time at all, he was making a speech about sexual politics, his specific point being, I think, that everybody's reaction to Marigold's outburst was patronizing, as if they (therefore we, the play, the director and the production) were saying, 'There, there, little girl. We all know women are prone to work themselves up.' As a matter of fact, I suspect Nick put his finger on the problem. The trouble was that he was more interested in continuing the debate, even though there was nobody really to continue it with, than with getting on with the scene. Harold, handling him with a potent combination of severity and diplomacy, said we would return to that particular scene tomorrow.

But this is certainly the most gruelling of my experiences in the theatre, not because it's more tense, but because the tension seems to have been going on much longer. Anyway, on this self-pitying note, I end, reminding myself that tomorrow, instead of doing half a day's rehearsal, which is what I had hoped, and then spending the rest of the afternoon at Lord's, we are going to do a full day. So I'll probably be able to get only an hour or so in at cricket afterwards. Not at Lord's in fact. The Oval.

Saturday, 23 June

Twenty-sixth day of rehearsal, I believe. And, my God, how deeply sick I've become of this diary, but, having gone so far, I suppose I'll have to go on to the end.† I haven't really anything to

---

* For this line in context, see Appendix D, p. 184.
† I reminded myself frequently that Simon Callow had reported himself – in his admirable book, *Being an Actor* (published by Methuen) – unable to continue his diary of rehearsals after the tenth day. This helped to keep me going.

report of great interest today. We were due to begin rehearsal at
11.15, back in the theatre. I arrived rather late because the taxi
chose to swoop with great rapidity to Notting Hill Gate, and then
take a number of rather eccentric detours around to the Lyric
Theatre. At the end, I ran up the stairs to the auditorium, my
heart pounding, to find that the little bit that I had particularly
wanted to see, which was the exchange in Act One, Scene Two,
between Martin and Stuart about Marigold's pregnancy, had
already been worked on, and that the actors were sitting around
waiting for the next bit of rehearsal. This didn't take place for
another fifteen minutes because the other actors had been given
the wrong call. Odd how valuable fifteen minutes of rehearsal
seems to be when it isn't being used. When they turned up, we
proceeded to implement a few notes, look at various passages,
particularly the passage we'd had to abandon yesterday because of
Nick's bout of disputatiousness.

I had suggested a slight addition so that after Marigold's
outburst to Humphry – 'You don't know everything. You don't
always know everything' – she could then retract slightly, saying
'sorry'. Nina tried it. Harold suggested that she make the 'sorry'
harder, more a dismissive 'sorry' than a request for forgiveness.
He went on, trying to explain what he meant about the difference
in tone to Nina, who sat staring at him like a bewildered puppy,
completely silently, without responding. He explained again, she
continued to look at him like a bewildered puppy, until he ran out
of explanation and stood gazing at her – like a bewildered dog
confronted by a bewildered puppy. Finally he said, 'Well, what do
you think?' and she said, 'Well, I think we'd do better without the
"sorry" if it's going to involve all that.' Her timing must have
been brilliant. Anyway, there was a lot of laughter.

The first act was very sprightly, so much so that I began to
notice actors' characteristics: Simon Williams has a habit, for
example, of sniffing between speeches; Nick's hands make various
courtly, expostulatory gestures, which I think are quite redundant.
Ian Ogilvy also sniffs. So there's a lot of sniffing going on and a
lot of unnecessary gesturing. But the fact that I was able to notice
it was, I thought, a fairly good sign, or so it seemed to me at the
interval, when I had to heave myself upstairs, carrying a chair,
with an Antipodean-sounding photographer from *Time Out*, for a

photograph to accompany the other day's interview. I was actually so tired and so busy thinking of sniffs and gestures, that I didn't give myself fully to the experience of being photographed. I sat in a kind of blankness, initially, and then found myself being commanded to lie on the floor with a typewriter beside me, amidst the wreckage of a table and spilled paper as a complement, I suppose, to the poster. I then went downstairs and had lunch with the rest of the company.

The whole cast was at the table, and a fairly jolly, perhaps too jolly, half an hour was spent before we went back to run Act Two, which therefore got off to a rather ropey start.

28 June

This evening Harold started on the lighting which at this stage is an interminable process. All the actors had gone. There were just the stage-hands on the set to give an indication of the effect the lighting would have. I kept Harold company until one of the PR girls came in and asked me if I'd do an interview for a BBC arts programme which should also be reviewing the play. I'm not at all keen. There is nothing more likely to make you look an absolute dolt and duck of a fellow than to give an interview in which you are encouraged to talk enthusiastically about your work, only to be followed by a review putting you emphatically in your place. Especially if the reviewer is someone I've come across once or twice, and is the author of quite a few unproduced plays. Of course much better writers than me can fail to get their plays produced, but given the way of the world I'd rather be reviewed by a greengrocer or even a professional critic than by an unproduced playwright, whose main thought during the evening is likely to be, 'Why him and not me?' Of course I may be maligning the chap in question. In fact, I hope I am. He may have several plays in the pipeline to the West End at the moment, or he may come to the theatre in the spirit of one anxious to salute a fellow vineyard-labourer who's had better luck than he's had . . .

I offered these ruminations to Harold, pointing out that we couldn't stop the review by either Raban or Raven (by this time I was against either of them) but that I could at least avoid the fall-guy interview, was in fact inclined to do so, what did he think? He said, 'I think you're quite right. Especially the way *you* do interviews.' This seems to me a bit hard, as the only thing I've ever believed wrong in my interviews is the interviewer. For example the chap from the *Daily Telegraph*, many years ago, who began, 'Well, Mr Gray, or may I call you Simon, is this going to be another of your disasters?' I told Harold rather coldly that I'd continue to think about it. Which reminds me that tomorrow I'm having lunch with Michael Owen of the *Standard*. At least that'll be an interview without a review. Altogether, tomorrow will be a long day. At two there is a technical rehearsal with the lighting, the doors, entrances, exits being worked through. It will probably go on until midnight. For me it'll be an unspeakably boring day. There is never any point in my being present at technical rehearsals, but I can never bear to stay away from them, convinced as I am that there will be lots of little things, important little things, to notice. And of course it's followed by the dress rehearsal, which is followed by the first preview – the first performance before an audience. So how can I possibly keep away? But what on earth is the real point of going?

Saturday, 30 June

Running four days behind on the diary, having been too involved in the previews and too exhausted when they'd finished, to make it to the tape recorder at night. I'll do my best to recall events as they happened, from the dress rehearsal through to last night's (Saturday's) preview.

Tuesday

Had lunch with Michael Owen of the *Standard*. A convivial man who seems to know a lot about my plays, and the sheer nobility of my life. There were two revealing incidents, however. We were talking about football, which he loves, and had got on to Liverpool's European Cup Final. Both our minds went blank. We couldn't remember who Liverpool had beaten and where they had beaten them, except that it had been on the opponents' ground. Michael Owen sudden remembered. 'Roma,' he said. 'Liverpool beat Roma', lifting his glass with rather charming insolence to the Italian waiter who had just come to our table. When the interview came out yesterday (Friday), this was reported as follows: 'He [that's me] raised a glass in an Italian restaurant to Liverpool's recent triumph in the European Cup and tried to remember which team they had beaten in the final. "Roma," said the Italian waiter icily, and turned on his heel.'

We also had a conversation about the Leavis/Snow controversy in which I quoted Snow's 'We die alone' and Leavis's rejoinder, 'Yes, but we also live alone.' In the interview both these observations are attributed to me, not so much out of context as in no context at all. 'We die alone and we live alone,' I suddenly and meaninglessly pronounce. Thus presenting myself, I think, as an impoverished but self-important philosopher. He also attributes to me two daughters, an error that my son, Ben, has taken badly, speculating on whether it constituted grounds for a libel action; which my daughter Lucy took badly.

After lunch, I went to the technical rehearsal, which didn't finish until midnight. All I remember about it was my relief at seeing the revolve work smoothly.

Wednesday

On Wednesday we had the dress rehearsal about which again I remember little except that we seemed to be in reasonable shape. Our main worry was Nick Le Prevost's voice, which didn't carry properly, even in the empty theatre. Also he was tending to withdraw from lines. I suspect that after so much work in front of the television cameras it will take him time to find a natural vocal level in the theatre. The last thing we want, though, is any projecting from the actors. I suspect Nick is too canny for that. Anyway, Harold and I decided to keep calm about it for the moment.*

---

* We probably both had in mind the first preview of another play of mine, when someone (connected with the management? a member of the audience? an usherette? – we never found out who) smuggled a complaint through to the cast during the interval about their audibility, or rather lack of it. Most of the actors, knowing the hazards of playing before an audience in the theatre for the first time, which includes not yet having discovered the right vocal level for that particular theatre, took it in their stride, either making slight adjustments or deciding to ignore the complaint until the problem could be considered next day, with the director. But one of the actresses, inexperienced, and convinced that the note had an entirely personal application, looked and sounded from that time forth like a participant in a speech-

Thursday

The first preview. Inevitably it was a difficult day to get through. There was a dress rehearsal in the afternoon (Nick's voice was OK) after which Harold gave his notes. The actors seemed fairly confident, some of them positively eager to get before an audience, and Harold is always supremely good at controlling the atmosphere, presenting an image of benevolent reassurance, though I sometimes wish he wouldn't wear his customary black for these occasions. I try to take my cue from him, not speaking unless I'm sure I'll be able to stop my voice from quavering, going in for little jokes and amusing asides, but of course, for most of the time, I'm sick with terror – at least until about an hour before the curtain goes up, when I become almost preternaturally calm, with a gallows fatalism on which not even whisky has an effect. Harold gives no indication of strain at all, although an alert observer might notice that his Adam's apple becomes restless, and that he seems to walk more upright than ever, sometimes even inclining slightly backwards. The truth is that both of us, I believe, felt quite proud of what we'd put on the stage, but had no idea what an audience would make of it. Over the weeks of rehearsals, lines and situations cease being funny or sad in themselves, first reactions to scenes are long forgotten.*

---

training experiment, walking stiffly around the stage, delivering her lines with a ghastly precision, not so much throwing her voice out at the audience, as throwing each word out, as if it were an egg that had to be caught, unbroken, in the stalls. However hard Harold worked to relax her every afternoon in rehearsals, the terror gripped her all over again every night. I don't think she ever succeeded in giving a natural performance. I learnt two things from that experience. Never let anyone get a note to actors during intervals of first previews (or any other previews or performances, come to that), using any weapons that come to hand to stop them. And never panic over inaudibility – deal with it in a casually matter-of-fact manner in rehearsal, with some such phrase as 'And, oh by the way, there might be a *slight* problem about whether you're actually being heard . . .'
* During the early rehearsals of *Otherwise Engaged* Alan Bates and Nigel Hawthorne were physically incapable of getting past a moment when Nigel Hawthorne, playing a minor-public-school teacher, had to step forward and announce aggressively, 'I am the latent pederast.' Both Alan and Nigel doubled up with laughter again and again. Weeks later, when the same moment arrived before an audience, they were bewildered by its reacting exactly as they once had done. Within a few nights they'd not only come to expect the response, but had incorporated it smoothly into their performances, and might even, if they had been less puritanical performers, have found themselves milking it by prolonging it a little.

I was sitting at the very end, right, of the first row of the dress circle. Harold was sitting at the very end, left, of the same row. Beryl and Antonia were down in the stalls. It was a full house, and it went OK for a first preview – more than OK. The first act had dead areas in it caused by, or I hope caused by, the audience not properly hearing Nick Le Prevost (which also meant of course they couldn't always make proper sense of what the other actors said when replying to him). But I reminded myself of everything Harold and I had reminded ourselves of about vocal problems, etc., and also took into account that the character of Stuart is in some ways a reticent one, and furthermore that for Nick there is the extra problem of having just come from prolonged television work, and in other words I wanted to kill him actually. I was convinced that he was reducing the value of the evening by about 50 per cent. But the curtain fell to decent applause, and Harold, running around the back of the circle to the exit before anyone else could move and I nipping out just ahead of him as I was right by the exit – it occurred to me subsequently that anyone in the audience seeing us would probably have thought that he was chasing me – made it to a little room on the side, which we'd marked as our hide-out, where there was wine and Scotch, waiting for us, and where we were joined by our wives. Gravely, over drinks, we anatomized the way it was going so far, with sedate references to the question of Nick's voice. We got back just before the curtain went up.

The second act seemed to go OK too, I thought, with Nick vocally fuller, the whole company gaining in command, and everything unravelling at the right tempo. There was laughter, sometimes scattered, sometimes collective – the line about Nick's offstage media rival ('Nappies' Harrop) leaving his television programme to become theatre critic on *The Sunday Times* where 'they seem to be impressed by his lack of qualifications' brought the house down. But I have to admit that I wasn't as touched by Humphry's death as I have been through virtually every run-through and dress rehearsal. Perhaps the first act wasn't sufficiently light and flowing for the darknesses of the second act to gather. We lurched, I felt, from mood to mood. But the audience was lively and interested, and there was a nice, full-blooded response at the end. I didn't notice anybody leaving before it, anyway.

We went back to the little room after the curtain, Harold and I again doing our Tom and Jerry to the exit. The mood in the room was pretty good, high-spirited, a general sense of confidence – the play obviously works, is there to be liked or disliked on its own terms – although with work to be done. What I really mean by this is that if we are going to be hated it won't be for having failed to realize what we wanted to realize. It would be genuine (or fraudulent) hatred for the thing itself. In fact, there was a muted air of celebration, much assisted by Beryl's and Antonia's pleasure in the evening. After the theatre cleared, we went to the bar to see the actors. I think their spirits had begun to rise after the first tentative few minutes, when they'd begun to take in that the audience was laughing thus establishing at the very least that the audience was listening. Laughs are a perpetual trap for actors. I hold primly to the view that any of my plays could be played without getting a single laugh, and still keep the audience's attention. But then I don't have to go up on stage and do it, do I? And I'm not sure that I'd like to sit through the experience in the audience, either.

Among the people in the business hanging about and having a drink was an actor of about sixty with whom I'd worked a few years ago. Good actor. Very good actor. He came up to me, puffing on his pipe and looking extremely wise, wisely worried was what he looked, and gave me a note about Nick's inaudibility, especially in the first act. He was forthwith replaced by another actor of about the same age, also extremely good and with whom I'd also worked, who gave me a note about Nick Le Prevost's inaudibility, especially in the first act. So these two sterling old pros confirmed what every member of the audience knew, that Nick Le Prevost had been from time to time inaudible, especially in the first act.

We stayed with the actors for a while, then went on to dinner at a restaurant near Hammersmith called the Trattoo. I was slightly drunk, as is usual at that time of night under these circumstances. Under most circumstances, in fact. I expect Harold was too. The alcohol that had made no impression on us up to and during, and even immediately after the preview (although we were adding to it all the time, in the interval and then in the room afterwards, and then at the bar) suddenly broke through the dam of terrified propriety and sluiced through all parts of the system. Or something like that. We went from feeling and seeming stone-cold sober to being and behaving drunkishly, only a few minutes after sitting

149

down at the table to a fresh bottle of wine. Neither Beryl nor Antonia was the slightest bit affected – by drink, I mean; they were probably affected by us – because (a) they're by nature more abstemious, and (b) are more sensible and grown-up and (c) for all their wifely devotion and sympathy, hadn't quite had the day we'd had, although I don't mean (c) to cancel out the tribute intended in (a) and (b).

I settled into a long compulsive whine about this and that, an actor here, a move there, a weakness in the text, what about the lighting in Act Two, Scene Two, and the music at the beginning and the end sort of stuff, until I noticed that Harold had gone absolutely still. Rigid. He looked either very ill or very furious, I couldn't make out which. Or was it both? I asked him what the matter was, had I said something? Certainly no one else had said anything because I hadn't given them a chance. He said, 'Nothing', grimly. 'Really?' I said, and proceeded to put that right with a denunciation of Harold for his glumness, and more than that, for his smouldering glumness, then loped off for a pee. When I got back he was delivering a series of pronouncements to Beryl and Antonia like a fighting general in the last stages of battle fatigue, dealing with two lady journalists down from the Hilton, then sat silently for a moment, then said he wasn't feeling too well, and had better go. He then left. Antonia, lingering only to mention that actually he'd woken that morning feeling rather ropey, followed. I turned my attention to my wife, with whom I was clearly still on speaking terms. At least *I* went on speaking. Analysing, worrying, complaining . . .

Friday

Hungover but back to work at the Lyric. Harold and I began by apologizing to each other. He attributed his condition to dyspepsia consequent on too much white wine. I've observed that quite a few people, amongst them myself, consider that white wine is an alternative to alcohol, which is probably a mistake.* For one thing, I'm certain it does far more damage to one's stomach than, for instance, Scotch does. The trouble with Scotch, on the other hand, is that it makes you drunker quicker, and it also makes you, or me

---

* Best exemplified by a young but well-known journalist. After, even by his own standards, a very heavy night, he was asked by his hostess what he wanted for breakfast. 'Oh, God,' he said, 'I'd better not have anything to drink. Just a glass of white wine, please.'

anyway, a great deal more volatile emotionally. By which I mean ill-tempered and unpleasant. When we'd done blaming our drinks for ruining our wives' evening out, we went on to consider a number of textual changes, small ones that had arisen where we'd felt the audience was failing to follow the story. We decided that clarifications were necessary all over the place, in fact, then discussed how to approach Nick Le Prevost on the problem of his voice, deciding finally to tell him that there were places where he wasn't being heard, and then specifying them. We had various other notes, Harold's recorded on page after page of the small Asprey's pad he uses, mine swimming about somewhere between memory and unconsciousness, to be groped for. Then we went to rehearsal, Harold opening with a small speech summarizing how he thought the evening had gone, then going on to the notes, and then running little passages where the text needed pointing, moves needed correcting, etc.

At lunchtime I had to give a brief interview for a television programme. The interviewer was a great friend of my younger brother, Piers. She has always struck me as an alert and intelligent young woman, but her questions, probably perfectly reasonable, really, seemed, at least when put to me on the set of *The Common Pursuit*, with a camera aimed at my large, not to say sumptuous nose, like a parody of all the worst questions I've ever been asked since journalists started asking me questions. There was, for example, a version of 'What does it feel like to work with Harold Pinter?' and a version of 'What gives you the idea for a play?', along with more specific probings – 'Don't you think people might find your preoccupation with five Cambridge friends incestuous?' With the first preview only some hours behind me, I still managed a more than passable imitation of La Fontaine's frog competing with the bull, swelling with fury and self-righteousness until finally bursting out with a statement to the effect that no one of any sense wanted to hear playwrights, or any other writers, talking about their work. The work was *there*, wasn't it? What could the author say that would change it by a jot? Or a tittle? The producer, roaming about behind the camera, raised his hand when I'd got to the end of this ill-natured bombast, declaring that here at last was something he could use. God knows how I'll turn out.*

---

* I didn't turn out, apparently. They cut the interview.

After this, lunch with Harold, Harold not drinking, my keeping him company with a glass of wine or two, then back to rehearsals, on to a second interview.

This was for the BBC arts programme to precede the review by the unproduced playwright. I was under the impression that I'd refused to do it, but one of the PR girls appeared, flustered, to say that the producer had arrived, and was waiting for me. I can't remember what he looked like, though I retain a vague impression of spectacles, a small, clean young face, a tie, and a recording device, which he tucked away on the promised dot. He had the great advantage of not having seen the play, and seemed healthily unfamiliar with my work. Most of his questions were of a general nature, and I didn't mind the interview nearly as much as the lunchtime caper.* On into the preview, after a brief exchange at the bar with Harold, still not drinking. Again, a good house, assisted by a vocally clear Nick Le Prevost. In fact, he was fully there, audibly with us, if sometimes only just. He dropped very few words, though he swallowed occasionally (this was the first time I'd really taken in the swallow) in the middle of a sentence or trapped himself in a slightly clogged rhythm, as if he were compulsively choking the words back, but these were moments apart, and he had great presence and style. I thought that the evening worked as a whole, probably for all kinds of accidental reasons – a second preview with the adrenalin still flowing from the first, along with the confidence engendered by the first having been reasonably success-ful. In fact it seemed to me an *almost* perfect account of the play, which is the most one can ever hope for. I was genuinely moved (as I hadn't been the night before) by the Humphry death scene, perhaps because this time the first act was fluent, the dramatic rhythms easing into each other, rather than alternating with each other. All in all I was quite pleased with myself, grateful to Harold, grateful to the cast.

Coming into the bar some way behind Harold, I passed a table at which a famous Noël Coward-type actress was sitting with a coterie of admiring johnnies that looked as if they were out of those pages in the *Daily Mail*, or wrote them even, one of whom was asking her, 'Well, tell us honestly, darling, what did you think of it?

---

* I didn't hear the programme, so have no idea how or even if I came out.

Did you enjoy it?' To which darling replied, 'Yes, I did. [Little pause, little *moue*.] *Quite*.' I reflected, as I unbunched my fist, that firstly this was a free country, secondly that she didn't know I could overhear her, and thirdly – and thirdly, I entertained people at the bar with my imitation of her, which was all the more effective, I believe, for the differences between our faces, hers being long and fine, mine being round and on the coarse side. I got the inflection on the '*Quite*' rather well and the pause before it, though I'm not too sure about the *moue*.

Harold and I stuck about a bit, talking to the actors, not drinking too much – he rather less than me, as he had nothing at all – then he went off to meet Antonia at the Trattoo (why?) and I had a quick dinner by myself down the road, during which I drank water and therefore returned home, to my surprise, extremely sober. Rather a wasted effort, in a way, as Beryl had gone to Guildford with Judy to see the touring production of *Butley* and she didn't get back until two in the morning, when I was in bed, deeply asleep in what no doubt looked like my usual hoggish coma. But really I'd had a calm and happy evening. We'd given a satisfying evening in the theatre, possibly even value for money. Anyway nobody, in my hearing, asked for theirs back.

Saturday

We met the company at two o'clock, to clean up entrances and exits, make a few minor adjustments to the text, etc. The two audiences had taught us a great deal, and as the actors were now completely at ease with their lines and their moves, they could make adjustments quickly. I am always deeply impressed by actors' memories, even more so by their ability to cancel memories. Moves and lines that, after six weeks of rehearsal, run-throughs and now performances, would have (I'd have thought) become habits were altered within seconds.*

We decided to leave the actors alone for the matinee, letting them

---

* A few hours before we opened *Butley* to the London press, I cut a substantial exchange, which involved Harold's finding new positions for the actors – and they'd been playing those lines, doing those moves, for three weeks out of town. But in the performance that night the exchange went so effortlessly that I couldn't remember quite where the cut had come. This has taught me never to believe a director who says it would upset the actors to make late changes.

play the play in the knowledge that they wouldn't receive a single note on it afterwards. I went for a walk in Holland Park, trying to look like a chap to whom sunlight and fresh air were a part of his daily routine, rather than a profound shock to his nervous system. The excitement of a production is a drug, and I'd become a junkie weeks before. Really I wanted to be back there in the dark, watching, thinking, getting exasperated; not rambling unsteadily among the Holland Park children and parents and nannies and squirrels and such. I dallied beside the pens, forcing myself to admire the peacocks, who at least had the grace to look entirely artificial, until the pubs were open and I could sit over a drink, smoke, jiggle my leg impatiently in a congenially foul atmosphere. I managed to hold out there until shortly before the evening curtain went up, met up with Harold in the bar of the theatre, went in.

The house was packed. It was very much a Saturday night audience, vastly less appreciative* than the previous night's, and the cast dealt with them as they (I hope) deserved, coarsely. There really wasn't much to be learnt from it. I sat there stoically, as did Harold. After a brief visitation to the bar, a few words with the actors, we went off to dinner, raised points about the acting, the text, in a desultory fashion. Then I went home by taxi (dropping Harold at his car *en route*) to an almost unendurably patient wife, and to bed.

Sunday

I've spent this morning struggling to recall the events from the first preview on until last night. Obviously there are blanknesses, but I believe I've recorded all I care to remember, and a bit over. I'll try from tomorrow, the last preview, to keep a daily account. There are only a few more days of the diary to go, anyway, thank God. It's a beautiful day. I'm now toddling off to the Oval to watch cricket.

Monday, 2 July

During the weekend Harold telephoned Nick Le Prevost, Clive Francis, Ian Ogilvy, and arranged to meet them in the theatre

---

* And were therefore either vastly more or vastly less discriminating, depending on your point of view.

cafeteria for private talks about aspects of their performances that had grown apace since the first preview that he wanted to eliminate before the first night. When I arrived he was just moving from Nick's table to Clive's, or from Clive's to Ian's, or from Ian's to Nick's, I can't remember from which to which, but he was passing in black from one to another like a salesman from Exit. I stood at the bar, trying to look as if all my interest was in the drink (white wine) in my hand. Then we went into the theatre for notes from Saturday's performance.

The effect of Harold's consultations and notes was evident in the show. Really rather a good performance, a distinct advance on Saturday night's, though probably lacking the *fresh* confidence of Friday's. In fact it was a consolidation, just the right sort of performance to give before an opening. I wish we'd had more of them, before the opening, to give. After the show we dallied with the actors at the bar, had dinner together, compared observations, went to our respective homes. I came into my study, Beryl asleep, the children asleep, to dictate this. Tomorrow is the first night, so I shall probably sleep well. I always do, before first nights. From which I deduce that I'll sleep my deepest the night before I'm hanged. I think this is what's called withdrawal.

Tuesday, 3 July

Woke realizing that I had done nothing about first night cards and presents. I hustled over to Notting Hill Gate and spent the morning controlling my panic by looking around the shops, until I found one that specialized in Victoriana. I chose some original Victorian greetings cards, all of them yellow with age but charming (I hope) and delicately coloured. In retrospect, I don't really know whether these make appropriate presents. If not perhaps they will suffice as *mementos mori*. I then spent a considerable time at W. H. Smith's unravelling a conspiracy to prevent me from buying the right-sized envelopes. Had lunch in an Italian restaurant where I wrote on the cards, thus destroying their value, and went to the theatre for the rehearsal, which had been called for 2.30. Harold went through his notes, changed some of the blocking on the first scene, then ran Act One, Scene Two, so far the most treacherous scene in the play. I watched it alone from the upper circle, cigarettes going as usual, doing my best to concentrate on what was immediately before me rather than on what was to come. It seemed to me, though, that it had taken on a great deal of authority, Nick Le Prevost flourishing in it. Usually one rehearses before the official first night in order to give the actors specific things to think about, in other words to help their nervousness. And one's own, come to that. On this occasion, the work was, I think, valuable in itself.

Afterwards, Harold and I went back to Campden Hill Square. We wanted to watch the end of the Test Match, but it finished virtually as Harold turned the set on. We missed Greenidge's magnificent 200 and whatever it was not out, catching merely a glimpse of the back of his head and his upraised bat as he entered the pavilion. Harold went up to have a bath and change, I lay on the sofa. I had come kitted out for the occasion. Dark suit, black shoes, and a dark blue tie (in my shoulder bag). I wish I had some of the bravura of the old-time playwrights. Carnations, walking stick, cigarette holders, tails, etc., or conversely, that I could start an entirely new trend, although I don't know what it would be.* Antonia appeared with Orlando, her seventeen-year-old son. They'd spent the afternoon at Lord's. Orlando, being a great fan of Greenidge, demonstrated some of the highlights of his innings. Antonia went up to change, Harold returned in his black suit, sombre and spruce, and watched attentively as Orlando demonstrated the Greenidge highlights again. When Antonia came back, we had a glass of champagne. No, *they* had a glass of champagne each, I had a couple of Scotches.

At 6.15 we set forth in the car that Harold had hired for the evening. The show, being a press night, began at seven o'clock. The traffic was appalling, a road somewhere having been blocked off, no doubt to assist the flow. We arrived at quarter to seven, later than we would have liked under the circumstances. The foyer was full of various first-night types. Critics, accident collectors, friends and relatives of the participants, unidentified groups who might actually have been there because they wanted to see the play, although anyone who really wants to see a play would do better to come on almost any other night. Beryl arrived a few minutes after

---

* Perhaps garments that harmonize with a pair of six-shooters buckled around the waist, a knife in the belt.

us, having also been held up by the traffic. She and I have shared this grisly experience so often that I've come to feel, if not reassurance, then a reassuring sense of alliance, the second I catch her face coming towards me in the crowd.* The four of us went to the little room, had a quick drink or two, went into the theatre. Harold and Antonia sat together at one end of the dress circle, I sat at the other. Beryl, who finds my first-night under-the-breath comments and frustrated gestures distracting rather than educative, sat by herself in the stalls. The lights managed to go down, the curtain managed to go up, the music managed to be at the right level, and I settled into the irascible stoicism that is my normal condition at any performance of my plays, especially on first nights.

The first act was the best it has ever been. It had authority, the consequence really of Nick Le Prevost's authority, and also seemed to have a lot of wit and charm much helped by Ian Ogilvy, at his most relaxed and sympathetic; furthermore (and more to the point) getting a decent response at the curtain. We spent the interval in our little room, where we were joined by the theatre administrator, Robert Cogo-Fawcett, and several of the theatre's guests, who inhibited conversation by (a) being introduced, and then (b) saying nothing. The silence, broken only by elliptical sentences and the sound of drinks being poured, became quite tacky, although Beryl, Judy and Antonia announced, at various points, that it was all going really rather well.†

---

* She was snowed up in Devon for the three days before the first night of *The Rear Column*. The *Daily Express* offered to helicopter her to London, but she made it to Axminster station on a tractor (though she didn't drive it herself) and arrived at the Queen's Theatre about ten minutes before the curtain went up. Michael Codron, seeing her enter the foyer, said: 'Ah, now I know everything's going to be all right.' Actually it wasn't, as the critics hated the play, but I didn't and still don't really blame Beryl for that.

† Better than the first-night interval in San Francisco but a few short months ago, when I was followed into the private room by one of those perpetually middle-aged American ladies, jaunty on high heels, bold under a blue rinse, crying, 'At least we get a drink!', jostling the director and myself away from the table to make sure that she, and her rather large party of friends, did, immediately. Our attempts to escape into a further room where drinks were also on display were blocked by that rare creature, a churlish Californian (most Californians are sunny to the point of imbecility) who informed us we weren't welcome in there because it was available only to people properly connected to the theatre. So we had to go back into the first room, having now made ourselves interlopers there, too.

As at the first run-through, the second act should therefore have been a disaster. As at the first run-through, it wasn't. It went rather better than the first act, in fact. The scene that for me has become the litmus test of the evening, reporting retrospectively on the first act and the first part of the second act – the Humphry death scene – was really touching. The reason for this must be, of course, the affection aroused by Clive's Humphry. What Clive gives us is a man deeply rooted, full of wit, and yet somehow poignant. The only tricky patch came in the Epilogue, when something went marginally wrong between Nick Le Prevost and Bob East. Some lines were either dropped or fluffed, I couldn't make out which. But, generally, every single member of the cast came through superbly, the production flowed smoothly, remarkably smoothly given the limited number of previews, in other words, the play was there, as a person or a building or a geranium or a toad can be said to be there, emphatically itself, to be liked or disliked on its own terms. Not to mince matters, from the playwright's point of view an extremely good night. Not least because the audience at the final curtain suggested that they thought so too. Anyway again nobody asked for their money back, at least in my hearing. More importantly, nobody asked for their evening back, at least in my hearing.

We went to our little room to wait until the critics, their partners and the other first-night perverts* had cleared off, and then went on to the party the theatre was giving in the circle bar. It was an unexpectedly lavish affair, with wine, spirits, sandwiches and celebrities all milling about. A PR job, in other words. Everybody seemed perfectly relaxed. Everyone but me, that is. I was depressed. No doubt post-coitally so, as I always am on first nights, my eyes going glazed, my movements wooden, my voice leaden with hopelessness.† But this time I couldn't understand it quite, as there was nothing specific to be depressed about, given how things had actually concluded only a short while before. But I *was* depressed. Perhaps it was just my usual paranoia about critics. I was already convinced from past experience that on the whole they wouldn't like the play and it was certainly in this spirit that I responded to

---

* I've left this in because, though no doubt unfair about first-night audiences, it's true to my *feelings* about them at the time.
† This is not, in fact, how I behave post-coitally.

Peter James, the artistic director of the theatre, who approached me full of confidence and congratulations. Almost simultaneously (I subsequently discovered) Beryl was dealing in the same manner with the theatre administrator, Robert Cogo-Fawcett, who, like Peter James, jubilantly refused to believe that the Lyric had anything but a hit on its hands.

In spite of my Cassandra self and my wife Cassandra, the party went swimmingly, the general buzz of success uncheckable by either of us. There was an odd moment when Ian Hamilton, the editor of the magazine on which the magazine in the play is based, met Nick Le Prevost, playing the part based on Ian Hamilton. Nick, about seven or eight years younger than Ian, looked as Ian looked seven or eight years ago; both their wives – Ahdaf, Ian's wife; Aviva, Nick Le Prevost's wife – are pregnant to almost, I should think, the same week, and both have teenage sons by their first wives. There they stood, the four of them, talking.

Around the walls of the bar was an exhibition of Clive Francis's cartoons, which were also for sale. They were of cricketers (a splendid Ian Botham),* tennis players, actors and actresses, a few old stars (Bette Davis). There was also, side by side, one of Harold and one of myself, the only two, as far as I could see, so far unsold. The one of Harold is actually anachronistic, as he's holding a cigarette, but otherwise catches him accurately in a mood of ferocious geniality. The one of me I frankly consider Clive's only failure, as he appears to have given me a rug (my hair is thick, and my own), a pair of bloated cheeks, and has the tip of my tongue, or it could be an extra layer of underlip, protruding lasciviously. I noticed that nobody lingered before this study.† At first I assumed because they didn't recognize me. Then I realized I was named on a placard beneath it. So perhaps they couldn't place either the face or the name.

I don't remember any specific conversations at the party, apart from the long one with Peter James in which I already appeared to be gloating over my bad reviews, and a number of short and gratifying ones with friends. But I enjoyed, cynically, a mite, the

* This now hangs in my study, next to Clive's study of Clive Lloyd (the West Indies cricket captain).
† Clive subsequently gave this to me. I still don't think he looks like me, though sometimes suspect that I am beginning to look like him.

spectacle of our son, Ben, moving with aplomb among the actors, paying out compliments as he knocked back the drinks and sandwiches. The affair came to an end when a cake in the form of a typewriter was brought out. I was ushered forward to assist in the ceremony by one of the PR girls, but modesty held me back a fatal trifle. One of the Friends of the Theatre, a severe, schoolmasterly looking woman, interposed herself between me and the cake, clearly under the impression that I was a close relative to the wino Harold had been taken for in the cold beef incident. By the time the misunderstanding had been sorted out, Harold had sliced the cake open, to the pop of flashbulbs from the Hammersmith newspapers, the theatre's PR people, and further Friends of the Theatre. I gathered that the woman who held me back had herself furnished, perhaps even cooked, the cake. Presumably she'd believed I intended to devour her masterpiece, or in some way demolish it, before it could be photographed for posterity to wonder at. While slivers of the cake were being passed around, Harold, Antonia, Beryl and I went off to dinner at Thompson's, the only restaurant I know that can contain in one sitting everybody in London I wish to avoid. This evening it was a good place to be. We've had so many of these first-night dinners, just the four of us, and while they are, in a sense, interludes, the work finished and behind us, the question of reviews and the future of the production still to be faced, they always seem to me the real climax of the experience.

Afterwards we went back to Campden Hill Square, for a last glass or two of champagne, and then Beryl and I came home to what, all in all, I consider to be one of the most hair-raising moments of our life together. Our answering machine signalled that we had a solitary message. What we got when I wound it back and played it was a baby crying, crying as if it were being tortured. I immediately thought of Lucy, who is fourteen, being reduced to gibbering terror by some psychopathic brute who'd kidnapped her.* Ben returned, I played him the tape, his face went white. Beryl said that before I phoned the police, the obvious next move, she'd better call her sister, Jennifer, in Exeter. Which she did. Between them they worked out the explanation. All that had happened was

* Lucy was in Paris at the time, on a school outing – a fact we forgot in the stress of the moment.

that Jennifer's baby who had held the receiver while Jennifer dialled, had suddenly started crying in the way that babies do. Jennifer had taken the receiver from her to speak into it, and hearing
the machine and having nothing particular to say, had hung up,
not realizing that the baby (Alice) had left a memorable message.

And so to bed, and a deep sleep. One of the better things about
getting older is that one gets more callused. I no longer dread the
trek down the stairs to the morning papers and the reviews until
after I've woken up.

Wednesday, 4 July

Woke up, took the long trek down the stairs to the papers, dreading the reviews. Nothing in *The Times* or the *Mail* yet. Billington's
line in the *Guardian* is that it's 'a good and intelligent play' but
not 'a great one', which he finds a pity as apparently I have the
capacity to handle 'large themes' (whatever they are). My major
problem, apparently, is that I lack 'magnanimity of spirit and
largeness of vision', as is evidenced by 'a running gag' about a
theatre critic and poet 'we could all put a name to'. Later Harold
phoned to report on the *Financial Times* review which gives a
robust and even seemingly enthusiastic account of the play, going
so far as to compliment me on my writing, then draws indirect
attention to 'Nappies' Harrop, and concludes: 'I can't say I
enjoyed any of it very much.' There's an agreeable, if low-key,
review by Milton Shulman in the *Standard*. A friend phoned to
report on the unproduced playwright's review. He'd spotted him
hastening from the theatre into a taxi, and guessed from the eager
expression on his face, what he was going to do. Apparently in
doing it he got the location of the play and bits of the plot wrong.
As I didn't hear it, I can't comment. Harold phoned again to say
that there was a very favourable review in the *Telegraph*. I think
this must be the first favourable review I've ever received in the
Telegraph. What's going on here anyway? So far the production
and the actors have come out of the reviews well. Harold clung to
the belief that the Sundays would do us justice. We agreed to meet
at the theatre and to do our best to raise the morale of the actors.

Shortly after, a friend rang to report that she'd got a friend who
works on *The Times* to read out its review, which would be

appearing tomorrow. It was unpleasant, she said, and again made a reference to 'Nappies' Harrop.

Met Harold at the bar of the Lyric just before six. Bumped into Robert Cogo-Fawcett, Peter James and David Porter. Robert Cogo-Fawcett said he was surprised that none of the investors had yet tried to withdraw their money, 'in spite of the reviews'. Three of them had called, however, to ask whether the play had any future, and if so where? I said, 'But of the reviews published so far, we've had one very good (*Daily Telegraph*), one good (*Standard*), one favourable if equivocal (*Guardian*), and only one bad (*Financial Times*), and the unproduced playwright who surely doesn't count.' I didn't mention *The Times*, my line being that we'd done better than I'd expected, at least so far. H said, 'Yes, I know. But they're not what *we* expected. We expected raves.' 'But Beryl warned you,' I began, 'And I warned Peter James . . .' At which point Harold, who'd caught fag-ends of the conversation and therefore its general drift, said grimly that it was time we went in to speak to the actors, to raise their morale. As it turned out, the actors' morale didn't need raising until after we'd done our best to raise it. They thought that the critical reception had been rather encouraging, couldn't quite see why we were so worried, lots of plays transferred, did well in the West End on far less, mild euphoria should surely be the order of the day. 'Yes,' we said. 'But—'

5 July

The *Times* review is apparently as unpleasant as it was reported to be. I haven't actually seen it, nor has Harold, as it failed to appear in our copies of the newspaper, mine in N6, and his in W8. The only person who appears to have read it is the friend who got the friend to read it out yesterday. She lives in SW6. She says it's so badly printed as to be almost unreadable. The reviewer responsible wasn't Irving Wardle. A pity, I can't help feeling, as at least I could have got him on the blower, for one of our ding-dongs.

6 July

No reviews, no news.

Saturday, 7 July

We were reviewed on *Critics' Forum*. I didn't hear it, but gather that it was generally unfavourable.

Nevertheless I spent a fairly pleasant day at home, walking up and down our strip of a garden with the shamble of a lifer patrolling his cell. ('Those lime-tree bowers my prison' came to mind, though, of course, we haven't got any lime-trees.) In the evening, before going up to the Chinese restaurant, I set the video to record a television programme on which a Cambridge professor of English was to talk about the poems of Bob Dylan, and then to review my play.*

Beryl and I sauntered contentedly around Highgate in the summer twilight, took our Chinese repast (among other delicacies, seaweed without the grated sea-slug), sauntered home in the darkness. As soon as I got in I made for the video, began to wind back, fast- forward, etc., then noticed a message on our answering machine. A friend to report on the Cambridge professor of English. He'd loved the Bob Dylan concert, hated *The Common Pursuit*, being particularly incensed at the jokes about Cambridge dons being unfaithful, getting themselves murdered, etc., though he conceded that the audience, 'the people' as he apparently called them, enjoyed it. I decided under the circumstances not to watch the programme, winding the tape back and setting it on play/record to cover the Cambridge professor. I'd no idea of what I'd recorded over him until Ben came in, a few minutes ago, in fact, and said, 'Ah, I'd hoped you were recording that film that Harold wrote, what's it, *The Servant*. He acts in it too, doesn't he? D'you mind if I watch it?' It's an ill wind.

I've just given Beryl stern instructions that, should she be awake before me, she is on no account to look at the Sunday reviews, but to plop the arts sections – we take the *Sunday Times* and the *Observer* – into a drawer in my desk; but please to leave out the news and particularly (with the McEnroe–Connors final coming up, and all the cricket currently going on) the sports pages. Actually, I invariably wake first, so take these instructions to be to myself rather than to Beryl.

---

* I've only met the professor a few times (years ago), but liked him for his vivacity. He was described by a TV critic – reviewing the programme on which he reviewed my play – as 'dazzling', for which I think I may take some credit.

Sunday, 8 July

Slept like a log, woke at ten. Beryl was already in the kitchen, the papers minus the arts pages waiting for me, along with the coffee. About an hour later Harold phoned, making it clear, in a few terse sentences, what he thought of *The Sunday Times* and the *Observer*. The *Sunday Times* reviewer was brief, hostile and referred to the 'Nappies' Harrop joke, identifying its butt as his predecessor, who is currently campaigning for the Chair of Poetry at Oxford.* The *Observer* piece was longer, equally hostile, but so perplexingly written, Harold said, that it was difficult to make out what his objection was. The *Sunday Telegraph* began by saying that *The Common Pursuit* was the wittiest play in London, but went on to hint that it lacked substance. All in all, he (Harold) felt so enraged that he'd decided that he wouldn't after all go and watch his club, the Gaieties, playing cricket, but would stay at home and regain control of himself. I think he found my tone – I was aiming at insouciance, but suspect I hit facetiousness – rather irritating, until I explained that it was somewhat like Hamlet's madness, 'north-by-north-west', feigned to prevent me from going mad. Also, I said, I'd had my breakdown when the reviews of *The Rear Column* came out, and couldn't afford another. At the moment it was only veneer, but I hoped to thicken it into a carapace, then reminded him of the buccaneering contempt he'd displayed when dealing with the first reviews of *Betrayal*. He said he understood, but begged leave to continue fulminating. I graciously gave it to him, and we agreed to meet on Monday, probably.

Several friends phoned during the day to register their outrage, thus giving me the opportunity to practise my flippancy. Now there are only the weeklies to get through, and this part of the experience of *The Common Pursuit* will be over.† What worries me

* This is, as I'm sure everybody knows, an elective professorship for which candidates are obliged to solicit votes from members of the university. The ex-*Sunday Times* theatre reviewer polled well and ran a good second, I believe.
† Not quite true. On Monday the *Mail*, which we'd all forgotten about, published what I can only call a rave. Of the weeklies, *Time Out* was very good, *Punch* was a mixture of praise and reservations, but was a bit of what's known in genetics as a sport, raising the 'Nappies' Harrop joke in order to relish it. The *TLS* had a review by the editor, complaining of weak characterization and ponderous ironies, but on the whole was favourable, concluding with the suggestion that T. S. Eliot and F. R. Leavis those well-known admirers of weak characterization and ponderous ironies

immediately is the effect the reviews might have on the management (Peter James, Cogo-Fawcett and Porter) who were so shell-
shocked on Tuesday. It occurs to me now that Harold and I would
have better spent our time rallying them, rather than the cast,
making sure that they get on with the business of looking for a West
End theatre to transfer to. What worries me in the long term is that
there has always been something wrong with this production. I'm
not talking about what's on the stage, but its career as a
production, its future in another theatre. Of course every production has its own life, seeming to become an organism quite
independent from the many people who contribute to it, and this
particular organism seems to me to have been poisoned at the start,
with all the initial muddle over Michael Codron, UBA, etc., and I
strongly doubt that it will survive. Oh, this is probably rubbish. I'm
merely going on in this vein because I'm rather enjoying sitting
here, at about midnight, drawing on a cigarette, sipping a whisky,
ruminating like some old campaigner.

Monday, 9 July

Harold and I met at the Lyric bar before the performance, to do a
repeat job on the actors, who again needed no rallying, having
regained their spirits after our last attempt. Not surprisingly, as
they'd all had excellent reviews in the Sundays, except for one critic
who referred disparagingly to Ian Ogilvy, Simon Williams and Bob
East as 'ageing boulevard actors'. This amused rather than irritated
Simon Williams and Ian Ogilvy, but left Bob East incredulous, as
well it might, as no equally talented actor with his sort of looks has
had less opportunity to get on the boulevard stage. The extremely
cheerful atmosphere was only lowered now and then by the
appearance of Cogo-Fawcett or Porter (Peter James having gone
back to Israel) who were both adopting the stance of men
struggling gamely but ineffectually against an unsolicited social

would have approved. The *Spectator*, by the man who compared *One for the Road*
with *King Lear*, was unfavourable, saying that my reputation was a mystery. People
always thought they quite liked my plays until they remembered that they didn't
really. I don't know of any others, but suppose that *City Limits*, *What's On*, *Vogue*,
Tatler, the *Harringay Gazette*, the *New Statesman*, the *Jewish Chronicle et al.*
carried reviews.

disease. The actors went off to get ready for performance, Harold left to play bridge, I hung about with a drink, wanting to leave but drawn inevitably to the performance. I didn't actually want to see it, but also I didn't want to spend the rest of the evening wishing I had. In the end, I went in, reminding myself that after all I hadn't seen the show since the opening night.

As it turned out, I wish I had spent the evening wishing I had been there. The problem, I suppose, was that the actors, after a day off but still not having played the play often enough to be completely at ease in it, were remembering effects and therefore exaggerating them. The performance lacked spontaneity, and furthermore I had the impression that their reception on other nights had led them to take the audience's enjoyment for granted. None of this was surprising, but I couldn't help being depressed at the interval; and further depressed when I returned to my seat and noticed, just as the lights went down, the distinguished grey head and noble profile of Michael Codron. He was sitting halfway down my aisle. The second act was no better.

In the bar after the show, I tried to have a quick word with all the actors. This was difficult, impossible actually, because they were surrounded by friends, the clusters lapping into each other to make up what was in effect something of a party. After a time, I gave up, joined the celebrations, came home.

Tuesday, 10 July

Phoned Harold and gave him my views of the performance. We agreed to go in and have a look at it together on Thursday.* Then Michael Codron rang. He addressed me in a tone of gloomy compassion, telling me he didn't really want to discuss on the telephone what he'd seen on the stage, but he did say that he found it an extraordinary experience, attending a play of mine that he hadn't produced himself, feeling both a part of it but excluded from it. We agreed to have lunch soon.† I said I was sorry he hadn't seen it at its best. Usual stuff.

---

* We did. The show was in excellent shape.
† This lunch did in due course take place; was extremely pleasant; and concluded with Michael's offering to produce my next play – if I write it, and he likes it.

Wednesday, 11 July

Went to the theatre in the afternoon, to attend a publicity session. Was slightly surprised to observe on entering that neither the *Telegraph* nor the *Mail* review had been blown up and displayed, nor were there any quotes anywhere to be seen. Mentioned this when I was in the office, was assured it was being attended to. Our plan was to put a large display ad in the *Guardian* and *The Times*, alternating favourable quotes with unfavourable ones. It was both fun and quite gruelling, but what emerged, to everybody's surprise – Porter, Cogo-Fawcett and two ladies from the PR office in attendance – was how many favourable, or favourable-seeming, quotations could be picked out of even unfavourable reviews. In fact, there is rather more going for us than we'd supposed. Porter and Cogo-Fawcett became quite animated, both showing a gift for juxtaposing abuse or downright nonsense with praise, so that the final version, which we reached late in the afternoon, reads like something from *Alice Through the Looking-glass*, anyway will, I hope, read amusingly in the *Guardian* and *The Times*, where space has been booked, though for tomorrow week, when we'll be halfway through our run. I asked why we were appearing so late, and as nobody seemed to know, suggested that we try for an earlier date. Agreed unanimously.* After the meeting, I hurried off to see the touring production of *Butley*, which arrived at Dartford last Monday, the producer wanting to bring it into the West End for a short season. The auditorium was vast and empty apart from a few OAPs who were sitting with heads bowed, reading their programmes presumably, or asleep or dead. The stage was very wide, very deep, as if designed for ice-skating exhibitions, and the actors, whose previous stop had been Guildford, which has a very compact stage, hadn't quite adjusted their performances. The few leisurely steps they were in the habit of taking to cross the room were now inadequate in this large space. They were virtually having to sprint to get to their usual positions, so inevitably they were speaking quickly as well, far too quickly. It was quite ghastly, in fact, the actors whizzing about, rattling off their lines as if controlled by a video fast-forward, the finger controlling the button belonging to someone who hated the play.

* I don't know if an earlier date was tried for. The ads appeared when scheduled, three weeks after we'd opened, three weeks before we were due to close.

Of course, I was in no condition to judge the production which I also suspect was in no condition to be judged. I tried to leave at the interval, but was intercepted at the doors – the theatre is a hideous edifice, by the way, wound about by ribbons of concrete leading to motorways, flyovers, vacant lots, etc., and, thank God, the railway station – by a rather farouche young man, unshaven, the bottom of his shirt hanging loosely around grubby trousers, whom I took to be a stray tramp, seeking succour, but was in fact the company manager.* He bought me a drink at the bar, and accompanied me back into the stalls for the second act. I stayed for ten minutes, slipped out, struggled across a pedestrian rampart to the station, waited nearly half an hour for a train, came home, dictated this. I don't feel quite up to appreciating the irony, that a travel-ruined production of an old play of mine that I don't believe anyone really wants in the West End may be going there, while a strong production of my new play that I believe quite a few people actually do want, may not.

The next few days were concerned with the Lyric's attempts to transfer the show to a West End theatre. I don't, of course, understand the business complications of transferring a play from a theatre where it is set for a limited run to a commercial theatre where it will run for as long as the management can keep it going at a profit. I gathered, though, during the course of conversations with Peter James, Robert Cogo-Fawcett and David Porter that it would cost about £45,000 to move the set from Hammersmith to Shaftesbury Avenue, and do a proper publicity campaign. This money would be provided by the shortly to become celebrated Lyric shareholders, who of course would have to be paid back before the play could run into profit. The choice of theatre is therefore clearly very important. If a play transfers to a big theatre, and does excellent business, it will run into profit quickly. If to a small theatre and does excellent business, then obviously it will take longer. If to a small theatre and does only good-to-average business, it might never run into profit at all, whilst to a big theatre

* When I came across him on subsequent occasions, in London, he was always immaculately turned out in a dinner-jacket. So either he was just showing the effects of a long and exhausting tour in a rather personal manner, or I was hallucinating him, too.

doing good-to-average business, it might *eventually* run into profit, etc. In London, shows that seem bound to make a loss (i.e. flops) generally close in about six weeks, which, compared to Broadway, is a lingering death.*

But back to the Lyric and our attempts to find a theatre to transfer to. There was talk of the Albery, the Fortune, the Phoenix, the Comedy, Wyndhams, the Mermaid, the Vaudeville. All, except the Fortune, turned out to be either hopeless commercial propositions, or to pass through swift reversals of circumstance in favour of the play in occupation. At Wyndhams and the Vaudeville, for instance, *Passion Play* and *Benefactors*, both rumoured to be about to come off, suddenly started to improve at the box office, as did *The Little Shop of Horrors* at the Comedy. The proprietors of the Albery, on the other hand, turned the theatre over to a consortium that intended to do plays of its own; while the Mermaid was deemed by the Lyric management to be too far from the centre of London to be of any use except for plays doing a limited season, and we'd already done ours at the Lyric; and the poor old Phoenix seemed to have become, over the last few years, the sort of theatre where plays looked as if they were on a squat, waiting to be forcibly ejected, rather than settling in for a run. Finally, although the Phoenix† and the Mermaid bobbed up until the last gasp, the only convincing possibility was the Fortune, the management of which were keen to have us, and on which Harold, Eileen Diss and I were more than keen, believing that its size – it seats about 450 – and the close relationship between the stage and the auditorium would perfectly suit the intimacies of *The Common Pursuit*.

Moreover, its stage could accommodate our revolve, if only just. We went to the Lyric, to talk to the management. The management hoped we'd come to a fairly swift decision, as there was another

---

* My first Broadway play closed after three performances – (see *Flops and Other Fragments* on page 189 for a description of this) – and I've heard of one that closed at the first interval, and of others that closed during previews. An actor friend of mine, an exceptionally handsome man with golden hair, shaved his head especially for a part on Broadway, and learned the morning after the first night that the play had already closed, just a few minutes too late to prevent his wife and children, who were coming over for the second performance, from boarding Concorde.
† The outside of the Phoenix has been refurbished since, and now looks both smart and welcoming. It is currently housing a Dario Fo farce and, I hear and hope, is doing very well.

play they were interested in bringing in. The other play was, inevitably, the touring production of *Butley*. We reported to the Lyric our view that the Fortune would be right for *The Common Pursuit*, and heard back from the Lyric management that their only worry was that the Fortune, seating so few people, would have to play almost to capacity, not only every night of the week, but on the two matinees, to keep us just above profit. The point being that unlike, say, the Albery, they hadn't the seats to recoup on good nights what they might lose on bad. Nevertheless, negotiations were going ahead. Something might be worked out.

I tried to concentrate on other matters in my life, looking for calm at cricket matches, and playing my annual game with Harold Pinter's XI against the *Guardian*. It was an experience I don't care to reflect on, even three months later. We batted first, and I was out second ball, prodding myopically forward to an offspinner that briefly visited the top of my bat on its way to second slip. The only reason I failed to drop a couple of catches when fielding was that I was running in the wrong direction when they fell. In the last two overs the *Guardian* needed about 18, I think it was, to win. One of their early batsmen, on 60 or so, hit the ball straight at me. The ball, like a savage rat, aimed itself at my throat, then kidneys, then ankles, before scudding viciously under my falling body to the boundary. When the batsman took guard again, he turned his face, crafty under its cap, towards me, singling me out as the fielder who was going to win the game for him, and hit another four right past me, then another one under me. The remaining runs were taken comfortably, and although I was responsible for only two of them, I think I can claim to have lost the match single-handedly. The following day, Monday, I spent keeping a low profile, dealing rather briskly with Harold who phoned to ask how I felt about the match.*

The next day I went to have lunch with an old friend, Tony Gould, who is the literary editor of *New Society*. We met at his office,

* I now recall that Harold, at slip, had dropped this same batsman when he'd scored about 16 or so, the ball bursting through his hands on to his chest, bouncing off his chest back through his hands, on to the grass. *That* was when the match was lost, I now believe. (NB For an apologia for my chequered cricket career, see Part 5 of this book.)

where there was a message from Beryl relaying a message from the Lyric Theatre, Peter James having at last returned from Israel, that there was going to be a meeting at Harold's studio at 5.15 to discuss the future of the play, with special reference to the possibility of a transfer to the Fortune. I phoned the Lyric to say I'd got the message. Tony and I had a leisurely lunch, after which sauntered about doing a bit of book buying, before picking up a taxi that got entangled in traffic jam after traffic jam, the driver seeming to have a nose for them or a yearning for them, seeking them out by detours, etc., so that I actually arrived ten minutes late.

Harold greeted me at his door with a look of utter astonishment, and asked me where I'd been. I said I'd been involved in the traffic, why, what are you worried about? He said, 'Oh, I thought – I just thought – that you hadn't actually – you didn't know where you were meant to be.' 'But didn't the Lyric lot pass on the message that I'd got the message about where I was meant to be?' He said, 'Yes, yes, I got the message, they passed it on when they got here, they're upstairs now, as a matter of fact. It's just that you're late.' He wasn't irritable or accusing, merely wondering, slightly confused, as if my presence was in a way as much a mystery as my absence had been. I was also confused. We stood quite a time on the doorstep, revolving the question of messages, presences, absences, lateness, a surreal conversation, in fact, with metaphysical over-tones. I think the truth was that neither of us really wanted to go upstairs and talk to Cogo-Fawcett, Peter James and David Porter. Finally he led me upstairs, to his sitting room, and there indeed were a whey-faced David Porter, unable to meet my eyes; a glum, inward-looking Robert Cogo-Fawcett, unable to meet my eyes; and an extremely tanned, just-back-from-Israel Peter James, unable to meet my eyes.

They had called the meeting urgently, Peter James explained, because they were going to go straight on from it to meet the shareholders of their production company, and wanted a little chat with us so that they could present the shareholders with our feelings. We talked for about an hour, or mainly Peter James did, during which David Porter contributed half a sentence but got whiter, and Cogo-Fawcett kept taking out of his pocket little bits of paper on which scraps of numbers appeared to have been written down and was occasionally invited to contribute some of these numbers to what wasn't so much a dialogue as a monologue from Peter James, who talked on and on in a soft, worried, compassionate fashion, there in his sandals, his grey hair falling to his shoulders, his decent, honourable, gentle face registering sorrowful emotions about nothing specific, something nebulous. Neither Harold nor I, while it was going on, could quite make out what his sorrowful emotions were about. And David Porter, as I've said, increasingly whey-faced, unable to contribute anything except the half-sentence I can't remember. It can't have been a relevant half-sentence, because I don't think it redirected Peter James's flow by as much as a pause. Then they left, Peter James saying he was glad we'd had 'this little natter' as it gave him something to put to the shareholders, especially the chairman of the shareholders. They looked, as they trooped out of the room, like an illustration out of the updated Bible. The three wise men, perhaps ducking out of a situation and on to the pavement.

'Who are these shareholders?' I asked Harold. 'They never said they had to consult with shareholders before.'

'No,' said Harold. 'They didn't.'

'And the chairman. What chairman?'

'I don't know.'

'Did you notice David Porter's face?'

'White.'

'Yes.'

'And he didn't say anything. What was he doing here?'

'I don't know. Perhaps they have a pact to do things like this together.'

'Yes.'

We discussed it for a time, both of us by now perfectly aware of what we'd been told, in spite of our not being told anything, and then I phoned Judy and reported our suspicions. She said, with Boadicean grandeur, that she would go immediately to the Lyric and try to be present at the meeting. If she failed she would confront the triumvirate, and the chairman of the shareholders if necessary, when they came out. I said I thought that was terrific. Harold took over the phone and said he thought it was terrific. While Judy charioted through the streets from Paddington to Hammersmith, he and I sipped a few more glasses of champagne, talking to no purpose about the perfidy of the human race, and of theatre producers in particular. Then I went to meet Beryl and Lucy, back from school for a few days, in an Italian restaurant in Highgate, and bored them – Lucy anyway – with an account of the meeting, doing imitations (my Cogo-Fawcett consulting his scraps of paper was reasonably well received) and paraphrases, and we went home.

There were two messages on the machine, both from Judy. In the first she said that she'd got to the Lyric just as Peter James, Cogo-Fawcett and Porter were coming out of the meeting. They reported that the chairman of the shareholders, and the other shareholders present, hadn't responded with much enthusiasm to the idea of the Fortune. They wanted the Queen's, the Globe, the Albery, anywhere central on Shaftesbury Avenue. But she would talk more in the morning. In her second message she said she was sorry about the first message, as the news was worse than she'd implied. In reality there was not the slightest chance that we would be going to the Fortune. We would speak in the morning.

My transcripts record that we spoke in the morning. Indeed over the next few days there were interminable conversations between Harold, Judy, myself and Peter James; or Harold, Judy, myself and Cogo-Fawcett; Harold, Judy, myself and David Porter; Harold and myself; Judy and myself; and no doubt Harold and Judy; but clearly the question of the Fortune was closed.

One morning, rancorous with disappointment, I went to Chelmsford, where Essex was playing Middlesex (I think it was), determined on tranquillity. With Gooch going strong on 36, I found myself haring towards a suddenly spotted public telephone to take Peter James through the matter yet again. Why, I put to him, with all the vivacity of a man discovering the question for the first time, had he insisted that the Lyric become sole producers of the play, cutting out such potential producers as Michael Codron, UBA, etc., without mentioning that the Lyric production company was itself owned by invisible but omnipotent shareholders? He didn't know.

On another occasion, in the bar at the Lyric, I put it to Cogo-Fawcett that he, Peter James and David Porter had already decided, before consulting the chairman of the shareholders, not to accept the Fortune's offer. He admitted that they had. I then hinted that therefore the meeting at Harold's had been a bit of a charade. He supposed it was. But really they just wanted to break the news as painlessly as possible, he explained, by indicating what might happen before actually making it happen.

However much we grilled and expostulated, we could never get an answer to our main question – viz. why it would be such a financial risk to go to the Fortune. Given the revolve, we virtually had a one set play; there were only six actors, the costumes would all be provided, surely we were cheap enough – if not how could *any* play that wasn't performed solo ever make it to the Fortune? The deal they were offered, they kept stonewalling, just wouldn't work. And there were mutterings, so casually muttered that we scarcely noticed them, about some of the actors being a trifle expensive. This led me to recall one of Peter James's humble asides (I think it was addressed to his sandals) at the meeting at Harold's. 'Don't forget', he'd said, 'that we're completely inexperienced in this sort of thing. Moving plays to the West End ourselves, I mean. We still don't know much about it.'

This was probably the nub of the matter. A month after *The Common Pursuit* had closed I learnt from a West End producer that a transfer to a theatre as small as the Fortune had been out of the question from before we'd begun rehearsals. Apparently the Lyric had committed itself, and whatever West End theatre it might move the play into, to paying three of our actors the kind of money normally only paid to one. 'The actors' agents ran rings around the Lyric,'* he ended, with a compassionate smile. I can't say his explanation cheered me up. I'd hoped for something more arcane, the kind of mistake that not just anybody could make. Our consolation, I suppose, Harold's, the cast's, mine, must be that *The Common Pursuit* provided Peter James, Robert Cogo-Fawcett, David Porter, their shareholders and the chairman of their shareholders, with invaluable experience.

But this explanation was, as I say, offered only recently. Back there in late July, after negotiations with the Fortune had finally spluttered out, two other theatres tantalizingly displayed them-

---

* In running rings around the Lyric, the agents had probably also run rings around their own clients, all of whom might have been happy to appear in the West End for substantially less than had been negotiated for them, given the chance.

selves as possibly available. One was actually in Shaftesbury Avenue. True, it had just moved in a thriller, but everyone, including the theatre owner, knew it was a bummer. The theatre owner claimed that if the reviews were as bad as he considered they ought to be, he would give notice to the show to quit immediately, and we could move *The Common Pursuit* in within six weeks. Would that suit us? It would, even if it meant a playwright waiting ghoulishly for a fellow playwright's catastrophe, actors waiting to replace fellow actors, a director picking up a fee or royalties a fellow director was going to go without. (*That*'s show business.) In fact, the reviews were almost as bad as predicted, but the producer, whom nobody had thought fit to consult, ruined everything by declaring that he had no intention of taking the thriller off, whatever the theatre owner's attitude. He would feed money into the box office, if necessary, to keep takings above the level at which the theatre owner had the right to close it.* The other theatre was down the road and around a corner or two from Shaftesbury Avenue. Its final excuse for rejecting us was that it wanted to be a permanent house for musical comedies. A musical comedy went in there, stayed a few weeks, came off. Its posters still don't quite cover the posters of the show that preceded it, or of the show that preceded the one that preceded that. The theatre, currently vacant, its recent and sorry past littering its facade, looks like some desolate image from *The Third Man*.

Given our preoccupation with finding a theatre it's odd that, as far as I can make out from the transcripts, I never got around to discussing with myself, late at night into the tape recorder, the kind of business we did over our six weeks at the Lyric. I can't believe I didn't take an acute interest in it. I do remember, though, that every time I went in myself during the run it seemed to be at least three-quarters full, once or twice completely full. Checking over her files and receipts, Judy Daish reckons we played to an average 60 per cent or more which she also reckons was pretty good, at least in a particularly hot August with most London theatregoers out of London, and American tourists not familiar with Hammersmith, let alone the Lyric, Hammersmith, and given

* It's still running as I write this.

the management's whimsical policy on publicity – i.e. none until it was too late. I also remember that at the fateful pre-shareholders' meeting in Harold's studio, I assumed from the management's attitude that we must have been doing badly. Peter James, however, explained that actually we were doing well. At least better than most new plays at the Lyric, and certainly better than any previously put on there at that time of year. However his, and I suppose Cogo-Fawcett's and Porter's, personal standards were rather high, their touchstone being Michael Frayn's farce, *Noises Off*, which had played to 100 per cent capacity before moving to the West End. The next new play at the Lyric, *Tramway Road* by Ronald Harwood, which had better and longer reviews than mine, at least in the influential Sundays, is currently doing somewhere between 10 and 15 per cent, at a more propitious time of year, but on the other hand deals with English ex-patriates in South Africa, which may not be a crowd pulling theme. The play immediately before *The Common Pursuit* – *Black Ball Game* – played to between 15 and 20 per cent, I believe. Presumably the Lyric's long-range scheme is to wait for another *Noises Off*, and transfer it. If their shareholders allow them to, of course.

Anyway, by the time Harold went off *en famille* to Portugal for his annual holiday, and I went off *en famille* to Italy, it had become clear that *The Common Pursuit* was to have no future, at least immediately, in London. There was nothing to look forward to on our return but its demise at Hammersmith. When I got back from rolling off rocks into the sea, eating, drinking, playing poker, etc., I phoned Harold, who'd got back from doing much the same. We agreed to bring our joint adventure at Hammersmith to as graceful a conclusion as possible by taking the cast out to dinner at the Trattoo (why?) after the last performance, and to invite the actors to invite a loved one as a companion. With Beryl and Antonia, there would be sixteen in all.

NB The following account is a combination of transcript and memory. The transcript being coherent at the beginning, but falling into passages of gibberish or measured nonsense, had to be structured by memory which is no doubt faulty in details. But what I've stitched from the one and the other is roughly what happened as I remember it, I think.

Saturday, 11 August

Went to the Fortune, saw a preview of *Butley*, the matinee.* Whipped around with a few notes, then scurried across London to the Lyric, arriving half a minute before curtain up to see, as I ran up the stairs, Peter James and David Porter at the bar. Peter James followed me up the stairs, and went into the stalls, I think. I went to my regular seat at the end of the front row of the dress circle. As I sat down somebody coughed behind me. A recognizable cough. Harold, smiling, holidayed, in black for last supper.

It was a good performance that would have been better if it hadn't been the last. The actors pushed slightly, trying to wring every nuance out of every line, every silence. We heard later that it had been going very well so naturally, with no more opportunities to come, the actors wanted to go a stage further, which is always one stage too far. Or so I felt.

During the interval we went, not to our old room, but to the bar where Peter James had laid on a bottle of champagne. I managed not to overhear the kind of comments I'm usually destined to overhear by adopting the simple tactic of talking and laughing very loudly myself. Thus, I suppose, presenting the image of the boastful playwright bent on hogging the interval too, and so didn't notice David Porter until we were all clearing back into the auditorium, still standing at the bar in much the same position as he'd been in at the beginning of the first act, a poignant image of solitude and exclusion, his tankard of ale in his hand. The same image greeted me when I came back down the stairs, the first out as always, Harold chasing me as always, at the end of the second act, although of course I couldn't tell whether it was the same tankard with the same ale in it. I was about to go solicitously over to him when Harold took me by the arm and led us back into the auditorium, on to the stage, where the stage management was holding a farewell party.

It's a true comment on the egoism and obsessiveness of my

---

* I had had to take the production over, the director having committed himself to directing something else before he knew *Butley* was going to the West End. It lingered at the Fortune for a briefer season than the brief season originally intended. It was an event almost without meaning, except (for me) in its contribution to the history of *The Common Pursuit*.

relationship with this production (with *any* production) that so far in my account I haven't as much as glanced in the direction of our ASM, Tana. From the first day of rehearsal right through to the last performance, she was devoted in her duties, discreet and efficient, a provider of comfort, coffee, tea, lost lines, necessary smiles and photocopies on photocopies of altered text. She had given up smoking at about the same time as Harold, and chewed nicotine gum almost it seemed, in rhythm with him. She also jogged, bicycled and did sponsored walks. I mention all this only to prove that I was actually aware of her outside her function, and I was very glad of the opportunity to raise a glass (full, inevitably, of wine she'd provided) in tribute. It was a nice party, the only intruders being a few friends, all of whom either liked the play or were happy to pretend that they did, and it was made specially pleasurable for me when David Porter put in a late appearance, relaxed and jovial, so putting an end to my anxious speculations about the personal griefs that might have kept him at the bar, away from the last performance of the play he'd co-produced and helped to cast.

The evening should have ended there, with our going our separate ways in our own little groups, the company breaking up for the last time. But life, 'old life itself', of which I'm so fond when I encounter it on the stage or the page, but less so when it turns up in its usual dishevelled fashion in old life itself was waiting for us at the Trattoo (where else?) in the small private room, with a round table large enough to accommodate all sixteen of us. The virtues of a round table for dining purposes are known to everyone. No quarrel need be confined to an area at the top, or the bottom, or the middle, as in a long table. By simply swivelling your head in the course of delivering a sentence you can see the face of everyone you're insulting with it almost simultaneously. In short you can get from tranquillity to complete uproar with a single ill-judged remark. Or well-judged one, depending on your intentions and mood.

I'd like to draw a veil over the dinner at the Trattoo, with the observation that never, in my experience, has a round table proved its value as did this one. But that won't quite do. The round table provided only the opportunity and the means; the motives lay elsewhere, in Harold and myself, quite indistinct to each of us, I believe, the result of months of tension, hard work, exhaustion, culminating in dashed hopes. In the cast, whose experience had been shorter, but just as intense – more so, at times. In the waiters, with their – I can't speak for the waiters, except to say that I blame them too, if not above all, for everything that happened. It's just that I haven't worked out any conceivable motive on their part, and indeed they showed, when the dinner approached its climax, an unseemly sense of panic, running in and out of the room as if we were members of a family from Palermo refusing to be calmed even when informed that we were merely celebrating *The Common Pursuit*. I don't know what they made of this, but I do know I've never been treated with so little ceremony by Italian waiters, not one of whom sang into my face when I left, or offered to help me into my coat.

Not that there was any actually physical violence at the dinner, merely threats of it, and those merely implied, as when Harold jounced an ashtray in the palm of his hand when replying to my suggestion, delivered with some vocal power and the flourishing of a steak knife, that he was an imbecile. Or when Actor A (unnamed because he can't really have meant it), glimpsing an opportunity for political suasion, made a grave speech on the difference between bad bombs and good bombs, bad ones being the ones that fail to go off and kill people, good ones being the ones that go off and kill the right people, i.e. those who disagree with him, which on a quick count meant almost everybody in the room. Or when Actor B (unnamed because he can't really have meant it) proclaimed – but I'm getting ahead of myself.

At the beginning there was no hint that anything lay before us except a somewhat lacklustre dinner, our real farewells having been taken, as I've already mentioned, at the stage management's party back at the theatre. The only perturbation came from the realization that the restaurant had opened many bottles of red wine, and spread them across the table, while there was no evidence at all of white wine, which everybody really wanted. White wine turned up in due course, if rather less speedily than required, and everyone fell to talking, rather listlessly perhaps, to those next to them. I don't believe a major dangerous exchange took place until after an hour or so, though I can't be sure of this as I fell into a light coma for a time. I was aroused by hearing Actor B exclaim that if a son of his had done a thing like that, he'd have broken every bone in his body and smashed out his teeth. He was talking, from the other side of the round table, to Beryl, who was sitting next to me. Thinking for a moment that this was his response to one of her affectionate descriptions of a boyish mischief our son Ben had got up to, I shook myself into battle position. But it wasn't so, he was in fact expressing his feelings about the three public schoolboys, from Stowe, I think it was, who had planted a dummy bomb in some nearby hall that the widow of the late Airey Neave, himself actually blown up by a bomb, was going to visit. I took the view that however disgraceful the boys' behaviour might have been, paternal bone-breaking and teeth-smashing weren't really the answer to their problem.

The conversation got rowdier, spreading around the table like the proverbial wildfire, until Harold, who had fallen into a coma of his own, reared into consciousness. His opening intervention was equally based on a misunderstanding: to wit, that Beryl and I were actually toasting the behaviour of the three boys (I wonder if it would have given them satisfaction to know that their dummy bomb, laid somewhere in the environs of Stowe School, actually went off weeks later in a fashionable restaurant in West London) and it was through a sequence of misunderstandings, as neither would allow the other more than a half-sentence in explanation, Actor A's sermon on the difference between morally good and morally bad bombs; further rousing descriptions from Actor B as to what he'd like to do to a son of his, etc.; some gruesomely inappropriate common sense from Beryl; some grossly redundant attempts at calm and clarification from Antonia – that we reached our climax and someone had to reassure the waiters, streaming in and out of the room aghast, that all this was merely in celebration of *The Common Pursuit*. They didn't of course realize that this was the title of a play.

The row subsided as quickly, as mysteriously, as it had arisen. There were two or three minutes of silence, during which Harold put down the ashtray and I wafted the echoes of my insults out of the room with lazy gestures, as if they were so many stray wasps. Then Harold made a speech about the experience of the production, I made a speech about the experience of the production, Harold paid the bill, and left,* and in due course, in bewildered

* I eventually paid my share, I'm anxious to report.

pairs, loved one with loved one, the rest of us left. And that, I suppose, was the end, the ceremonial end, anyway, of the adventure of *The Common Pursuit*.

But life, 'old life itself', going through one of its shapelier phases, hadn't quite finished with us. A few days later, *Butley*, the play with which Harold and I had begun our association, opened at the Fortune, the theatre which we had once hoped would house *The Common Pursuit*. And a day or so after that, returning from Judy's office in a taxi at about six in the evening, I found myself wheeling around just off Holland Park and running parallel with Harold, who was walking across the street, carrying a copy of the *Standard* in his hand. I think, in the course of our fifteen years' association, that this is the only time I have come across him accidentally. I whistled through the window several times. He didn't hear me. My taxi slewed around and went up towards Highgate. He walked steadily on towards Campden Hill Square. We each maintained a dignified silence for a few days, until I sent him a note, he made a telephone call, both suggesting lunch. We had it in a restaurant situated in Holland Park itself, overlooking the nannies, parents and children among whom I'd stumbled one afternoon between a preview matinee and the evening preview. It was sunny now as then, this being one of those summers that turn up from time to time, though mainly in literature or in memories of childhood.

The lunch got off to an inauspicious start, with my waiting downstairs in the bar for him, while he waited upstairs at our table for me. I sorted that out by reminding myself of Harold's punctuality, and going upstairs to check. There he was, in black, framed against the large, sunny window, and there was I, bag swinging from my shoulder, a glass of half-drunk champagne in my hand. Both of us, I suppose, at our most characteristic, so how, under the circumstances, could the lunch not be like all the lunches we've had down the years? We agreed that at the Trattoo the demons that had pestered *The Common Pursuit* from the start had finally taken a brief but full possession of us, and then dropped the matter in favour of the things we cared to remember, of which there turned out to be quite a few, though not many of them, I now realize, reported into my tapes. Perhaps the problem with keeping a diary, and the reason I'll never keep another is that one records only the things one would prefer to forget. At least if one has a temperament like mine.

Appendixes

Appendix A

NICK: (*Enters, coughing slightly, looks around.*) Where's Stuart then?

MARTIN: He said to wait, they'd be right back.

NICK: They – oh, of course, Marigold. Well, isn't there any coffee on the go or anything? I've got a hangover.

MARTIN: Really? How did you get it?

NICK: Drank too much. In fact, look, what's that stuff, slimey, thick and yellow?

HUMPHRY: That covers a large number of revolting substances.

MARTIN: Oh, it must be advocaat, mustn't it? You know. Egg Nog.

NICK: That explains it. I'm allergic to eggs. Probably allergic to nogs too. If they're what they sound like. It was that bloody girl from Girton – Muriel what's-it?

MARTIN: Hoftstadt?

NICK: Yes, she produced it. I was perfectly all right until then.

Appendix B

HUMPHRY: Can we have some music instead. (*Little pause.*) If we're going to wait, could we at least do something worthwhile.

NICK: I advise you not to resist him. He has a powerful personality. (*He goes to the gramophone.*) What would you like to hear?

HUMPHRY: Wagner would probably be the most inappropriate. So let's have him.

NICK: I don't know if Stuart goes in for Wagner. (*Hunting*) Or anything musical, really. Except for reverie and romance. Ah – here's some. (*He puts the record on the gramophone.*) Mainly snatches from the great tunes, from the look of it. I hope it'll do. (*He sits down.*)

(*Wagner fills the room.* NICK *lights a cigarette and coughs.*
HUMPHRY *listens.* MARTIN *assumes a listening posture.* PETER
*listens idly, smiling pleasantly. They remain in that position as
the set revolves off, the music still playing, while Stuart's office
revolves on,* STUART *at the desk, for Scene Two.*)

Appendix C

Martin has just attempted to persuade Stuart not to resign from his
publishing firm. One of the inducements he offers is that Stuart will
edit Humphry's long-awaited book on Wagner, and suggests that
Stuart should go up to Cambridge to talk to Humphry about it.

STUART: Of course I'll talk to him. And there's nothing I'd rather
read than a book by Humphry on Wagner. Almost. But I won't
edit it. I have *got* to quit, Martin. You see, the real thing is –
well, last night, just before you and Marigold got back from the
concert, I was sitting in the kitchen drinking coffee and
watching Martina strutting about on the counter. Then she did
one of her things. You know, squatted on her haunches, arched
her neck, stretched her legs. Went into a kind of trance of
concentration. Aimed herself at the top of the fridge. And
missed of course. No, she didn't. She caught the corner and
ricocheted off, to the floor. And then she strutted away.
Looking pleased with herself. And instead of finding her funny
and endearing, I found myself thinking that either she was a
freak – because a clumsy cat's a contradiction in terms, isn't it?
Or she's a pervert. Because she *prefers* getting to the floor by
way of a ricochet off the fridge. And I actually found myself
loathing her as a – a – oh, obviously as a symbol of my – my –
anyway, I went from loathing Martina to loathing it. My life I
mean. And so back to first causes, and remembering that I only
came in with you – well, you know why. To have children.
Comfortably. You see. At your expense. I now realize. And
there's quite a lot wrong with that on any terms, but especially if
there aren't any children. To justify it. Partially.

Appendix D

STUART: Actually, let's face it, or let me face it, at last. It's probably the right decision. The fact is that the magazine doesn't really matter, to anyone except me. As Nick pointed out. (*Little laugh.*) To do him credit.

MARIGOLD: Yes, it does. It matters to lots of people. Hubert Stout* among them. Or he wouldn't have given you his six new poems, would he?

STUART: He only gave them to me because I gave him that bloody party, which was finally what bankrupted us, as Martin has always refrained from pointing out, although he came close a little while ago. Anyway, the Stouts will get themselves published somewhere far more public, and for real money, instead of promises of it.

MARIGOLD: But you're not seriously talking of giving up! Not now! You can't. He can't, can he?

STUART: Oh, yes I can.

MARIGOLD: But – but it's not fair. (*She gives a little laugh.*) It's actually not fair.

STUART: Being fair has nothing to do with it. The printers want their money, and why shouldn't they have it, they've worked for it? The landlord wants his rent, and why shouldn't he have it, he owns the place? I can't pay the telephone bill, the electricity bill, I can't even pay for the issues of the magazine I fail to bring out. If fair means anything it's not fair on them. And above all it's not fair on you. It probably never has been. But certainly not now. Come on, Humpty. Let's hear the truth.

HUMPHRY: But you've just spoken it. Almost. Even if you get the grant doubled you'll be having a version of this conversation a baby or two from now.

STUART: Yes, well trust Humpty to go the unpalatable stage further. But he's right. In the end it won't survive.

MARTIN: It will. If you come in with me –

MARIGOLD: You don't know everything! You don't always know everything! (*To* HUMPHRY)
(HUMPHRY *looks at her, makes to speak, doesn't.*)
I – can I – look, do you mind if I – well I want to talk to our editor, the literary gent, you see. Sorry. (*Little laugh.*)

---

* In the published text Hubert Stout appears as Hubert Parkin, but I have kept the name we changed to in rehearsals to avoid confusion.

2

Further Experiences in
An Unnatural Pursuit

Flops and Other Fragments

There was a party at Sardi's to celebrate the opening of my first play on Broadway. The producer, whose only venture into the theatre this was to be, sat sobbing at the end of a long table in an upstairs room that had emptied with the arrival of the *New York Times* review (epoch of Clive Barnes).

GRAY: Oh, come on now, no need to cry now. Only a play! (*Little pause.*) Old chap?

PRODUCER: Only a play? When I invested all my wife's money in it? And I haven't told her yet?

Early the following morning, my wife and I stole with our luggage through the hotel lobby, to avoid the manager who had given us cheap rates, a high standard of service and mysteriously obsequious smiles because, as we'd also learnt at the Sardi's party, he too had invested money in us.

Back in New York some months later, with a new piece. Standing in a bar next to the theatre during the interval of the second preview, my third large whisky smouldering in my mitt. A friendly figure hovers beside me, orders himself a drink.

FRIENDLY: (*After a pause, turns.*) Saw the same guy's last. That was crap too.

GRAY: (*Shakes his head gloomily.*) State of Broadway.

FRIENDLY: Somebody ought to give him the bum's rush. Got enough crap of our own. Don't need his.

GRAY: Yeah.

This piece first appeared in Ronald Harwood (ed.), *A Night at the Theatre*, London, Methuen, 1982.

A smooth theatrical production, though, interrupted only by life itself. Our youngest actor mugged twice in his dressing room during the first week of performance. One of the understudies raped in a car-park during rehearsals. Our leading lady held at knife-point for two hours behind the theatre. Flying home after a week of previews, I phoned from the airport.

STAGE MANAGER: Hello.
GRAY: Hello. Simon here.
STAGE MANAGER: Oh, hi, Simon, what can I do for you?
GRAY: Just wondering how it went this evening.
STAGE MANAGER: The first act went pretty well, I thought.
GRAY: Good. (*Pause.*) And the second act?
STAGE MANAGER: There wasn't a second act.
GRAY: Oh. (*Pause.*) Any particular reason?
STAGE MANAGER: The company went to see *Hello Dolly*.
GRAY: Instead of doing the second act, you mean?
STAGE MANAGER: Right.
GRAY: Oh. (*After a pause.*) Any particular reason?
STAGE MANAGER: Somebody reported a bomb in the theatre.
GRAY: Oh. (*Attempts lightness.*) Which?
STAGE MANAGER: (*Laughs politely.*) Ours.

On my third visit to Broadway, all went well apart from the discovery of the wardrobe mistress's body in the wardrobe an hour before curtain up on the first night. Natural causes, however, which in New York, opening doors on to inexplicable mysteries, are more alarming than the run-of-the-mill foul play.

In Berlin the German translation of my first play was almost a complete triumph. At curtain call the cast received a prolonged ovation. The director, one of the Grand Old Men of the European theatre, was summoned to the stage, and cheers sounded; which continued as he beckoned me up to join him. Two usherettes led me through the wings, and out, centre stage. I tipped myself forward, shyly.

GRAY: (*After several bows.*) Why are they booing?
GRAND OLD MAN: It's normal, you see.
GRAY: (*Bows again, to increased boos.*) Well, who exactly are they booing?

GRAND OLD MAN: You.
GRAY: I see.
GRAND OLD MAN: You must take another bow, please.
GRAY: Why?
GRAND OLD MAN: Because it is bad manners if you do not.
GRAY: But if they're booing me . . .
GRAND OLD MAN: (*Irritably.*) It's quite normal.

In Rome the theatre burnt down a month before we went into rehearsal for my fifth play. Or so the Italian translators claimed.

One of my plays had its première at the Charleston Festival (twin to the Spoletto Festival) while the wardrobe-lady-dead-in-the-wardrobe play was still running on Broadway. I made Charleston headlines with 'Gray hits town' which I took to be a set-up for reverse headlines when we opened a few days later. The humidity was such that every morning, in my air-conditioned hotel room, my clothes were soaking before I put them on. Either humidity or the usual terror. Unusual terror, actually, as I kept receiving messages, delivered by hand to reception, from a member of the cast, a swarthy and muscular youth who, in the course of the play, was called upon to garden-shear an old man to death in a fit of pique. His messages, scrawled on scraps of what looked like lavatory paper, were rambling but unmistakable threats against my person, brought on by my interference at rehearsals. One evening I returned to find waiting for me at reception the messenger himself. I fell instinctively into my favourite defensive posture, the academic stoop, which I at once realized made me resemble his nightly victim. Readjusting myself perhaps excessively upwards, I strutted the two of us to my room, and woofed him disdainfully into a chair.

GRAY: So. What's the problem?
YOUTH: You're killing me.
GRAY: Ah. How so?
YOUTH: The way you keep trying to make me hold back. I got something special to give the audience. Something special. You got to let me give it.
GRAY: (*Reverting to academic.*) Well, you see, what I feel is, you see, is that this is a shy inhibited boy, the part I wrote, who

can scarcely talk to other people, as I mark clearly in the text, I feel you'll agree, or even look at them except humbly and gauchely.

YOUTH: Jeez!

GRAY: But you, you see, you come bounding on stage, you see, and furthermore, I know I've mentioned this at rehearsals, forgive if I'm labouring, woof woof, and you stand there ogling the audience if you follow, and doing that odd business with your eyebrows I've mentioned woof woof, and bellowing and leaping about, sometimes you give the impression woof woof that you're about to do a cartwheel or sing or take out a guitar and strum it. (*Pause.*) Woof.

YOUTH: OK. (*Pause.*) Right. (*Pause.*) OK. (*Slides his hand into jacket pocket, where* GRAY *suddenly observes a lumpish object, clearly lethal.*)

GRAY: Now. Woof. Now – (*Calculating: too small to be garden shears themselves. Knife? Pistol? Dusters? Clublet?*) Why not a drink? (*Moves smoothly to telephone, picks it up suavely, trembling.*) Call down for (*Help! But calm, keep calm!*) Scotch for myself, d'you fancy anything?

YOUTH: Got one. (*Takes can of Charleston beer out of jacket pocket, rips it open.*)

GRAY: Woof. Send up Scotch please or some such. Woof woof. Now?

YOUTH: The tradition I work in, you see. Commedia dell'arte. That's where I am. Commedia dell'arte. (*Settles powerfully forward in chair, expatiates on commedia dell'arte, his talent for it, my suppression of it, while supping down Charleston beer, until –*)
(*Telephone rings.*)

NEW YORK: Just to confirm, Simon, that you're coming to the Tony awards next week, Simon right?

GRAY: Hadn't thought to, actually.

NEW YORK: Now look, you got to come, Simon.

GRAY: Why?

NEW YORK: You've been nominated!

GRAY: Yes, I know. But I'm not going to win. That play about people dying nobly of cancer is going to win. So there doesn't seem much point in coming all the way to New York, and

being locked in a large room, and being shown on television
for a few seconds watching somebody else winning instead of
me if you follow – (*To* COMMEDIA DELL'ARTE) Excuse me.
NEW YORK: (*Passionately*) Who says cancer is going to win,
Simon? Who says you're not going to win, Simon?
GRAY: Well, everybody. Including me.
NEW YORK: Well, I'm not allowed to say who's won and who
hasn't, but what I want to tell you Simon, is this, Simon, that
there are a lot of people in this town who think you're going to
win, and are rooting for you to win and are going to be very,
very surprised if you don't win, Simon.
GRAY: Well, I still think – (*To* COMMEDIA DELL'ARTE) I'm *very*
sorry –

On the day of the Tony awards I left Charleston, where the
commedia dell'arte youth had stolen all the notices – he was
welcome to mine, as they weren't up to much – and flew to
Washington, *en route* to New York. Or London. My tussle was
even shorter than Robert Frost's in the snowy woods. I watched
part of the awards programme on television at the airport, and
noted that the noble-death-by-cancer winner expressed profound
surprise at his success. So perhaps he'd been rooting for me too.

A small, plump, engagingly camp American who once wrote
campaign speeches for a famous but no-hope Republican candidate
moved to London with a dream: to produce a play at the
Haymarket Theatre, London. A play of mine, small, domestic and
mildly troubled, was put in his way. Stopping only to pick it up,
and certainly not finding time to read it, he raced with it towards
his dream. And lo! lo! it came to pass that he stood at the famous
doors, in white tie and tails, and welcomed in the elderly
fashionables and the usual gang of critics, etc. About three weeks
later he phoned me.

PRODUCER: What do you think went wrong?
GRAY: Oh. Play too small? I suppose. Or theatre too large. (*Pause
for thought.*) Both, probably.
PRODUCER: Yes. Well, you did your best.
GRAY: Thank you.
PRODUCER: Thank you.

GRAY: Not at all.
PRODUCER: (*After a pause.*) And we did it at the Haymarket.
GRAY: Absolutely. That's where we did it!
PRODUCER: Thank you.
GRAY: No. Thank *you*.
PRODUCER: (*Whinnies. Pause.*) Be in touch.

He hasn't been. Although I've heard that he's back on the American election trail, campaigning for another loser.

My first and still my favourite flop was at the Aldwych, about twelve or thirteen years ago. Rehearsals went well, as they're wont to do in the real flops. There was a great deal of easy, after-rehearsals talk about the transfer, its venue and date and even, reaching ahead to the end of the first run, about replacements. Wood was, of course, touched, and other superstitions honoured, but nothing, it was felt all round, was likely to go wrong. Four weeks of work, and there wasn't a single fragment of the play – and each fragment was being meticulously polished up and polished up – that didn't seem exactly funny, exactly sad. What conclusion could be drawn from this, other than that when the fragments were aligned, the whole would be exactly right? Perhaps the truth is that at that stage we – the two producers, the director, the cast and I – had quite different versions of the play which none of the fragments, still invitingly open-ended, could contradict. It was a tribute to the *camaraderie* of the company that we listened to each other's versions in a spirit of friendly, though sometimes impatient, disagreement.

So it remained until the first real run-through, which took place in Sadler's Wells, at about six in the evening, some twelve or thirteen years ago.

Few buildings are as desolate as an unused theatre, which seems to exude all the cold shadows of its past failures. One of the producers turned up, previously a chain-smoker and now a gum-chewer, and isolated himself in an aisle seat to the front of the stalls. I remember peering towards him when the lights went down but before the stage was lit, and noting that, with his face rising attentively out of the collar of his overcoat, and with his jaw flickering, he looked like some strange reptile, a lizard of the dark;

and then looking around at the rest, scattered at intervals in the ghastliness – gargoyles, undertakers, murderers from Victorian novels – a brotherhood from Hieronymus Bosch.

Some three and a half hours later, again frailly human in the lights of the pub around the corner, we tried to speak of what we'd seen – all those fragments, still with their polish on, but resting inertly next to each other. Continuity, which was to give us our whole at last, had in fact emptied the fragments of all their possibilities. Four and a half weeks of rehearsals had provided us with seven or eight little corpses of seven or eight little plays. Such an entertainment had at least found, in that theatre's ambience, its appropriate audience.

Desperation set in at once, and our voices were calm with it. Most of our sentences began with, 'No, all it needs is . . .' or 'What we've got to do really, is just a matter of . . .' though I also have the impression that the word 'life' figured significantly; as in, for instance, 'No, what we've got to do really is just a matter of giving it life.' 'That's right, you're quite right, a bit of life is all it needs.' Well, we were right. Does any corpse need more?

In the following run-throughs in London, then between audiences in Brighton, we worked for life. Our attempts took various forms, and were ingenious. The director thought out new moves and assisted the cast into new readings. I rewrote incessantly, adding scenes here and cutting monologues there. We changed the ending, sometimes twice in a single conversation, and of course and almost by the way, we continued to polish up and polish up. Ultimately, because nothing pays off like hard work and a willingness to adapt, we were rewarded. We established connections, we achieved coherence. Our little plays joined themselves into one whole play. Our little corpses swelled and joined into one big corpse.

About halfway through the Brighton run we had an illumination. Our key phrase became suddenly to do with the need to salvage the 'real text' – although I think we suspected that none of us any longer knew what this was. We had made so many alterations, insertions, revisions of alterations, and addenda to insertions that probably the authoritative script was buried deep in the collective unconsciousness. Still, we must feel our way back to the 'life' of the 'original'. But each struggle with our now immaculate corpse simply produced increasingly complicated arrangements to its limbs – fresh ways, in fact, of laying it out. Which eventually gave rise to yet another proposition (for what could be manipulated could also, in a sense, be said to 'work') – that though we had to pursue our quest for its life, we nevertheless mustn't lose what we had already got. So we watched the audience fall as if palsied before our piece, and laboured in whispers to reconcile our two quite opposite intentions – to preserve our articulating corpse, which at least kept people in their seats; and to recover that forgotten impulse that might actually make them sit up. Once again, but with a proper reverence for the dead, I rewrote; again the cast relearnt; and again the director redirected; and again our corpse walked, corpse-like.

Midway through our second week at Brighton I sat in the foyer of one of the grand hotels, half an hour or so before curtain-up, and wondered, as I nursed my fourth refill, whether I could make it to the theatre. A new guest arrived, a smart, plump, on-the-town sort of johnnie. As he signed in he spotted the small poster on the desk advertising the play.

GUEST: Ah, that looks good. Think I'll pop in on that.
RECEPTIONIST: (*applying right thumb and forefinger to nose, squeezing it, while jabbing left thumb down brusquely.*)
GRAY: (*Decides he can make it to the theatre after all.*)

At the interval a wizened and effete novelist from a bygone age, famous for his vivacity, introduces himself into the familiar cluster of demoralized author, despondent director and hopelessly brave producer. He makes to speak frankly of what he's so far seen, is cut off by a swift introduction to myself. Upon whom he fixes a gaze of malevolent compassion, and proceeds to speak of his cats and his garden and other wholesome topics until the bell releases us back to our torment.

It was an odd thing about the play, that though the audience clearly loathed it, and though Brighton is celebrated for the sound of up-tilting seats at almost every stage of every performance of any play ever performed there, nobody actually walked out on us, or even left us at the interval. Nor did they cough, shift irritably or applaud at the end, though there was always a rather eerie rustling when the curtain dropped as of spectral hands or autumn leaves.

Perhaps we sapped their will, or they felt that having looked in by mistake on a corpse, they were obliged to keep the vigil with us.

A director friend of the director was summoned to Brighton to save us. He came straight from the station to the theatre, and afterwards, over a fish dinner, told us that all we needed, really, was a bit of life. Yes, ah yes. And a lot – lots and lots and lots – of colour. Ah. Ah–hah! Yes! And you also need – don't you? – more movement? With his fresh eye and unshattered morale, we saw through the haze of our fatigue a small light dimple. Work began on the set the next day. It was halved in size and coloured up until it began to look like the interior for a naughty postcard. The cast were given some new moves, which they were asked to execute on the run; and some new lines, which they were asked to deliver on the run, but which were actually only a down payment on a whole new folio of rewritten scenes I provided over the next few days, also to be performed on the run.

The transformation from Brighton to London was miraculous even to those of us who had worked the miracle. Our Lazarus hadn't come back from the dead, of course, but with his cheeks freshly waxed and rouged, with his false nose and funny trousers, he was up and about his newly half-sized grave, up and about and on the run. Galvanized himself, he succeeded at last in galvanizing our audiences. Groans of irritability, early and resonant departures, angry complaints at the front of house, full-throated comment at the interval – he conjured up all the recognizable components of a swiftly recognized flop. We allowed him a limited run at the public before performing the last rites and piling the earth on top of him. But he managed to keep rearing up, vivid in an endless sequence of obituaries. The dailies were followed by the weeklies, the weeklies by the monthlies. The chappie in the *Daily Mail*, a scourge of our times, based on it, in a full-length feature, his whole case for bringing booing back to the theatre. Should I be around some night when the graves give up their dead, I know which corpse, capering festively, funny trousers flapping and false nose pointing, will head straight towards me.

A few months ago the telephone rang.

WEST END: Ah, Simon? Just to make sure you'd be coming to the theatre awards next week.

GRAY: Well, Eddie, I hadn't really —

WEST END: But you're up for four. Best actor, best actress, best director and best playwright.

GRAY: Really?

WEST END: So you've got to come. Haven't you?

GRAY: Why?

WEST END: Because of all your nominations.

GRAY: Yes, but as we're not going to win — that play about the deaf-and-dumb girl is going to win. So there doesn't seem much, well — in coming all the way into town, and being locked into the Café Royal, watching somebody else winning instead of me, if you follow.

WEST END: (*Suavely*) Simon. Let me just say this. Nobody knows who's going to win.

GRAY: I do.

WEST END: *Nobody* knows. But — if you won't come — let me put it this way — who do you want to pick up your award for you?

We went, my wife and I, and watched the actor and actress pick up the awards for themselves, as well as for the author, expressing on each occasion, in prolonged passages of deaf and dumb, their delight and surprise. So . . .

So. I can claim after fifteen years in the theatre that I've learnt only that I've learnt as little from my few correct decisions as from my many mistakes. In that respect too, it has been a second home.

Confessions of a TV Playwright

I became a writer of television plays entirely by accident, before I was in possession of a set or thought of television as anything other than a magic machine that transmitted cricket and football matches into the living rooms of friends; who were thus victim to unexpected visits during, and to deft cultural jokes between, important internationals. I didn't know – wouldn't have been caught dead knowing – who Honor Blackman was; had never in my life clapped eyes on a ballroom dancer, at least in action; and wouldn't have believed that people actually wrote plays *for* television. Now, a mere two and a half years later, I can usually identify by name the second villain in *The Avengers*, feel that my judgement ought to carry weight in the ballroom competitions, and have once or twice been overheard saying a soft goodnight back at the closing-down announcer. I am an addict. The only respect in which I haven't changed is in my ignorance about the nature of television plays, although this ignorance is now a complex and active state.

The first play I did was an adaptation of a short story I had had published in *Voices*. The BBC offered to buy the rights, and my agent was anxious to sell them, but there was never, in the early stages of negotiations, any intention on either side that I should do the adaptation myself. But when the script editor revealed in a slip of the tongue that the rights were worth less than the work of adaptation, I became both thoughtful and bold. I told my agent that I was sure I would soon 'pick it up', my agent presumably told the BBC that I had already picked it up, who courteously but presumably with qualifications agreed that I might at least be allowed to try to pick it up. For the next few days I worked at

This article first appeared in *The Times Literary Supplement* on 19 September 1968.

visualizing the story in television terms. When on the bus or in the bath I would project it on to an imaginary screen; I went to the public library and scrutinized a book with a title like *Writing for Television*; and I struggled to realize a weak recollection of having once seen a television script, while struggling to forget that I had had to put it away from a dizziness induced by phrases like 'boom-in', 'angle right cam', 'angle left cam', and 'tracking shot'. I still have no idea whether these words actually exist in the television vocabulary, but I became frighteningly convinced that they or something like them did, and that it was the merest part of my function to know when they should be employed. I didn't, of course, know what a television camera looked like, but another recollection of certain films suggested that it was sat on by an expert in headphones who drove it backwards and forwards, sideways and in circles, in accordance with this crucial code. So my visualizations became now feeble, now frenzied, and my library pursuit of knowledge became more eccentric (to the point, actually, of reading Gilbert Harding's autobiography; for his was a name I did know), and in other words I did everything that I thought might assist me write the script except arrange to watch a short play on television. I suspect that in those two weeks I did as much genuine research as I had ever done while a registered Ph.D. student, and to approximately the same effect. In the end there was nothing for it but to sit down at the typewriter and begin.

It took me about four hours to produce the script (it was a half-hour play); for my approach, when the chips were down, was simple to the point of imbecility. I eliminated all the prose between the dialogue – of which there was, thankfully, a great deal – and then replaced the prose with terse but masterful instructions. So instead of describing the way in which a character entered a room, I wrote:

JOHN: (*Opens the door, comes into the room, walks towards the sofa. Stops. Turns. Sits down on the chair.*) Good God are we really . . . etc., etc.

Occasionally and experimentally, as for instance when I couldn't think of anything to go in parenthesis, I wrote in 'close-up', or 'hold camera', or 'track significantly'. When I had done this, I typed the whole out again and, with the confidence of a man who is in possession of thirty neat pages, had them delivered to the BBC. The script editor telephoned the next day to say that everything was fine, although there *was* a problem.

The problem was that the play was to be done 'live'; by which was meant that the play was not to be taped or filmed; which in its turn meant that I would have to think again about continuity; which finally and specifically meant that a man who is in the bath in one scene cannot be expected to appear fully clad and halfway through a cigarette in the next (which I in fact had expected of him) and vice versa (which I had also expected of him). *So*, the script editor said, if I could just think of ways around this problem. I thought of them immediately, for I was not afraid to draw on all the resources that I assumed were at the disposal of so technologically complex an organization as the BBC, only to hear, in amazement bordering on contempt, that these vaunted experts could manage very little in the way of expertise after all.

'You mean you *can't* superimpose water on an actually empty bath in which a nude man is sitting (who have you got for the part, by the way, have you toyed with Gielgud?), *but* cutting off his head so that Gielgud's head *looks as if* it's on the top of his neck – a perfectly simple trick shot I should have thought, actually (what about Olivier?).' At the end of the conversation it was agreed that I would rearrange the scenes; a matter, I was comfortably told, of only a few hours' work.

It was a matter of only a few minutes' work. I moved another scene in between the bath scene and the dressed-with-a-half-smoked-cigarette scene, thus allowing Gielgud or Olivier a full 75 seconds to change into a suit and get into his fag; and I retyped two other pages that had become grubby in transit, and I sent it in again, and it was accepted as the final version. I had written a play for television.

I had never before attended rehearsals for anything, although (again) I had seen enough films to know what authors looked like when they did so. I took my posture from Henry Fonda – an authorial hunch, a humane smile, an air of inner grace. I paused, for a second, before the door behind which the first reading was to take place, checked a minor lesion of confidence, then stilt-walked inside. A number of instantly familiar faces turned towards me, smiled courteously, turned away from me. I found an empty chair and, with flaming cheeks and lowered head, tried to become deaf to my own dialogue. I don't believe that, in the six or seven rehearsals I attended after this, I exchanged more than a few phrases with any of the actors, who were unfailingly but mutely polite, as if there were water between us. The director, on the other hand, warm and loquacious, contrived to use effusion as a means of evasion. I was thus kept isolated, by two contrasting types of charm. It wasn't until I had experienced the same thing in longer plays that I came to realize why this happens. The writer, until he becomes hardened, is acutely embarrassed at hearing his lines said aloud by people who are publicly stuck with them; the actors are acutely embarrassed at possessing voices, faces, even personalities, that they suspect are deeply at odds with the lines they have to say, which they also suspect they haven't understood anyway; the director is hysterically alert to any whiff of conspiracy between the author and the actors. He knows (quite falsely) that the overriding ambition of any author is to direct his own work, and that, foiled in this, his next immediate ambition is to direct the director by taking over the actors. But during rehearsals for that first small play of mine I had only the desire (too modestly held even to pass as an ambition) to be allowed to mingle with actors I had admired in the cinema, and perhaps to pick up pieces of praise from here and there. To have a small part, in fact, in the whole magic process.

Oddly enough I made more real contact with the actors on the night of transmission than I did on the occasions when there was no immediate strain. I was escorted down to the dressing rooms by the script editor, instructed in the etiquette of well-wishing (hugs and kisses for the ladies; powerful hand-clasps and confident smiles for the men) and in each room I found, not an egomaniacal star eagerly awaiting the moment when he or she could hog the cameras, but a diffident, sympathetic and extremely nervous person who would have given a great deal to be somewhere else, about to do something else. Up to this moment I had myself been unimaginatively confident (after all, *they* were professionals, even if I wasn't) but before so much bravely contained panic it was impossible to be anything but sick with fear. I was shown around the set, which had cost some £6,000 to construct, and which seemed an extraordinary chaos. The studio itself was a muddle of trailing cables, abandoned cameras, and meaningless (to me) steel constructions that rose, with sinister imprecision, to a roof so high that it was almost out of sight. Here and there a cool fellow in jeans loitered, negligently. Dumped arbitrarily, or so it appeared, in all this vastness was the set; a clutter of fake rooms, fake offices and fake corridors, the totally fake and yet hideously extravagant realization of those peremptory phrases – 'Goes down a corridor, enters office, proceeds through it to bar' – that I had thrown so casually down on paper. The original story, from which all this had blossomed, had taken a day and a half to write. The television script a few hours. The scene changes a few minutes. My total expense could not have been more than sixpence and the story anyway had never seemed more than a trifling exercise between important literary adventures. And here were the consequences of that cool frivolity. Six thousand pounds of debris, six terrified actors, and a host of ace (judging by that negligence) technicians. I could see only two possible conclusions. Either denunciations from press barons and money chancellors, or universal recognition for a genius whose throwaway jokes, even, had to be brought to the attention of the widest possible public, no expenses spared.

I trudged beside the script editor, up to a little glass box with a television set and two armchairs inside it. This room gave on to a window-lined corridor from which I could take in a descending panorama – by way of the director and his assistants in a kind of science fiction control room immediately beneath – down to the floor of the hangar below. I had, under the pressure of reality, abandoned my Henry Fonda imitation in favour of a country-bumpkin-in-the-big-city bewilderment – a role that on the whole better suits my *fils du peuple* face. I made incomprehensible conversation with the script editor and kept my eyes off the clock.

What started at ten precisely was both agonizing and amazing. By walking a few feet out into the corridor my gaze could rest, first on the director, who sat at the centre of a large desk, with subsidiary directors beside her and a row of television screens, all giving off different pictures, in front of her; then I could shift my gaze down to the muddle of the studio – over the cables, the struts, the blank spaces that surrounded the set; then across to the set itself. There, with cameras aimed at them, the actors were at last at work, live. They bobbed out of balsa-wood doors to reappear in balsa-wood corridors; they whipped around untelevised corners to saunter smoothly into roofless bedrooms; they stood frozen with tension before relaxing into abrupt expressions, emitting easy bursts of laughter that were followed by swift sprints to seemingly arbitrary spots where they froze again, into perhaps postures of rage. I remember particularly the leading actor, sensual in a bath, replete, smiling; then out of the bath, behind a camera, thrashing himself into shirt, trousers, tie, jacket, and a half-smoked cigarette that was passed smoothly to him by a lady in a smock with a script under her arm.

On the other hand, by returning to the glass box, I could watch a polished little piece (I refer only to its visual appearance) in which men and women moved up and down the halls of a modern office block or in and out of the boudoirs of Hampstead Garden Suburb. I could watch this and marvel. Yes, marvel at my own mastery.

When it was all over, at 10.30 precisely, the script editor led me down to the dressing rooms again. This time I needed no instructions. Intoxicated, I embraced the men, shook the ladies warmly by the hands, preened among the experts, who still loitered negligently, and modestly allowed myself to be escorted up to the BBC bar and bought drinks. I deserved them, for had I not peered into the abyss, and seen not simply order, but an order composed of brilliant and witty surfaces, conjured out of it? I rode home in a BBC taxi, my self-esteem burgeoning naturally out of the morrow's headlines. As I glanced out of the windows into the London night, I knew what the nation was talking about. The morrow's papers, which dealt in idiot detail with some Cabinet crisis or foreign war, failed nevertheless to mention my play. I was never mentioned at all in the press, to my knowledge; which was vast, as I was still scanning the television columns ten days later.

But if fame was still deep in the bushes, its scent had reached my nostrils. I made my first move down the trail by hiring a set from a shop in Kilburn, and my second, more important move, when I telephoned the script editor with an idea for a new piece, one that would last for a memorable length of time. The script editor, who had just been transferred to the *Wednesday Play* series, listened attentively, jotted down some details, and telephoned a few days later to say that I could go ahead. Before I had even begun to think properly about the project, I was in receipt of the first half of the fee. It was then, on my way to the bank, that I knew finally that I had jumped from having written a television play to becoming a television playwright. There was nothing in the experience that has not been repeated, with varying degrees of intensity, on every subsequent occasion – the sensation of confidence, a temporary impersonation of the wealthy man, followed by a vertiginous descent into a depression that was marked by a compulsion to telephone the script editor, my new agent, the publishers of my novels. But what distinguished it radically from the previous experience was simply that I did not have thirty pages of dialogue with adaptable passages of prose to start from. I had only the memory of a scrappily written and hastily read account of a murder committed in the 1930s, and the knowledge that this time the result was to be taped. The first draft amounted to about a hundred pages, which seemed to me just right. The script editor, however, explained that by this reckoning my first draft would run to a few minutes under two hours. Could not the normal limits of the *Wednesday Play* be expanded somewhat? I reckoned back at him, to accommodate every pause and pan that I was prepared to burn at the stake for. They could not. A *Wednesday Play* was one and a quarter hours long. Mine was to be a *Wednesday Play*. It was to be one and a quarter hours long. Furthermore, there was no stake to burn at. Only the chance that the play wouldn't be done, the second half of the fee wouldn't be paid, and fame would continue to lurk free in the bushes.

I sent in the second draft, which amounted to some seventy pages, confident that *now* everything was just right. This time it was the director, calling in person at my flat, who explained what was wrong. The problem amounted to a curious legacy from the half-hour live play. Whereas in that piece I had allowed the scenes to follow on in the manner of the original short story, with no worries about the consequent difficulties for the cast, I now made absolutely sure that none of my characters ended a scene without being able to step naturally into the next one, or, if that were impossible, had at least a five-minute break in which to slip out of an overcoat. The result made for a chronological coherence that in no way compensated for the disordered dramatic logic that puzzled everyone who read it. Each scene went on for too long, very little seemed to happen in it, and yet there lay behind it some curious atmosphere, really, of purpose.

There was a tentative suggestion from the director that perhaps I had not thought about the visual freedom of television, a suggestion I indignantly repudiated. But in the course of the ensuing apology and counter-apology I suddenly found myself in possession of two crucial facts. One: in a taped play one could jump from here to there, from now to then, because the production could be stopped and started at will (not quite true, as it happens; there are prescribed major breaks and even prescribed minor breaks; but true enough to make all the difference between live and taped). And two: that one was permitted eight minutes of film that could be incorporated into the tape during performance. I approached the third draft with a sense of freedom that could well have culminated in disaster, but the methods I had already and mistakenly confined myself to held the play in a secure grip. I could change and cut, let things happen as they dramatically ought to happen, without being able to distort the basic structure. And so I completed the third and final draft.

Again my relationships with the actors failed to develop until the play had been performed, and again the director manoeuvred charmingly around me, and again I felt as if I were present as either the poor relation or the bailiff. But this time I did have at least the wit to watch what everybody was doing. At first sight they were merely rehearsing in a large, draughty hall owned, I think, by one of those military groups that people like the Duke of Norfolk are constantly appealing to the nation to keep alive. Photographs of uniformed men, massed together and staring hopelessly, hung about the walls between insignia, paintings of cannon, and hand-written directions to the lavatories and snack bar. The wooden floor was marked at intervals by chalk lines on which the props or their substitutes were placed, and here, oblivious to the cold and to the sad, unused spaces around them, the actors were acting with passion and intelligence, and the director was directing them with passion and intelligence and something more. Crouching over a chart with squares and numbers on it, or crouching a few feet away from the actors, boxing off his vision of them from now one angle, now another; pouncing forwards or leaning sideways, he was clearly practising at once the most secret and the most significant part of his craft. What he was doing, as I found out at the post-performance party, was calculating possible shots for the television screen; being, in fact, the camera.

While I, taking up an inconspicuous position at a convenient distance from the actors, was being a theatre spectator. It never for an instant occurred to me that the whole of what I was seeing was in bulk much more (and in significance much less) than what would finally be taped. This seems to me a crucial point, not only against myself in my naivety but about writing for television in general. The audience of a television play has no choice at all, far less even than a cinema audience has. For the fact that the television screen is very much smaller than the cinema screen means not that the effects are merely smaller, but that they are totally different. All through those rehearsals I behaved like a man in the front stalls, with a view of the stage or screen that was certainly comprehensive but could be made selective. Sometimes, as at a film or a play, I watched one actor's face, sometimes another's; sometimes I focused on a detail – the accidental movement of hands or feet. And it became apparent to me, when I read the script again the other day, that I had written out of the same misconception.

I *saw* the characters in their physical completeness, embracing each other or standing away from each other, and assumed, in my quite potent ignorance, that this would be how the final audience would see them. But of course on the television screen there is room only for either a diminutive version of everything or a larger version of something. It is the director's responsibility (and ultimately the writer's also) to ensure that what fills the screen is what is dramatically most necessary. Which is precisely television's strength, for the continuous act of concentration and exclusion amounts to a positive discipline. A television play, in fact, is not a play done on television. Nor is it a film for the small screen. It has its own laws. And this is after all another way of saying that the medium has created a form, flexible and generous when explored imaginatively, inhibiting and even destructive when accepted grudgingly.

When I sit down to a television play now, I do so in a very different spirit from when effecting that first casual adaptation. I know that I am involved in a different mode of realization, one in which the exchange of dialogue is more likely to be the starting point than the conclusion. But at the same time – as I confessed at the beginning – I know nothing about the real nature of television plays, what it is, for example, that distinguishes the writing of a good one from the writing of a bad one. That secret is as inaccessible as the secret of writing good films, good novels and good stage plays; as inaccessible as the secret behind all art. A familiarity with the possibilities of the medium makes the beginning merely a beginning, just the same. And although the bushes still rustle, and my nostrils still twitch to the scent, there are many days when I would gladly exchange all my experience for that time of innocence, when ballroom dancers danced in a million homes, but did not dance for me.

I should like to make it clear that I do not hold myself responsible for any inaccuracies in this account of my early experiences as a television playwright. I have merely been as faithful as possible to what I now think it probably seemed like.

3

Culture and Environment

The Pursuit of F. R. Leavis

One of my abiding memories of Cambridge is of a walk I took, one brilliant winter morning, with my current research supervisor. He was a celebrated literary critic, both the author of a number of distinguished books and a well-known reviewer in the Sunday papers. He was also an influential figure in English Faculty politics. He had an easy, anecdotal manner, always treating me with consideration, never bullying me for work, and on our infrequent meetings I found myself liking him a great deal.

As we passed along the Backs he raised for the first time in our relationship Leavis's name. What did I think of Leavis? I tried to tell him, beginning with the effect on me of *The Great Tradition* and *The Common Pursuit*, going on to discuss the influence of his seminars and lectures on my intellectual development – my supervisor listened with his usual inattentive courtesy. 'Yes,' he said fretfully, when I'd nearly got into my stride, 'I do wish he'd hurry up and die.'

His impatience may of course have been with my labouring literalness. After all, I was threatening to answer in detail a question that was probably intended, in the Cambridge manner, to answer itself. Even so, I'd clearly goaded him into a literalness of his own. He hated Leavis, as did many of his Faculty colleagues. Frequently there was a personal history to account for the hatred. For instance, I was subsequently told that my research supervisor had begun as a great admirer of Leavis, had once gone around to visit him with his just published book on a subject Leavis had also written about, had slipped it shyly on to the Leavis dining table, and had had it returned the following day with a covering note from Leavis saying that he could only assume its author had left it there by an oversight, as it could be of no conceivable interest either to his wife or to himself.

During my decade or so at Cambridge I heard many such stories, some of them no doubt apocryphal, but there is evidence in Denys Thompson's collection of *in memoriam* essays to suggest that rather too many of them were true. Leavis wounded his colleagues (though never his students, as is universally acknowledged) where people least like to be wounded, in their vanity. The pain must have been worse for those who'd previously thought that they were his natural allies.

I suppose that in some respect his sense of his own integrity was rather like Coriolanus' sense of his own honour, as dangerous when flattered as when abused. The most poignant epitaph in a collection full of epitaphs comes from Leavis's old collaborator, D. W. Harding. 'I am left,' he writes, 'half wishing he had been different enough not to have had to endure, and to cause, so much unhappiness.' But as Harding recognizes in his next sentence, Leavis *couldn't* have been different, if he was to do the work he set out to do. This double note sounds through many of the essays in the book.

Another note that sounds, sometimes faintly and sometimes distinctly, is that it was not really Leavis, but his wife, who was the cause of all the trouble. It was she who snuffled out unintended offence, unsuspecting traitors, blameless enemies, and obliged Leavis – desperate to preserve marital harmony – to wage the public battles and to continue the private acrimony. In this reading Leavis becomes a grimly active variation on the henpecked husband, bullied by his wife's sense of grievance (amounting almost to paranoia) into an aggression quite foreign to his nature – his innate courtesy and charm are reported in essay after essay.

My own limited experience would seem to confirm this view of Queenie. She struck me as formidable and discomforting. In her company Leavis frequently seemed to fall into a kind of wry trance, his eyes flickering with what I took to be an ironically simulated vacancy between his wife – who would usually be enthusiastically demolishing the reputation of a colleague, or an ex-friend or a famous writer – and myself, who would be nodding hypocritical agreements, anxious only to leave. I took what I was sure was his side, of course, and felt a disagreeable pleasure when, after Leavis's

This review of Denys Thompson (ed.), *The Leavises: Recollections and Impressions*, published by Cambridge University Press, first appeared in *The Sunday Times* on 21 October 1984.

death, stories began to leak out that Queenie was claiming that Leavis plagiarized her work. It seemed in character – at least in the character I'd attributed to her.

But several of the essays also mention that when Queenie married Leavis she was promptly and permanently disowned by her Jewish family, in whose love she had always felt secure. After such a profoundly scarring experience she might well have been on the look-out for betrayal from every quarter, even – perhaps especially – from those who came closest to her or to her husband. It was her way of protecting them both, perhaps.

And there are glimpses in the book of a spirit very different from the one I'd seen, the excellent cook overwhelmingly hospitable, the busy housekeeper warmly interested in children (though she seems to have frightened some of them or their parents, with her educational intensity), and towards the end (in a touching essay by Nora Crook), a kind and companionable sort of aunt to a young mother bewildered by Cambridge life. So some of the virtues that survived that traumatic maiming were, ironically, the recognizably Jewish ones. One can never speak confidently of marriages, but hers and Leavis's was an exceptionally long one that perhaps – that one hopes – had at its centre a sustaining love.

Almost all the essays in Denys Thompson's book offer moving little insights into either Queenie or Leavis, or their relationship, and almost all of them capture some elements of Leavis's genius as a teacher, or pay proper tribute to Queenie's gifts as a scholar. I'm deeply grateful for them. Leavis is the only great man I have met, so I suppose it's not surprising that the sentences that have already begun to haunt me come from Michael Tanner's description of Leavis dying:

he was sunk in unapproachable and terrifying gloom. I can't imagine seeing anyone look so desperate. All he said was 'I'm not feeling chirpy.' Not long after he became completely quiet and docile, and spent nearly all the time in bed dozing. I would go round and see him occasionally; he seemed to like to have someone sit with him, and Mrs Leavis did all the time. His death was a relief.

My Cambridge

When I was three I was evacuated to Montreal with my slightly older brother, to live out the war with our grandparents, then in their late sixties. Our grandfather was a businessman who spent the weeks in Toronto and only the weekends at home. My grandmother, an alcoholic, was mainly confined to a large, musty room at the back of what remains in memory a large, dark house. Occasionally she emerged, smelling strongly of peppermints. There was also an aunt, in her early forties, who had long before resigned herself to looking after our grandmother – her only child, so to speak. It was an unhappy household. My father told me, many years later, that his father remained passionately in love with his mother, who had never loved him. Thus, his weekly absences; thus also, perhaps, her addiction to drink; and our aunt's servitude. Whatever their feelings about each other, their interdependence was so complete that when my grandmother died – some twenty years ago – my grandfather and my aunt followed within a few months. The causes of their deaths were medically different, of course, but in reality they had long since come to form one organism.

However these three actually viewed their responsibilities to the two children that war had thrust upon them, they quickly simplified them into catering arrangements. They fed us with all the foods that were to remain unobtainable in England for another decade. They made sure we had clothes, clean sheets and were well shod. They made sure we went to bed at night and got up in the mornings. But they never played with us and only rarely spoke to us. In other words, they treated us as members of the family.

This piece is taken from a collection of reminiscences entitled *My Cambridge*, introduced by Ronald Hayman, London, Robson Books, 1977.

As soon as we were old enough, we were sent to a local school where, after an introductory month during which we were beaten up when we arrived in the morning, beaten up in the first break, beaten up at lunchtime, beaten up in the second break, and beaten up on the way home, we were accepted into one of the gangs, and joined in beating up less adaptable children. After school and in the holidays we hung about street corners, or went down to the drugstore for sodas and cokes, beat up the sons of the two French Canadian families in the street, and three Jewish brothers, one of whom was called Harvey. We read and exchanged comics and smoked fairly heavily. By my eighth birthday I was on ten cigarettes a day. Our grandparents gave us pocket money, but not enough for our style of life, so we stole more from them, or from the parents of other members of the gang. I also practised on my own a form of begging. I would write on an envelope an address in England I'd copied from one of the letters that arrived for my grandparents, take up a position by a post office, and cry. On being asked what was the matter, I would explain that I'd lost the stamp money for my letter to Mummy and Daddy, and so would collect in the course of a session anything up to two dollars. I only stopped when a middle-aged plain-clothes policeman told me that if he hadn't been on his way home, he'd have taken me down to the station. He said that from then on he would have me watched by other men in plain clothes. There are moments in my life now when I believe he still does.

We had left England with the moppet hairstyles, the piping accents, the submissive feelings and no doubt manner, of the nanny-trained, middle-class infant. We were returned to it with crewcuts, harsh North American accents and (in my case – I can't speak for my brother, a lawyer) criminal habits. In our grandparents' house there had been several photographs of our father, their son, whom we failed to recognize from our own past. I don't recall any photographs of our mother. We were therefore as horrified by the powerfully built man and the tall, vivid woman who claimed us from the ship at Southampton as they were by their two overfed sons, with their cropped heads, jug ears, and cunning eyes. We were far too old to be the children of such young parents, and they, who had no doubt often dreamt of clutching again the mere children who had left them, were ashamed of us. I don't recall the trip from Southampton to Hayling Island, where my father had become a GP before the war, and where he had now settled again to become a pathologist, but I do recall our bath, that first night. We were put in together, and our mother washed us. She had us nude and defenceless, but we were no babies of hers. At least, not yet. This was known on both sides.

Our re-education began at once. Our mother gave us elocution lessons (the key words were 'water', 'tomatoes' and 'laugh') and we were sent to the only girls' school on the Island. I suppose that if our mother was to achieve that hold on her two sons that is the inalienable right of middle-class Englishwomen, she had at short order to induce the correct sexual confusions. Two years there were followed by three at a boys' boarding school in Portsmouth, which were followed by two at a prep school in London, where we'd moved after the Portsmouth contribution and at which I was alternately fondled and caned by an extremely possessive pederast; which were followed by five at a famous public school! – Westminster for me, St Paul's for my brother – as day boys. At eight and nine we had been acceptable, indeed dominant, members of a Montreal street gang. At thirteen and fourteen we appeared to be acceptable, indeed dominant – because we were both good at sports – members of our years at our respective London public schools. At seventeen my brother had decided on Sandhurst and a career in the British army; at sixteen I had settled for Oxford and the intellectual life. I remained, however, something of a thief (at fifteen I'd been almost expelled for a sustained fraud on the London underground, which had led to an appearance in juvenile court) and a total liar. I was determined never to fuse my life at school with my life at home, and so told lies in each about the other, and told lies in each about everything else as well. I can't explain, of course, what it was I was protecting, but the habit of fluent evasion (my lies not being simple denials of actuality, but complicated alternatives to it) marked me out at school as a clear scholarship candidate.

The intellectuals at Westminster in my time had been comprehensively prepared in Latin, Greek, English and English manners. My Latin and Greek were feeble, my English essays designed to conceal that I'd only partially read, if at all, in the subject on which I was writing authoritatively, and my English manners, being acquired by observation and imitation, could be rapidly adjusted to circumstances. My little peroration at the juvenile court hearing elicited more than one appreciative nod, for instance, just as my General Paper essays in the History Sixth were acknowledged as models of that cultivated but not disturbing originality that wins scholarships.

While in the History Sixth I had a passionate friendship, which never became quite an affair, with a more clever and daring boy who was frequently and romantically ill (he died at Oxford in his early twenties) and I dramatically renounced all games and corps, in order to devote myself more fully to an intellectual life that was all the more shapely in form and epigrammatic in expression for being barren of content. I really did know *almost* nothing, which was exactly enough to spread through the Oxford scholarship papers. If my performances were confidence tricks, then my expensive schooling had given me the confidence to pull them off. I had infiltrated Westminster, in the decreasing though continuing expectation of being found out. Through Westminster I would infiltrate Oxford. It was all quite easy.

Unfortunately my expensive education had drained my father's finances. Just as I was poised to slide out of Westminster and up into Christ Church, the means test, the hospital politics that evolved out of the National Health Service, and a new set of taxes, compelled him to emigrate back to Canada. My distress at having to sacrifice my heritage was alleviated by the realization that I would at least be escaping National Service. I had long suspected that nothing in my nature or education had prepared me properly for that.

Nobody who came across me during my four years in Halifax, Nova Scotia, would have had reason to believe that this was, for me, a return visit. There was anti-Semitism in Halifax, and a general dislike of French Canadians, but there were no street gangs that, for safety's sake, I needed to join. It was a coastal town, clean of air, with vast beaches and a pervasively moral atmosphere. Along the main street there were almost as many churches as there were banks. I allowed my hair to hang to the nape of my neck – in my first week a policeman stopped traffic in order to wonder aloud at its length – and my Westminster drawl contrasted pleasingly, to my ears anyway, with the nasal Scotian twang. The irony of a chap destined for the Oxford quads actually finding himself on the Dalhousie campus was one that I further enjoyed by bringing it pointedly to the attention of the natives. I sauntered about the college (which now houses the largest collection of Rudyard Kipling in the world) with the poems of T. S. Eliot in one pocket and a pencil and a pad of verses in the other. I saw myself as a boulevardier fallen among provincials, and discovered only after I'd left that I'd been seen in my turn as the campus pansy. My career as a student was a succession of triumphs. I was treated by Anglophile professors and associate professors and assistant professors of English with reverence. Quite a few of them were New Zealanders; others were underqualified Englishmen, or mere Canadians even; too nervous of being seen through themselves to dare to see through me. My essays were passed about the department, and sometimes on into other departments. Once a professor (or assistant, or associate) of Economics searched me out in the library, where I held court by isolating myself in a far corner, to congratulate me on a slimy pastiche of James, borrowed from an equally slimy but more skilful pastiche by Beerbohm. In seminars I could force abdications with a phrase. Fellow students scribbled my rehearsed throwaways into their course notebooks. Those teachers in whose eyes I caught any glimpse of the sardonic, I boycotted for fastidious reasons that helped guarantee my reputation while satisfactorily undermining theirs.

I also made two close friends, one the son of a rabbi, the other of the principal of a Baptist theological college, with whom I read Shakespeare, Plato, Aristotle, Kant, Heidegger, Sartre, Camus, and one or two medium-to-light weights; with whom I went to Westerns and gangster films, discussed life and sex (we took them to be synonymous), and to whom I showed my poems and various novels; in collaboration with whom I founded a literary magazine in which we published my more major works and anonymously, for fillers, some of my minor ones; and from whom, therefore, I received whatever in Halifax, Nova Scotia, I did receive of an education.

I also had one or two experiences with girls – those who were of an intellectual bent themselves, and therefore thought there was some cachet in cuddling the campus pansy (who also, by the way, had a weight problem, owing to a secret addiction to candy bars, hamburgers and Coca Cola); but on the whole kept sex down to those conversations about life, or firmly back in the head from which I frequently expressed it into socks and handkerchiefs, in the usual manner of adolescents, which I no longer was. The campus pansy/intellectual was in one or two respects, perhaps, a mite regressive, though in fact heterosexual enough for two – the penalty, I now see, of insisting on remaining an English public schoolboy (which, you must remember, I'd never properly been).

But otherwise I grew, and not only fat. I'd started my career at Dalhousie by presenting myself as an English boulevardier. I concluded it as a citizen of all civilization, known as France. As soon as I'd taken my degree (a most distinguished one romantically marred only by a couple of failures in compulsory courses that demanded, along with application, knowledge), I departed for Clermont-Ferrand to teach as an 'assistant' in its *Collège-Technique*. I was going there to be, not just a Frenchman, but (from the Anglo-Saxon point of view) a thoroughgoing frog, which would entail losing some inches in height, changing the colour of my eyes, wearing a beret, stinking of garlic, despising the English (this I'd managed in advance), acquiring a mistress a decade older than myself and, if necessary, picking up some of the language. By the end of my first week I realized, as I sat in a café puffing Gauloises and sipping marcs with the five or six other outcast English students who infested the educational institutions of that magnificently provincial city, that I was already on the right lines. But during my year I didn't advance much beyond that first circle, except into several official *vins d'honneur*, from one of which, through an excess of wine, I failed only by inches to make it out of the door over which I vomited, and thus had the honour of hearing myself described by one of the thoroughgoing frogs at the back of the room as a *sale cochon anglais*.

At Clermont-Ferrand I became close friends with the English *lecteur* at the university, a man of twenty-six who had been doing the French circuit since coming down from Downing three years before. He introduced me to the novels of D. H. Lawrence and the critical writings of some Cambridge don called Leavis, about whom I'd once read an article in the *New Statesman*, I think it was, by J. B. Priestley, it must have been, and of whom I therefore also had the measure (as, by the way, I had of J. B. Priestley, having read a

Leavis or Leavisite reply the following week). I spent the next two months on the bed reading Lawrence, and then Leavis on Lawrence, and then Leavis on George Eliot, Henry James and Conrad (the Great Novels course had included *Adam Bede*, so I'd got the measure of her; and *Lord Jim*, so I'd got the measure of him; and *The Ambassadors*, the victim of my plagiarized pastiche, so I'd got the measure of him), and then I read George Eliot, and then Henry James, and then Conrad; and then Leavis on all of them, all over again. My real introduction to English literature was thus made in a bedsitter in Clermont-Ferrand, with five years of an English public school education, and three years of a Canadian university already behind me. And my introduction had come through an accidental encounter with a teacher whose writings showed me I still hadn't learnt to read. It became a matter of great importance to get to Cambridge as quickly as possible, for Cambridge – in English studies at least – was evidently Leavis.

I wasn't in Cambridge long before I discovered that Leavis was hated by many members of the Faculty who, if they didn't as a whole take literature seriously, took seriously any of their colleagues who did. Not that Leavis was yet as isolated as he was to become. He still had his Fellowship at Downing, still gave his weekly seminars and lectures, and had a self-appointed coterie of Downing graduates and a girl or two who had fallen in with Downing graduates. It must be admitted, however, that these chaps and their girls weren't, except when viewed from a distance, much fun. They spoke in almost inaudible voices (the girls didn't speak at all) and were masters of what I can only describe as moralizing *longueurs* – i.e. sustained passages of silence, which were boring even though one knew that adverse judgements on oneself were being formed in and expressed through them. Febrile personalities (such as mine) could be panicked into hysterical utterance, by which they stood further condemned. In my first year as an undergraduate I bumped into one of the Leavisites in a pub. (But what was *he* doing there? Unless waiting for someone like me.) He was a chunky fellow, broad of shoulder with a broken nose and the characteristic mumble of profound seriousness. He greeted my greeting with a small movement of the mouth, which inevitably impelled me into an extravagant dilation on some film or other I'd seen that week – it might even have been that day; there were long periods of my life when I went to the cinema twice a day; one week, by a judicious use of taxis, I got it up to three times. When I'd come to my throbbing conclusion, he regarded me for an hour or two with an expression of pondering or ponderous humility, muttered 'I see' and departed. I later heard, as one always did hear these things in Cambridge, that he'd finally forced me, in some pub or other he'd caught me in, to expose myself as a 'brute'. A brute. The campus pansy had found his balls, at last.

The only time the Leavis circle – in which, by the way, I never saw Leavis himself – came to life was when it was debating such matters as whether it was the cleaning woman, or Dr Q. D. Leavis, or Leavis himself who'd hung up the washing that had been observed flapping from the garden line shortly after breakfast, but which had been taken down (by whom?) some time before lunch. Inaudible or even silent on so many topics, they were dreadful gossips – in the double sense – on any aspect of the Leavises' domestic arrangements. They were, not to mince words, a pretty grisly gang; but time, thank God, has wreaked its usual shapely havoc. I've heard reports of one who, famous for his scathing silences from which he fired questions so remorselessly personal that they can only have been intended to elicit angry stammers from men and tears from women, or both from both; who shrouded his own movements in such mystery but to such seemingly sinister purpose that his was the face I always conjured up when asked to imagine the traditional knock on the door, at three in the morning, in Kafka and other police states; who seemed so totally without warmth, or even intellectual sympathy, or any but the vilest curiosity – I've heard reports that he has long since sunk cosily into a provincial nook, where, a gentle but bonhomous homosexual, he dispenses hospitality and kindly advice to all who need it; and doubtless to quite a few who don't.

I myself started at Cambridge as a postgraduate. I concocted in Clermont-Ferrand, with my Downing friend's help, a specious outline for proposed research on Henry James, which was accepted by whatever board was responsible for those matters; then, having gained my entrée, insinuated myself back to undergraduate status – I was anyway only twenty – and settled down at Trinity to my two years (my three at Dalhousie being assessed by Cambridge as worth one of Cambridge) of life and literature. Of life through literature.

Those two years, of the in fact eight I spent altogether in Cambridge, ended in the usual unnatural fashion with the Tripos examination. In preparation for it I had only one supervisor, who did me no harm and almost certainly meant me none. We walked in the Fellows' Garden in good weather, or sipped coffee in his college rooms in bad, and we gossiped of this or that great writer, soothingly. He was intellectually versatile, with a grasp of different disciplines – law, philosophy, modern languages, classics, even mathematics – and also an elaborate traditionalist. When I once turned up for a supervision without a gown, he sent me back – a matter of a mile or two – to get it; and on another occasion, when I confessed I was desperate for a cigarette, he pointed out to me that I was having a supervision, and was therefore obliged to wear a gown; and that undergraduates were not allowed to smoke while wearing gowns; then resolved the problem by informing me that he was about to leave the room, and that as long as he was out of the room the supervision was not taking place; and that therefore as long as I took my gown off, and kept it off while he was out of the room, I could smoke my cigarette. He may, of course, have been something of a comedian as well as a traditionalist.*

The only lectures and seminars I went to were those given by Leavis. This was not because I was unduly discriminating, but because in the gap between being a child and having children I found it difficult (having little reason) to get up before lunch; on top of which we weren't allowed to smoke in lectures, a prohibition less disabling to my career as a student than it is now to my career as a lecturer.

As for Leavis's teaching – well, whatever I learnt from it, I carefully refrained from summoning forth during the examinations, for which I trained myself up on the side, so to speak, of my interest in literature and in which I employed the techniques I'd acquired at Westminster, in the History Sixth, with the Oxford General Paper in view. I suppose that my predictable success (I'd predicted it, anyway) was an agreeable late return to my father for the money he'd invested in my public school education, but I mustn't completely disclaim my own contribution – that part of my nature

---

* He also, by cunningly indirect routes, taught me more than I had the grace to acknowledge when I wrote this piece.

which had combined smoothly with circumstances to make me, from an early age, an accomplished liar. I wrote all my papers with a fraudulent fluency that could have taken in only those who were bound by their own educations to honour a fluent fraud – at least to honour him more highly than any churlish Leavisite whose sense of the texts depended on close and therefore uncertain readings. The rewards were considerable. A first-class degree, and the pleasure of knowing that if I hadn't got the measure of Leavis himself, I'd got the rest of the Faculty dead right.

My moral and social education (they were, in important respects, synonymous) proceeded along the same lines as my intellectual one, to this extent at least: that in public I was a fraud, of ever-increasing fluency. I had polished opinions on novels, poems, plays, films and all pieces of music, including those I hadn't read, seen or heard (I am almost tone-deaf). These opinions, however phrased – and the phrasing was all – could be reduced to one uncomplicated formulation: *overrated*. Everything was overrated. Except by me, of course. I went of an evening to the rooms of friends in their colleges, and drank whisky, and curling my voice as a way of curling my lip, delivered my opinion for two hours or so. Then, with the air of a man with more stimulating assignations to keep, I made my exit on a valedictory sneer, then slunk anonymously through the dark streets to the cinema where I sat completely rapt before films that nobody, including their writers, their directors, or the rest of the audience, would ever overrate, or rate at all. After the film, I would go to the rooms of friends in their colleges, with an air of having kept some stimulating assignations, and join in a poker game that often lasted until two or three in the morning. We played for sums we couldn't quite afford, and so frequently ended up, all our cultivated urbanity corroded by whisky and fatigue, in squalid squabblings over our winnings and losings. I remember that one night a man who had lost hand after hand to the tune of ten pounds or so, collected two shillings and sixpence on a straight flush. I drew no conclusion from this, or indeed from any other event in my nightly life, which in retrospect seems to have been one long night, although the routine must quite frequently have been broken by circumstances, if never by inclination. After the poker game, my mouth burnt out with cigarettes, my head aching with whisky, and my stomach dipping from both, I went to bed. At least I suppose I did. I have little recollection of the period between the last dead hand and the first cup of tea in the morning.

Being a sort of alien, with a distastefully complicated background, I wasn't offered rooms in college. I lived in a boarding house with a couple of aspirant politicians from Ghana or Tanzania; an extremely old mathematical historian of twenty-six or seven who was engaged on a work so comprehensive and detailed that he couldn't see his way to begin the actual writing of it for another decade, at least; and a straight up-and-down sort of open-faced chap who was doing one of those fringe courses set up by the Colonial Department a year or so before the Department was wound up, along with a large part of our national history and influence, for ever. We were, in other words, and in our different ways, all aliens. As was our landlord, an extravagant Pole who dressed and spoke as if he ran a tenement in the Bronx. His wife, however, was a sweetly plump, soft-spoken little Englishwoman whom one from time to time suspected of spooning rat poison into the sugar bowl. She served the breakfasts we all ate together, uncommunicatingly; and she made the beds we never shared; and she made sure the water was hot only between 7 and 7.13 in the evenings, as it was her boast that her lodgers could have baths as often as they liked – which, under the circumstances, wasn't anything like as often as they needed them. I have no inclination to go into the room now, small and dreadful as it was, having had to go into it when it was my home, with such despairing regularity, twenty years ago.

My daily life, those long stretches of it that weren't spent with my supervisor or at the Leavis seminars, or lying in bed with a hangover, passed in a kind of blank fretfulness. I did some reading, of course, in my calculatingly selective way, dully, with a pencil to hand for the notes that would (and did) recall it all in the week before the Tripos, but many of my afternoons drifted by in the cinema, or as I tramped and tramped the Cambridge streets. I went to Boots a great deal, passing aimlessly between the counters, or mulling listlessly through the books in its subscription library, turning the pages of the identically spined and coloured volumes in its Western, Thriller and Romance sections, following fragments of the different stories until they cohered into one dully lunatic, unconcludable epic. Sometimes I went to Lyons, and sat over a cup of tea, reading the *Standard* and the Cambridge *Daily News*. Once I stood in the Market Place, in the rain, for about an hour, unable to decide where to go until I became so wet I had (thank God) no choice but to return to my room and sit shaking before my meter-operated gas fire. It seems now, in recounting it, like a kind of madness, and perhaps it was. I have no idea what my soul was up to, although its sporadic yearnings were not unlike the continuous, unassuaged yearnings of my body. Perhaps I was just waiting, getting through the hours until my first public appearance and the first airing of my single opinion.

I was saved by the vacations, part of which were spent back in Halifax, Nova Scotia. In the summer I swam in its great cold harbours, and worked with undistracted if cynical clarity for the Tripos. The winters were bitterly cold, and yet I could trudge the almost snowbound streets with a dizzying sense of purpose and even a future, as if Cambridge had been only a long dull dream from which I had awakened at last.

To which I inevitably returned. But as the Tripos loomed nearer, so did my concentration achieve a focus. I still put in my opinionated public appearances, still played poker, went to the cinema, and did my Boots–Lyons circuit, but for shorter periods, and always with a redeeming sense of something that had to be got back to. In the last weeks of my second year, in the general atmosphere of examination terror, I came to terms with Cambridge for a brief spell at last, positively enjoying even its beauty, which I seemed to see for the first time as I walked to the examination hall in the bright morning, and away from it in the soft afternoon. When the examinations were over, I lay on the Backs in the sun and celebrated my imminent triumph, while simultaneously swearing that when I left Cambridge in a few weeks it would be for ever, and that I'd never open another book; except from interest, disinterestedly.

Next year, lodged as a fraudulent research student (I'd resubmitted my Henry James piece) I organized, in a magazine I edited with a friend, an examination of the examinations. We debated whether the questions they contained could successfully provoke anything but fluency and fraudulence. It's a tradition of English life that though we might sometimes be compelled to bite the hand that feeds us, we never bark at it in public places. Among elderly Faculty members we were dismissed as 'bounders' (the word was actually used), while in the *Cambridge Review*, edited by younger Faculty members whose primary qualifications we had denigrated, we were described as 'psychopathic hoodlums' which my co-editor, a mild-mannered man of disinterested intelligence who'd anyway read History, could well have been; and which I, in spite of my most secret inclinations, had so far found myself unable to be. The *Listener* took up the matter of examinations, as did the *TLS*; and found against us, as did the *TLS*. I should like to claim that from then on my life as a research student was made insupportable by vindictive dons of all ages, but it wasn't so. I was allowed to stay on, and on; and long after I could stand it, on. I had early been alerted to the fact that by changing my research subject every year, I could jostle back to the beginning all over again. When I finally managed to leave, eight years after arriving as a first-year research student, I was still in my first year of research, which I still hadn't begun.

But of the six years that followed my degree I remember little more than the little I've already recorded. Often, when I lie sleepless at night, I need to invoke certain scenes from my past (a late cut executed in the middle of my fifteenth summer, say; or a coolly taken goal, lifted with the toe over the heads of the backs and into the left-hand corner of the net – that, in my great Junior Colts season) in order not to be invaded by those many other scenes I wish absolutely to revoke. But of the new or ancient shames that bring me out of bed and downstairs for tea, cigarettes and monotonously unconvincing justifications, none belongs to or points back to my Cambridge years – not even my undergraduate ones. This eerie infertility may be the result of my having written two novels about being in Cambridge while I was still there, so that I'd seen the experience not only published but in part remaindered before being completed. Or it may simply be that those eight years contained nothing of any consequence, except in their inconsequential passing. From the brightest perspective eight years can be judged as no time at all, especially if one doesn't remember noticing them going by; and could therefore be described as a period of unruffled calm, or happiness perhaps.

But here are some facts. Having begun by not being offered rooms in college in my two years as an undergraduate, in all subsequent years, as I became more deeply habituated to the seedy bedsitters from which I could conduct my furtively independent existence, I declined them. In my last years, and from a panicky sense that loneliness had become an unendurable addiction, I moved into a cold little warren of rooms above a coffee shop which I shared with two other outcasts, one of whom, a Classical research student from King's, was a friend with whom I could eat, for instance, a Christmas dinner of sardines on bread. One winter it was so cold that we wore overcoats in the sitting room, and I had to take two blankets to my favourite cinema – at which, on midweek evenings, I was the only patron. Back in my first bedsitter I used to be kept awake by two young men from Trinity, I think, who quarrelled shrilly beneath my window. One of them committed suicide by tying his head into a plastic bag. The other then went down, or was sent down, or possibly simply followed suit. There was a man from Sidney with alopecia, three tufts of hair growing from a thin blotched head, whom I saw on the streets regularly every year except my last when, instead of dreading the sudden sight of him, I found myself eagerly looking out for him. There was another man, from Trinity again I think, an asthmatic whom prescribed drugs transformed in a matter of months from youthful slenderness to bloat decadence. He also took his life. There was a small, elderly Scots tramp who ran about the town shadow-boxing (like so many of the rest of us) until one term I realized that he too had gone. There were May Balls, to which I always seemed to go in the company of girls who'd waited until the last minute to be invited by other men, with whom they nevertheless succeeded in meeting up after about the third dance of the ball itself, and on my ticket so to speak, and danced my dances with them before allowing themselves to be led off by them (while still morally on my ticket, so to speak), just before dawn, to somewhere that was far beyond the reach of my glaring eyes and acquiescent smile. There were quite nice afternoons on the river with friends, but far better ones alone in the cinema. I drank more and more as the terms succeeded each other with less and less definition. After taking my own degree, I supervised undergraduates. I wrote two novels and began a third, which I concluded after I'd got away at last, to London. And yes, of course, the bells. The bells rang incessantly, tolling my terms in, pealing to my departures, from which they tolled me back again. The winter light always seemed to dim by three in the afternoon, just as the crocuses on the Backs invariably came up earlier that year. Those are some facts. But even recording them doesn't help me to remember them, except thinly.

I have an abiding impression, though, that something was continuously, undiagnosably unpleasant all the time I was there – apart, that is, from myself. An impression that becomes vivid on those occasions (as few as I can make them) when I go back. There is the moment, as the London train slides along the interminable Cambridge platform, when my stomach lurches, and I violently wish I were visiting somewhere else I used to live; or even better, somewhere I've never lived at all.

4

Real Life

My Place in Cricket History

I didn't see my first cricket match until I was nearly ten. My brother and I had been evacuated to Canada during the war, and our Montreal leisure activities had consisted of smoking, pilfering, comic-reading and general thuggery. The only outdoor sport we knew was a kind of street baseball, played for money and frequently – especially in its later, violent stages – without a ball.

When we got back to England, we were unprepared for any aspect of English life, particularly cricket. But our mother, who had sent off a pair of Christopher Robins and got back a couple of Bowery boys, was determined to rehabilitate us, and at speed. She worked unremittingly on our accents and our table manners, and furthermore she knew – her father had been something of a cricketer and a devoted cricket-watcher – the part that cricket played in the formation of the English male psyche.

So one afternoon on that first summer of our return, when our hair had had a chance to grow out, and our ears had resumed a less grotesque relationship with the sides of our skulls, she took us to Lord's. She prepared for this ritualistically, with a packed lunch of bread and marge, three eggs set aside from the rations, and a thermos of tea (to which we'd only just been introduced, and which we hated).

Our immediate impression of the game of cricket can best be expressed in one image. There, on a large stretch of grass, an elderly 'chappie' in white clothes was imbecilically lolloping a red ball at another, much younger chappie in white clothes, who, stooping imbecilically over a large bat, paddled the red ball either straight back to the elderly chappie or to one of the other white-clad chappies who stood imbecilically about. In fact, it took us something less than two minutes to realize that, like most things English, cricket was boring and preposterous.

Also, like most things English – except the women – it was unmanly. We spent the afternoon improvising some rather more virile games of our own, pausing occasionally to observe our mother who – adhering poignantly to her education plan – clapped or called out 'Good shot, sir!' and 'Well played, sir!' in the manner, I suppose, of our maternal grandfather. I've often wondered since what match was in progress. Perhaps Middlesex were playing Gloucester – Goddard being the elderly ball-lolloper. The chappie with the paddle might even have been Compton, though I doubt this. When I next saw Middlesex play, Compton was at the crease, and it was love at first sight.

Of course my attitude to the game has changed a trifle since then. I won't go into my own triumphs as a batsman – not even to linger over a perfectly executed late cut in my fifteenth year that I still evoke when I want to remind myself that life isn't all dross; nor how, in the next season, I swept an ex-England spinner for four when opening for my school. I'll merely record that my development took a classically English line (and bound to, after such an alien beginning) from cavalier smiting and reasonable scores, through coaching and the close study of manuals to creasebound inhibition, declining scores, and a premature retirement.

I play an occasional game now, but I read about cricket and watch it incessantly, and in wangling myself membership of the MCC I've already gone further than my maternal grandfather. In fact, my one contribution to the highest reaches of the game came on my first afternoon in the Lord's pavilion, when, demonstrating to some old stray with watering eyes and the usual veins on his nose how Doug Walters *ought* to be playing the cover drive in English conditions, I stepped back and trod on Doug Walters's toe just as he was clattering his way through the Long Room to the crease, after lunch. He was out almost immediately, having been going, before lunch, threateningly well for about the only time in the series.

I doubt, though, whether my mother, who would have been out of tune with so much in the modern game, would have been proud of me. But then, as we all now know, ritual can blind us to realities, especially in cricket. I suddenly recall that my mother had forgotten to boil the eggs on the evening before that afternoon, thirty-four years ago.

This article first appeared in *Wisden Cricket Monthly*, October 1979.

Memories of Lopez

I'd been batting with my usual fluency against the faster bowlers, including the fifteen-year old who was already reputed to be the fastest bowler in the school, and had rattled up an easy twenty or so runs. The fastest bowler in the school, who I think was called Kemp, and who I know was exceptionally tall and thin, with a long, fearsome and gangly run-up, took himself off after I'd scored three successive fours by simply playing the ball gently and almost, but not quite, straight back at him. I felt pretty good. In those days, until a few minutes later that day, I always felt pretty good when I was batting; and was generally able to attribute my downfall, when I gave the matter any thought, to an act of negligence, unconstrained violence, or to a ball that somehow and unaccountably got through. I was always completely in, in fact, until the moment when I was suddenly out, and that was that. But then the bowlers I always faced simply bowled as fast and as straight as they could, Kemp-like.

So Kemp, who was also the captain, replaced himself with a chap I'd vaguely seen around the school and had heard was something of a bowler, but apart from reputation and a certain foreignness of appearance, was not in the slightest worrying to a boy who'd never been worried at the crease. His name was Lopez (Lopez!) and at fifteen he was slightly balding, and he was sallow. I looked forward to his first ball.

I spent quite a time looking forward to it, because it was quite a time coming. Not that he had much of a run-up, Lopez. There was a short amble from behind the umpire, a stutter of feet as his left

This piece first appeared in Michael Meyer (ed.), *Summer Days: Writers on Cricket*, London, Eyre Methuen, 1981.

elbow came up, and all the time in the world to watch his right arm
come over. And then more time as the ball rolled gently through the
air, and fell within easy reach of my bat, somewhere just outside the
line of my off-stump. As I'd located it so early, I myself had lots of
time to gather myself up before scampering powerfully out to smash
it where I would. My bat curved through the air, there was a scuffling
and a shuffling from behind the stumps, and if the wicketkeeper
hadn't made as much of a hash of it as I had, he could have stumped
me three times over.

I decided I'd better watch Lopez's next more carefully. This time I
took in that actually he was coming from the wrong side of the
umpire – i.e. bowling around the wicket – and this piece of information, which I hadn't bothered to register when he'd bowled his first
ball, lodged like a piece of grit in my mind all through the ball's flight,
and indeed long after it had passed my bat and was being tossed from
fielder to fielder back to Lopez. I pondered the implications as he
appeared yet again, raised his elbow, stuttered his feet, brought his
right arm over, etc.; then turned his back, not even bothering to
watch as I picked myself up out of the tangle I'd made of myself just
inside the crease.

Nothing like this, I must repeat, had ever happened to me before. I
can understand now, having first watched and then listened to Jim
Laker on television, that Lopez was a precociously expert bowler of
off-spin, with no doubt a master plan for each over and a separate
policy for each ball, along with a shrewd insight into the psychology
of each incoming batsman, even if he'd never seen him before, and by
the time he bowled his fourth ball I had at least grasped that his
action was so casual only because it was so accomplished. But the
real devastation, of which Lopez was only the efficient cause, was the
result of my seeing myself suddenly and for the first time in a different
light. It was as if my feet had swollen, my pads grown almost to my
chin, and my bat become both so heavy that I could scarcely lift it and
too small to make contact with a ball that strayed wilfully in and out
of my line of vision, without seeming at any moment to hurry itself. I
survived to the end of the over, ran my partner out in the next over,
and was out – I can't remember the details, but I have a clear
impression – presumably a moral one – that I was lbw, caught,
bowled, stumped, and made to hit wicket all at once – off the first
ball of Lopez's next. For the first time ever, I welcomed my end.

I went to the boundary, some distance away from where the Junior Colts had dumped the pads and the scorer, and watched a chap of no known class – he'd only been picked twice for the team that term – attempt to cope with Lopez. He did somewhat better than I, eventually perishing nobly in the covers off a stroke that at least looked like a stroke. Some of the later batsmen, including one of the tailenders, actually knocked Lopez about a bit. But then they probably had no idea what they were up against.

Those seven balls from Lopez marked a change in my life. From then on I never faced a halfway decent slow bowler with anything like composure. The ball ceased to be something I hit, and became a revolving tangle of contradictory opportunities – play forward; play back; get to the pitch; smother; *hit him off his length!*; use your pads; get your pads out of the way – that were invariably not taken or taken simultaneously, and either way left me stretched in some ignominious posture astraddle the crease. I think it is true to say that post-Lopez, though I continued to love cricket, I never enjoyed playing it again.

Nevertheless, by application – I took to wearing a cap, the peak of which I jerked before the bowler began his run-up – I managed to make it in due course to the school's First XI, as an opening bat. I survived there for a while because I could still usually see off the fast bowlers, but it was eventually noticed by the captain and the sportsmaster that my departure invariably followed the first bowling change. 'It's a matter of your feet, Gray old chap,' the sportsmaster explained quite sympathetically, as he pinned up the Second XI list, with my name on it. He was quite wrong. My feet were perfectly nimble. It was my mind that it was a matter of.

My slide into the Second XI was the first stage of my slide out of cricket altogether. Having been defeated by thought (my own, or Lopez's) at the wicket, I began to take it up in the classroom, and was thus able to claim that the demands made on me by essays on existentialism, *The Republic*, the French Revolution, and such, made it impossible for me to fritter my afternoons away on a cricket field. I withdrew into the library, emerging only on the occasional golden afternoon as a supercilious spectator who had outgrown even memories of the game, and I made sure always to take a book (Kafka, perhaps) with me, to help me make a telling image on a distant boundary.

Some years later, after periods in Canada and in France, I became, by a process too subterranean for me to be able to mark its stages, a cricket addict again – but only as a spectator, naturally. I spent almost as many hours as I do now watching to or listening to the Test Matches. Any game in a park, even between squabbling children, would bring me to a long halt, and I read the newspapers mainly for the county scores. I also had opinions, strong ones, on Test selection, and must have composed at least 500 unsent telegrams to the selectors, all of them abusive. My interests became known to my students – I was supervising at Cambridge – and one of them invited me to a knockabout at the College nets. I refused, of course, with just the right amount of flirtatious shyness, until properly persuaded; and one evening proceeded, in the manner of a chap bent on humouring his juniors, to an evening session.

It was as if I went straight back to a time before Lopez and other disappointments had touched my life; or rather as if I'd really spent those seemingly drab years somewhere where I'd discovered a far more skilful cricketing self. I had, for one thing, mastered a curious but effective top spin, holding the ball in a grip that must have come from imagination or pre-natal memory, and by flicking my wrist and twisting my fingers at the arm's arc, at different points of the arm's varying arc, I became my own kind of Lopez to the best batsmen in the College's Third or was it Fourth XI? Furthermore, within minutes of my starting to bat a small group had gathered around my net to note my off-drive (and its follow-through), my on-drive (a stroke I'd found unplayable during my immature prime) and my wristy little turn to leg. At the end of the session I was invited to play in next week's game. Flushed with success, or the folly that frequently follows it, I accepted.

I was put on to bowl first change, the two opening batsmen proving efficient and stubborn accumulators, though not actually dangerous – at least, until confronted with my flickering wrist, twisting fingers and my arm's varying arc. The captain, in whom a spirit of scientific curiosity, or perhaps mere good manners, at that stage prevailed, kept me on for three overs in all, and so was as responsible as I was for changing the course of the game. In one of my resting overs I also managed to drop a catch; a slightly more difficult one than the catch I dropped almost immediately after I was taken off.

My batting was worse because it lasted longer. I played immaculately down the line of the fastish, fastish-medium, and mediumish, so tapping the ball straight back to the bowler, or in the direction of fielders it just lacked the power to reach; or in the case of the slow bowlers either missed the ball completely in my innate style, or had it skid off the bat's base to slips, third bounce. This little swine of an innings – or lengthy swine of a little innings – was complicated by my complete inability to judge a run, which meant that I remained moribund in my crease while my partner, every time he hit the ball, spurted yelping a few yards from his, only to be checked by my imperiously raised hand, and dignified instructions to no, go back. I eventually adopted a bit of a limp, to explain the inexplicable, and tried to deafen my ears to the perturbations from around the pavilion, and the increasingly hysterical gestures from a captain now no longer scientific or polite. I decided to settle for an honourable draw. As long as the next eight men could hold up the other end, I could hold up mine. But the man currently at the other end summoned me to a mid-wicket conference, in which he laid out certain facts hitherto (so I still believe) kept from me. This was a limited-over match, in the newfangled mode. There was either victory or defeat, with nothing except a tie in between. 'But a cricket game', I attempted to philosophize, 'that couldn't end in a draw was scarcely a game of cricket. For one thing –' 'Look,' he said, 'you've either got to run or to get out.' With my concentration thus disturbed, I was bowled a mere four overs later, which even so wasn't quite soon enough to prevent our having to concede the game through a series of suicidal run-outs and scything blows that were taken both adeptly and fumblingly on the boundary; with two wickets still standing.

This game, played some seventeen years ago, and some fourteen years after the Lopez match, ended my career as a practising cricketer. I draw no conclusions from either game, or even from both taken in relation to each other, except to affirm that for me, I now realize, cricket has been too much life itself ever to serve as a metaphor for it. Just as Lopez's off-spins altered my development at school, so did that last innings lead, and not too indirectly, to a bizarre outburst at a Cambridge literary party that blighted several delicately forming (in the Cambridge manner) friendships and love affairs. I have a fairly recurrent daydream, though, in which I replay my last innings with a full swing of the bat, in the cavalier spirit that was my own true self, I know, before Lopez robbed me of it; and another in which Lopez himself, still balding, sallow and fifteen years old, appears from behind the umpire, around the wicket, and I dance down to cover-drive him off his length – a dream that I can revive almost at will, even though I've long known that Lopez died by his own hand shortly after leaving school, a victim of depression and, I suppose, circumstance.

Index